W9-CXN-801

Diplomacy
&
Diplomats
in 19th Century
Asante

Diplomacy & Diplomats

in 19th Century Asante

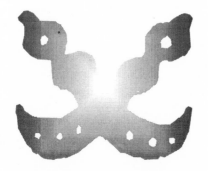

Joseph K. Adjaye

Africa World Press, Inc.

P.O. Box 1892

Trenton, NJ 08607

P.O. Box 48

Asmara, ERITREA

Africa World Press, Inc.

P.O. Box 1892
Trenton, NJ 08607

P.O. Box 48
Asmara, ERITREA

Copyright © 1984 Joseph K. Adjaye

First Africa World Press Edition 1996

Cover Design: Aaron J. Wilson

Library of Congress Cataloging-in-Publication Data

Adjaye, Joseph K., 1940-
    Diplomacy and diplomats in nineteenth century Asante / Joseph K. Adjaye.
        p.   cm
    Originally published: Lanham, MD : University Press of America, c 1984.
    Includes bibliographical references and index.
    ISBN 0-86543-504-9. -- ISBN 0-86543-505-7 (pbk.)
    1. Ashanti (African people)--Politics and government. 2. Ashanti (African people)--History--19th century. 3. Diplomatic etiquette--Ghana- -Ashanti Region--History--19th century. 4. Ghana--Foreign relations administration--History--19th century.   I. Title.
DT507.A34 1996
327.2'09667'09034--dc20   96-18448
                                                                            CIP

To my Parents

KOBENA ADJAYE-FRAIKUE and ADWOA ASOBO

Contents

Preamble

In recent years there has been an increasing demand for copies of this book, which was first published in 1984. On several occasions I have been invited to speak on other campuses or locations on various topics, only to be approached by a number of individuals who enquired as to how they could obtain copies of my book on Asante diplomacy, which is now out of print. It is partly in response to this continuing interest that this second edition is being produced.

Indeed the original publication of *Diplomacy and Diplomats in Nineteenth Century Asante* (University Press of America, 1984) was in general favorably received. J. E. Flint, reviewing for *Choice,* described it as a "well-written and fascinating work [that] adds a new dimension to the rather sophisticated studies of pre-colonial Asante," adding: "One hopes that this book will be read not just by African specialists, but by all who are interested in diplomacy and international relations. The evolution in Asante of a bureaucracy for external affairs shows astonishing parallels with the emergence of similar institutions much earlier in Europe, despite the fact that Asante was a state organized along very different lines and with a different social formation." David Killingray (in the *Journal of African History*) described it as a "useful and thorough study" and concluded that "the arguments and examples are clearly presented, making this study an important contribution to an aspect of West African history that hitherto has been little studied." In her review for *The International Journal of African Historical Studies,* Donna J. E. Maier similarly concluded that "the entire book is well documented and researched" and that "scholars in general should all be concerned and interested by the implications of the highly developed sense of diplomacy in Asante and the extensive diplomatic activity which Adjaye documents so well." To these and many others who thought so well of my book, and to the selection committees that honored me with a *Choice Outstanding Academic Book* award (1985-86) and the status of a *Herskovits* finalist (1985), I am most grateful.

In producing this edition, I would like to seize the moment to re-state the book's central concerns and thrust for the benefit of the reader. The study takes its premise from the general recognition that, like all autonomous polities, Asante did maintain external relations and did have techniques and mechanisms for operating and adjusting those relations. The study thus goes beyond the macro-spectrum of foreign relations into the micro-study of the body of functionaries who served as the vehicle for the maintenance of those external relations and examines their functions and operating procedures. Three interrelated issues are therefore of central concern here: the institutions, personnel and mechanisms of Asante diplomacy. Hence the governmental bureaus and various officials who specialized in diplomatic communication are analyzed, as are the principal instruments of diplomacy. A fundamental thesis is the postulation that the demands of foreign policy in the nineteenth century created an increasing emphasis on skills and roles that resulted in the emergence of an Asante corps of functionaries who specialized in diplomatic activity and whose work came to be guided by established procedures.

In a study focusing on diplomatic history and practice, it is inevitable—even expected—that social and economic issues would be of peripheral concern unless they directly influenced specific diplomatic missions, appointments or policies. Even so, they were not ignored, nor were issues relating to the cognitive and material dimensions of the Asante experience, status, and class. The reader will therefore find interesting and fascinating discussions of issues and subjects like the *nkenkwaa,* the King's household attendants (chapter 2), women and minority groups (chapter 4), capital punishment (chapters 4, 7), and the economic determinants of Asante diplomacy (chapter 7).

The reader may be forewarned that I consciously avoided the common practice of some African scholars whereby they present their studies by first formulating a Western theoretical model and then proceeding to interpret their African case studies within these alien models, because I do not believe that African institutions and developments should necessarily be patterned after foreign constructs. I happen to belong to the African historiographical tradition that finds it objectionable to seek to interpret the African experience in strictly Western models. Nonetheless, I did indeed find useful and did apply a number of comparative theoretical models. However, my preferred approach was to integrate such relevant comparative perspectives into the study rather than establishing a foreign model and then proceeding to interpret Asante diplomacy within that alien construct.

The comparative frameworks that were applied to this study came from four broad traditions. First, I found my relative familiarity with diplomatic concepts in the Islamic world useful, especially concepts derived from Shaybuanui's *Siyar* (the Islamic law of nations, as expounded by Khadduri 1966, for example), and the relationship between the *dar al-Islam* (the Islamic world) and the *dar al-harb* (the world of "infidels"; ref: Cardahi 1938). A second and more compelling source consisted of ideas and concepts derived from Roman diplomacy and especially the Italian ambassador during the Renaissance period. In this respect, I benefited tremendously from Don Queller's authoritative work on the Italian ambassador (1967) as well as from personal discussions I had with him in the late 1970s while we were both at the University of Illinois at Urbana-Champaign. Thus I was influenced to extrapolate concepts like the ambassador-at-large and the resident ambassador, not because they were Asante models—as indeed there are no Twi terminologies for these concepts—but because I believe that the functions performed by men like John Owusu Ansa Jr. and Kwame Butuakwa, for instance, were identical to those performed by such Italian diplomatic officials. In the same vein I found useful concepts like *plena postestas* and mandate, which I modeled after Roman procuration, as well as other analogies to, and parallels with, Roman private law (e.g., Sohm 1970).

Comparative influences from two African sources were also applied: African customary law (Elias 1956) and African diplomacy in general (e.g., Smith 1973). I believe that for the true contribution of a development like Asante diplomacy to be assessed, it has to be weighed against similar developments in other parts of the world, but the Asante contribution does not necessarily have to be made to fit those foreign jackets. All these comparative sources were cited in the original bibliography.

A number of important studies on Asante history have been published since *Diplomacy and Diplomats in Nineteenth Century Asante* first appeared in 1984. These include Tom McCaskie's *State and Society in Pre-colonial Asante* (1995), a deeply profound historical reconstruction of the Asante state centered on an analysis of the Odwira festival and of key Asante concepts and ideas; Jean M. Allman's *The Quills of the Porcupine* (1993), a richly textured political history of the National Liberation Movement in pre-independence Ghana; and Larry W. Yarak's *Asante and the Dutch 1744-1873* (1990), a study of the nature and development of the pre-colonial Asante state with wider historiographical implications for an understanding of African institutions. Of these, only Yarak's directly advances our understanding of Asante diplomatic history through his analysis of the resident ambassadorship of one senior diplomat, Kwadwo Akyampon. Mention should also be made of Ivor Wilk's *Forests of Gold* (1993), a collection of his previously published essays, one of which expands our knowledge and understanding of the pioneering career of Asante's foremost female diplomat, Akyaawa Kikwan.

Yet, inasmuch as our understanding of the complex nature of nineteenth-century Asante government and society has been advanced by these and other recent studies too numerous to mention here, *Diplomacy and Diplomats,* even with its limitations, remains the only full-length study of the personnel, institutions and instruments of diplomacy in Asante, or, for that matter, in any pre-colonial, traditional African state. It is largely for this reason that this second edition is being made available for the benefit of the student of Asante and African history as well as the general reader.

Pittsburgh, Pennsylvania
January 1996

Preface

This work is intended to contribute to our growing understanding of the structure and functions of pre-colonial African polities and their reaction to the configuration of external politics. Centered on nineteenth-century Asante, the study examines the personnel responsible for diplomatic communication and their operating procedures, reconstructs the structure of the administrative bureaus that specialized in the maintenance of diplomatic relations with foreign government officials, and analyzes the instruments and mechanisms of inter-comminucation as well as the adaptations that occurred in the institutions and strategies of diplomacy. In no sense the final word on the subject, it is hoped that this work will provoke or stimulate further investigations into indigenous diplomatic practice in Asante and other African traditional societies.

Over the past years that I labored on this manuscript and the Ph.D. dissertation upon which it was based, I have derived varied forms of assistance from a number of individuals and institutions without whose support this work could not have reached fruition. While admitting the impossibility of identifying every single source to which credit is due, I would like to acknowledge my gratitude to the Program of African Studies, Northwestern University, Evanston, which generously awarded me in the summers of 1976 and 1977 research grants that made possible my initial field work in England and Ghana. I am equally grateful to the community of historians of Asante and scholars of Ghana studies at Northwestern University, the University of Ghana, and elsewhere, in whose association I derived invaluable insights and intellectual stimulation, both direct and indirect. I particularly benefitted from my participation in the Asante Collective Biography Project (Northwestern), to which source I am further indebted for biographical information on several Asante functionaries.

In addition, I owe a debt of gratitude to a number of Asantes too numerous to mention—Joseph Agyeman-Duah, the late Barima Owusu Ansa, Asomfohene Kwaku Kankam II, Nseniehene Kwasi Addai III, Yaw Kobi, Agya Atwi Kwaku, Francis Ofori and others who generously gave of their time in my field interviews, taught me *mpaninsem* (that is, the wisdom and knowledge of the past acquired through the elders), and in some instances initiated me into the inner workings of various traditional institutions. Without their obliging time and assistance, a great deal of oral data would have been unavailable to me.

xiv

Finally, I am specially thankful to Professor Ivor G. Wilks for his direction and guidance over the years, and to my wife Dinah for the support that sustained me during the long and arduous period of writing.

Madison, Wisconsin
May 1984

CHAPTER 1

Introduction

The Supremacy of Diplomacy

While some of the observations and conclusions made in this study of Asante diplomacy might in some respects be seen as falling in line with procedures that are known to be either akin to contemporary diplomatic observances or of universal application to diplomatic practice everywhere, certain pertinent observations must be made from the very beginning. Firstly, there is no attempt to recreate for nineteenth-century Asante an ideal picture based on current procedures which may not necessarily be consistent with the known historical evidence. Secondly, the art, skills, and techniques of diplomacy were known to and practiced by the Asantes themselves in the nineteenth century. The dual premise upon which this study is predicated, then, is the contention that diplomacy à l'Asante, as described below, is neither an invention of the twentieth-century mind nor a conceptualization of the nineteenth-century Western observer; diplomacy was indigenous to Asante.

The moment effective contact occurred between European and Asante officials in the early nineteenth century, it became abundantly clear to the former that the latter were guided in their relations with foreign powers and even their provincial states by established diplomatic procedures. The use of envoys in diplomatic communication and the resolution of differences by peaceful negotiation and other diplomatic instruments constituted the cornerstone upon which Asante's foreign policy was built. During his discussions with the Asantehene in Kumase in 1817, Thomas Bowdich, the official representative of the Africa Company of Merchants that administered the British coastal settlements, noted that "however assured the King of Ashante may be of the flagitious actions or expressions of any tributary or chief, it is always the form to affect a disbelief of the report, and to send two or three state officers to see if the offender persists or recants." [1]

Three years after Bowdich's visit, another British officer—Joseph Dupuis —had the opportunity of observing the workings of the Asante bureaucratic system in Kumase. Through the diverse discussions that Dupuis had with the Asante government over the readjustment of its relations with the British and the southern provinces, the British Consul similarly concluded that Asantehene Osei Tutu Kwame "took particular pains to ingraft an impression upon my mind, that it was a maxim associated with the religion he professed, never to appeal to the sword while a path lay open for negotiation."[2] This view was corroborated by both private Asantes and non-Asante Muslims that Dupuis came into contact with during his stay in the Asante capital. The philosophical principle underlying the preference which the Asante monarchs showed for diplomatic mechanisms as opposed to military instruments approached a government ideology. And, as Dupuis further observed, the policy of the utilization of diplomacy was embedded in the very historical tradition of the Asante kingship. Indeed, Osei Tutu Kwame "maintained that he would defy even his enemies to prove his assertion" that he as well as his predecessors were committed to peace and diplomacy.[3]

The belief of the Asante kings in diplomacy was reinforced by their faith in the sanctity of international agreements. Though head of a preliterate society, Osei Tutu Kwame in 1820 emphasized that his government and people regarded that "oaths of friendship written in a book were sacred" as much as the traditional oaths which Dupuis called "Fetische." Thus, despite the apparently repeated violations of existing agreements on the part of the Fante and the British, the Asantehene (Asante king) preferred to work out peaceful resolutions of their differences. Hence, although he contended that he could easily destroy every fort on the Cold Coast, he pointed out that "it neither suited his inclination nor his policy" to resort to this course of action.[4]

Besides, it should be borne in mind that diplomacy was not a skill that was acquired and employed by government officials only. The art of diplomacy was a craft which was mastered by the society at large and therefore ingrained in the Asante nature. Daily interpersonal exchanges, relationships between the citizenry and those in authority, and the reception of private guests were considerably regulated by established procedures that were very much in the diplomatic vein. "In such a land as Ashantee," observed Reade in 1874, "every man... from an early age" as well as "the king and chiefs are profoundly skilled in the arts of diplomacy. "[5] Viewed from this perspective, international diplomacy was, to Asante, local diplomacy writ large.

Asante believed not only in the theory and practice of diplomacy but also in its style. The consummate diplomacy was that which was conducted in a most impressive and grand style. The dignified bearing of the envoy, the size of his retinue, the slow pace at which large embassies moved, and the use of a whole spectrum of diplomatic paraphernalia were all influenced by a grandness of taste and style that was intended as a pointer to the wealth and power of

Asante. When the Okyeame Boakye Tenten mission of 1881 arrived in Cape Coast, for example, British Governor Samuel Rowe considered it the most impressive embassy ever received from Kumase.[6] When notification of the embassy that was to be dispatched to London in 1894 appeared in the Gold Coast press, it was indicated that the party would arrive in Cape Coast "with a retinue of about 500 all told and in grand state."[7] The 1881 and 1894-5 missions to the British, as manifested in their grandiose scale and majestic style, represented the epitomes of a national policy dedicated to the maintenance of external relations by diplomacy.[8]

When Osei Tutu Kwame signed the peace treaty of 1817, the Asantehene did so in the firm belief that the agreement would regularize the vague relationships that had existed between his government and the British and Fante. The history of the period immediately following 1817 was to indicate that the hopes the Asantehene had reposed in the Bowdich Treaty had been misplaced. Yet, exemplifying a firm commitment to a policy that called for the resolution of conflicts by negotiation, Osei Tutu Kwame sought to settle apparent violations of the agreement by dispatching four successive missions to the British administration in 1819-1820.[9] When an impasse was imminent, following the failure of the peace missions, Osei Tutu Kwame again availed himself of the opportunity provided by the visit of Joseph Dupuis to Kumase to review the whole issue of Asante-British relations. The diplomatic discussion protracted for several months, and as Dupuis, who was apparently beginning to show signs of exasperation at the inconclusive nature of the talks threatened to leave, the Asantehene's reaction evidenced his firm commitment to the settlement of disputes by peaceful agreements:

> Do not leave me; you cannot go now, for you must make me
> a book to be good friends with the King of England, as the
> other book tells lies.[10]

Osei Tutu Kwame's zeal in seeking the external goals of his nation through peace and diplomacy was by no means unique to his administration. The history of Asante in the nineteenth century gave ample evidence of a nation seeking to adjust its external relations by internationally accepted diplomatic methods. Asantehene Osei Yaw Akoto, his successor, acquired a pacific reputation even before his accession to the *Sika Dwa* (Golden Stool) in 1824. Reports circulating in British quarters at the time of the death of Osei Tutu Kwame characterized the *abakomdwa* (heir apparent) as one who was "against hostilities in principle."[11]

Following the uncertainties of the 1820s, which witnessed two major Asante-British military confrontations, Osei Yaw Akoto succeeded in executing with British Governor George Maclean in 1831 a document whose importance was significant. The 1831 peace treaty became the primary document that regulated Asante-British relations for the succeeding four decades. Far more important than that, the spirit of the 1831 agreement lived on and influenced in varying degrees successive Asante governments until the end of the century. As late as 1881, for instance, when it became necessary for Asante to dispatch a mission to Cape Coast to assure the British administration that no hostile actions were being contemplated against the coast, the headship of this mission was strategically entrusted to a man who had acquired recognition for his espousal of the doctrine of peace and diplomacy. Addressing the British administration in Cape Coast, Ankobea *okyeame* (counselor) Kofi Bene "reiterated several times that he was the late King Quako Dua's man who was celebrated for his peaceful disposition...."[12]

That the success of the 1831 agreement is attributable in part to the forthright application of its stipulations by Governor George Maclean was argued by Metcalfe as far back as 1962.[13] What did not receive adequate attention until 1974 was the fact that much of the success of the 1831 landmark agreement was due also to the pacific disposition of Asantehene Kwaku Dua Panin.[14] The simple fact is that this Asantehene practiced a lifelong policy of commitment to peace, negotiation and other peaceful approaches, for which reason his memory in Asante oral tradition remains that of the most pacific Asantehene.[15]

Asantehene Kwaku Dua Panin summed up his ideology of peaceful and diplomatic coexistence to British Governor Stephen Hill in 1854:

> I have not the least spark of anger in me, I am glad to be always at peace with you, as the late Governor Maclean does with me that in his time, no disturbance at all; I hope you may go on so with me the same, and I shall accommodate you anything likewise you shall want from me.[16]

But even before then, the British administration had itself recognized the peaceful disposition of this Asantehene: "I believe that the present King of Ashantee is averse to war."[17]

Asantehene Kofi Kakari (1867-74) followed the well-trodden path of peace and diplomacy established by his nineteenth-century predecessors. Those who might hold a contrary view of this Asantehene should be reminded that the campaigns of 1868-69 and 1873 were brought about by the need to suppress provincial insurrection. In the interest of peace with the British, this Asantehene several times showed a willingness to forgive and forget Fante and Asen molestations of Asante envoys and traders by his affirmations of "let bygones be bygones."[18] When direct Asante-British military confrontation seemed imminent in early 1874, Kofi Kakari's preferred course of action was to exploit to the fullest extent negotiation and other diplomatic instruments. The missions he dispatched in rapid succession to meet with British General Sir Garnet Wolseley, who was advancing on Kumase with his forces, is a matter of record.[19] Repeatedly, the Asantehene professed to Wolseley: "I have no quarrel with the white man."[20] It was, however, the British who turned down the Asantehene's unmistakable peace entreaties of:

> My ancestors never struggled with any European Power,
> and I cannot do it if your Excellency do not mean to fight
> me....[21]

Asantehene Mensa Bonsu (1874-83) was similarly a firm believer in the doctrine of peace and negotiation. In a time of incessant provocation from Dwaben in the mid-1870s, he showed great restraint, for as he explained to the British Administrator, he wanted to prove to him that "I keep fully to the oath that my predecessor swore." [22] Through diverse approaches he "endeavoured to open negotiation"with Dwaben, resorting to war only as an eleventh-hour measure.[23] The events of 1881 were to provide further illustrations of diplomacy in operation. In a period when extreme suspicions of Asante motives were being engendered in British circles in Cape Coast, Asante made a supreme investment in diplomacy by dispatching several high-powered embassies (including the one which was led by Okyeame Boakye Tenten) to negotiate with the British.

There was no departure from the policy of negotiation during the administration of Asantehene Agyeman Prempe I. As Asante's susceptibility to British colonial advances during this period placed increased stress on its relations with the British, the Asantehene intensified his efforts to seek a settlement of differences through diplomatic channels. When diplomatic cooperation with officials on the Gold Coast repeatedly proved futile, Agyeman Prempe finally decided to take diplomacy Asante style to the very doors of the British Government in London. The justification for the appointment of the 1894 embassy to England was lucidly laid bare before British officials in Cape Coast:

> Considering the unfriendly attitude already assumed by her
> Majesty's Government on this Coast to the Kingdom of

> Ashante ... it is impossible that mutual sympathy and under-
> standing could be looked for or arrived at in the Colony for
> prevention of war and bloodshed and that therefore special
> embassy should be sent to England to lay before Her Maj-
> esty and Privy Council this and other matters connected
> with peace and progress of Ashanti Kingdom and its coop-
> eration with settlements of Her Majesty the Queen .... [24]

The persistent efforts of this mission to seek official audience and its long battle for diplomatic recognition were clear demonstrations of a supreme faith in the use of diplomacy as opposed to military approaches.

It is also worthy of remark that the Asante government's policy towards the British at the close of the century was a reaffirmation of that by which the century had begun. Agyeman Prempe could not have drawn the line of continuity any clearer:[25]

> I am always ready and willing to receive my friends (the
> white men) at my capital whether visits of pleasure or on
> political matters, and I think I am justified to say, that as
> my late grandfather, King Kwaku Dua I, was so friendly
> with Sir George Maclean, then Governor of the Gold Coast,
> so likewise I imitate the footsteps of my late grandfather, that
> I am a peaceful King with Her Majesty the Great Queen of
> England.

While the dispatch of embassies may not in itself be directly equated with a policy of peace, it is significant to note that the Asante administrations generally showed a preference for the use of diplomatic instruments. Further, the nineteenth-century Asante monarchs desired peace not because they were pacifists; their preference for peace and negotiation emanated from calculated strategic considerations that were linked to national security and development. As Agyeman Prempe I lucidly outlined in a letter to British Governor W. B. Griffith in 1894, it is only when "hostilities go away from her (Asante), that the evils which the constant wars has (sic) brought upon her, like destroying our jewels, may die everlastingly from her" and he would be in a position to promote "good order in my Kingdom and to restore its trade and the happiness and safety of my people generally."[26]

The Myth of Militarism

"Asante Kotoko, wokum apem a apem beba" (" 'Porcupine Asante,' if you kill a thousand a thousand more will appear"), so the old Asante national war cry goes. This is a maxim that has evolved out of a histori-

cal tradition of military feats and accomplishments, a reputation that Asante earned through proven military superiority over its Gold Coast neighbors. Yet, a close examination of the historical evidence indicates that the incidence of warfare involving Asante in the nineteenth century, for example, was not that high by the standards of the time. Indeed, if we were to examine Asante-British military confrontations, for instance, it would be seen that the times of major wars were limited to only six for the whole century. These were in 1822, 1824, 1853, 1863, 1873-4, and 1899. Contrary to popular belief, there was no Asante-British war in 1807, as the British gave in to negotiations at the last minute. Again, for those occasions cited above, it should be remembered that direct Asante-British warfare was avoided in 1853 and 1863.

Given the relatively low incidence of large-scale warfare, the issue of Asante's militaristic reputation needs a reassessment. In the first place, adequate emphasis has not been given to the fact that Osei Tutu Kwame in 1806 and 1822, and Kofi Kakari in 1869 and 1873, for example, undertook offensive action against the coastal states only after their persistent diplomatic efforts had been exhausted. Secondly, a distinction has to be drawn between the military character of the Asante campaigns of the eighteenth century and those of the nineteenth; whereas the wars of the eighteenth century were principally campaigns of conquest and annexation by which the Asante empire was established, the military actions of the succeeding century were caused by the need for Asante to suppress provincial rebellions and to enforce existing diplomatic agreements. Thus, when Osei Yaw Akoto declared war on the Wassa, the Fante, and the British in 1824, he did so because they were accused of "perfidy, infractions of treaties, violations of public faith, treachery, cruelty, etc."[27] Similarly, Asantehene Mensa Bonsu took pains to explain to the British administration that in waging war on Dwaben in 1875, he was "not trespassing upon the Treaty, but simply making it to be respected and observed strictly."[28] Thirdly, the contrast must be made here between the actual incidence of war (which was low by the yardstick of the nineteenth-century) on the one hand, and, on the other, a military tradition that has been bolstered as a national ideology to foster internal unity and deter Asante's potential adversaries.

There is reason to believe that war was never resorted to without just cause. Dupuis' comment on the subject, that the British residents on the coast admitted that "Ashantee has never engaged in war with the maritime states from sheer caprice and rapacity," is emphatic. In support of this claim, Dupuis cited the words of Mr. Nollan, a British official at Cape Coast at the time, who was quoted as declaring that "he never knew the King to make palaver without cause, or violate this word."[29] Given these considerations, there is reason to suggest that, within the Asante-British axis at least, the Asante monarchs of the nineteenth century deserve their militaristic reputation only in part.

The Study

In 1894 the Asante Government dispatched an embassy of seven to present its case—the preservation of Asante independence against British colonial advances—before the Government of England. The embassy's commissioning instructions clearly spelled out its mandate and delineated the credentials of each member. As one of the two leaders of the mission, John Owusu Ansa Jr., was authorized to present before the English government "divers matters affecting the good estate of our kingdom and the well-being of our subjects with full power for the said Prince Ansah as our ambassador extraordinary and minister plenipotentiary to negotiate and conclude all such treaties."[30] The embassy marked the climax of a century of intensive diplomatic activity which had resulted in the development and standardization of procedures associated with diplomatic appointments, representation, and communication in Asante—matters which this study seeks to examine more fully.

The subject of this investigation, then, falls within the area of Asante diplomatic history. It seeks to identify the distinguishing features of the procedures and practices that became standard in the maintenance of external communication between the Kumase-based administration and the outside world. It is a two-part study; the first analyzes the personnel who specialized in diplomatic communication, while the second both reconstructs the structure and functions of the bureaus by which Asante sought to maintain its foreign relations and examines the mechanisms of intercommunication by which those relations were maintained and adjusted. The approach results in the depiction of what may be seen as corresponding to "the Asante ambassador in the nineteenth century" and "the Asante Chancery," respectively. The connecting link between the two parts is a section providing a detailed analysis of a sample of specific embassies. There is inevitably a relatively heavy reliance on evidence derived from the Asante-British spectrum because of the dominance of British relations in Asante's foreign policy, although illustrative cases are drawn as well from Asante's relations with its Arabic, Dutch, and Danish-speaking neighbors.

The project takes its premise from the general recognition that like all autonomous polities, Asante did maintain external relations and did have techniques and mechanisms for operating those relations. This exercise, however, goes beyond the macro-spectrum of foreign relations into the micro-study of the body of functionaries who served as the vehicle for the maintenance of external relations and seeks to examine their functions and operating procedures. The cornerstone of the thesis is the postulation that the demands of foreign policy in the nineteenth century created an emphasis on skills and roles that resulted in the emergence of an Asante corps of functionaries who specialized in diplomatic communication and whose work was guided by established procedures.

Following this introductory chapter, each of the succeeding six chapters is designed to examine a distinct aspect of the study. Chapter Two analyzes the various functionaries who provided the corps of Asante's envoys. These include the *nhenkwaa* (household servants), of whom an important component, from the point of view of this discussion, is the *abenase* (wardrobe) department; the *afenasoafo* (swordbearers) and *nseniefo* (criers), the principal agents of external communication; and the *akyeame* (counselors) who served as leaders of major missions and whose heads (*akyeamehene*) in a number of instances performed the roles of Ministers of Foreign Affairs" and "Chiefs of State Protocol." Though these functionaries are viewed as initially performing diplomatic assignments as extensions of their domestic roles, attention is drawn to the development that progressively emphasized the professional character of their work as agents of external communication. A discussion of the classification of ambassadors follows, with illustrations identifying their distinguishing characteristics. Other issues discussed in this chapter are the ranking of envoys; skills and other eligibility criteria; questions of mandate, credentials, and diplomatic representation; and the scope of functions performed by nineteenth century envoys.

Chapter Three focuses on issues connected with the conduct of embassies and Asante diplomatic practice in general. The principal issues discussed include appointment and commissioning procedures; the composition, size, conduct and duration of embassies; formal audience procedures; and the remuneration of ambassadors. Other major questions delved into relate to the inviolability of envoys, misconduct and attendant penalties. Throughout, the discussion appropriately draws upon parallels and contrasts with present-day practice.

The next chapter essays a detailed analysis of several major embassies. The concern is to provide an in-depth picture of the operation of large embassies, with a view to substantiating the characteristics of embassies identified in the previous chapter.

Chapter Five argues the creation of an Asante Chancery as an office responsible for the preparation, preservation, and retrieval of diplomatic and other official documents. Within the comparative framework of a general discussion of the structure of the entire chancery, the operating procedures of the component bureaus, namely, the Arabic, Dutch, Danish, and English, are analyzed. The background and skills of the official who is traditionally known as *ohene krakye* (king's secretary) are examined, as is his role in the maintenance of external diplomatic communication.

Chapter Six provides a functional analysis of the Chancery, thereby complementing the preceding chapter. Procedures relating to the preparation of documents are examined, and emphasis is placed on the measures that were employed to ensure accuracy in the transmission of oral messages into the written medium. Types of chancery documents and chancery styles are also discussed. Through a comparative discussion of the written and oral modes of communication, an attempt is made to assess the extent of use and effectiveness of the mechanisms of external communication. The emphasis in this chapter is two-fold: first, an examination of the role of the Chancery in diplomatic communication; and second, a study of chancery documents as an index to identifying the thrust of Asante's diplomatic relations.

Diplomacy

The maintenance of neighborly peaceful or friendly relations is perhaps as old as man himself and is traceable to as long as human communities have existed. Herskovits points out that "non-literate peoples, in their dealings with each other, had and still have techniques of settling differences." [31] But diplomacy is not to be confined simply to the resolution of disputes. It involves the art and "method by which these relations are adjusted and managed," and encompasses all that goes for "the management of international relations by negotiation." [32] Hence, diplomacy has often been conceived of as being synonymous with "foreign politics." [33] Viewed from the broadest perspective, diplomatic practice embraces the institutions, instruments, and mechanisms by which nations or communities carry on their affairs with others or their official guests. It is in this broad context that the term diplomacy is used in this discussion relating to Asante in the nineteenth century.

Ambassador

A problem that the student of nineteenth-century Asante diplomatic history has to grapple with is that of distinguishing the status of the various officials who served in diplomatic capacities. There is no doubt that the primary sources of the period show some recognition of differences in rank within the diplomatic corps, hence the use of a title like "messenger" as opposed to "ambassador." However, the use of titles based on a consistent application of criteria does not become discernible through a reading of much of the primary material. What has obscured a clear identification of the individual status of Asante diplomats in the European sources is the tendency of the authors to approach the subject from Western perspectives. Thus, attempts were made to rank Asante envoys according to the size of their embassies or the functions they performed on missions. Besides, the tendency on the part of the nineteenth-century British administrators, for example, to view embassies led by *ahenemma* (sing., *oheneba:* princes or princesses) as being of the highest rank—a disposition that was based on the false assumption that the sons and daughters of kings commanded the highest status in the diplomatic corps—again underlies their lack of understanding of the local situation. Another cause of ambiguity is the fact that oftentimes the European authors did not make any effort whatsoever to identify the exact rank of visiting Asante diplomats, preferring to lump many of them together as "messengers." The Western viewpoints of many of the writers have inevitably created ambiguities which hinder an understanding of the sources. Unlike the Western approach, the primary Asante criterion for classifying diplomats will be seen to have been based less on the functions performed than on the rank of the official at home.

A major complication arises from inconsistencies in the application of titles. Although European colonial administrators, diplomats, generals, and other officials who visited the Gold Coast were conversant with the prevailing nomenclature of nineteenth-century Europe, their use of titles like messenger, emissary, herald, courier, resident, commissioner, and ambassador with reference to Asante diplomats was not characterized by any degree of consistency. If a "messenger" is to be understood in the European context as a diplomat of the lowest rank and with limited powers, then Dupuis' description, for example, of Adu Borade, who was sent on a mission to Cape Coast in September 1819, was certainly inconsistent with the status of a "messenger."[34] Adu Borade's mission was preceded by incidents involving, firstly, the spread of false rumors by coastal peoples of a Gyaman victory over Asante during a protracted Asante-Gyaman war 1819),[35] and, secondly,

Komenda assaults on Asante envoys who were sent to the coast with jawbones as evidence of victory, following the conclusion of the campaign. Adu Borade, who was evidently empowered to recapitulate the Komenda affair, convincingly argued his government's case against the British administration and the people of Cape Coast and Komenda for violations of the Bowdich Treaty of 1817. His conduct throughout the discussions indicated that he was permitted some exercise of discretionary powers and that he was evidently of a rank higher than a mere "messenger." Elsewhere, Dupuis' contradictory description of Owusu Dome as a messenger but "in the quality of ambassador" provides yet another indication of the ambiguity which characterized European attempts at designating Asante envoys.[36] Again, a contradiction becomes evident in Beecham's description, following Dupuis, of the Asante envoys sent to resolve the Asen crisis of 1806 as "royal messengers" but their missions as "embassies."[37] However, the same author preferred the title "ambassadors" for the Asante diplomats who were to have accompanied Dupuis to England in 1820, thus implicitly raising the question of whether the use of the word "ambassador" was perceived to be dependent on the host being of sovereign status.[38]

The Asante approach to the issue, however, posed no difficulty. The common Twi expression used in referring to the dispatch of missions translates as: "the king has sent out an *obofo,*" *obofo* being a generic word for envoy. When the need for specificity arose, the Twi language provided an effective way of resolving the issue: the individual domestic titles of the officials, as *afenasoafo* (sing., *afenasoani*: swordbearer), *nseniefo* (sing., *esen* or *nsenieni*: court crier), and *akyeame (*sing., *okyeame*: counselor) were used.

It was therefore the individual domestic title of the official that generally determined his diplomatic status. Within the domestic rank order, the *akyeame* were of a status superior to the *afenasoafo,* whose status was in turn higher than that of the *nseniefo.* Besides, it is to be noted that, within individual *nfekuo* (sing., *fekuo*: department), rank systems existed which made it possible for functionaries to rise to the headship of their divisions. Additionally, one measure of status was the degree of authority with which an office-holder was commissioned for his diplomatic assignment. Therefore, to forestall ambiguity, the Asante system of identifying functionaries by domestic titles and roles will be followed. Where English titles are used for convenience or to avoid repetition, the word "ambassador" will be used to denote the highest ranking diplomat, usually the leader of a mission, and, unless employed in a generic sense, "envoy" will be used in the context of a senior diplomatic official below the rank of an ambassador.

No serious attempt to identify Asante envoys by their proper titles becomes discernible through a reading of much of the European sources for the greater part of the nineteenth century. "Messengers" and "ambassadors" were often used interchangeably in descriptions of visiting envoys, as if the two were the same. Notwithstanding these ambiguities, there was no uncertainty in Asante's perception of its envoys as official diplomatic representatives of the Asantehene and his government. Though envoys differed in status and role, their basic functions remained the same. They were diplomatic representatives of the Asantehene, and their juristic authority rested on the fact that they stood *in loco principis.* Thus, they were the instruments and channels through which the foreign representation of the Asantehene-in-Council found expression.[39]

Asante Diplomacy and the Literature

When British Consul Joseph Dupuis visited the Asante capital of Kumase in 1820, he found in existence a well-organized kingdom with an elaborate bureaucracy. Yet an in-depth analysis of the workings of that government beyond a superficial narration was to wait for well over one hundred years. At the close of the century the literature on Asante remained no more than accounts of military campaigns or travelers' impressions.[40] When Ellis published what can probably be described as the first history of Asante (and the Gold Coast),[41] it did not substantially alter the trend—narratives of European activities and Asante-British wars. Reindorf's publication was in a sense a "pioneer work," based as it was on interviews with over 200 persons. Yet it was history as the author saw it: a "methodical narration of events in the order in which they successively occurred,"[42] and lacking any systematic analysis. By his limited use of British parliamentary sources, Claridge gave a new dimension to Asante historical scholarship. The work is indeed "monumental," consisting of two volumes of over 600 pages each. However, it lacks the "nice sense of proportion" that Hugh Clifford attributes to it.[43] For it is essentially military history, the author devoting, for example, about 200 pages of the second volume to the 1873-74 war alone!

No major studies on Asante were published until Rattray's works appeared in the 1920s. Essentially a product of the new anthropological school born out of the belief that anthropology could be utilized to serve the needs of colonial administration, Rattray's publications[44] were works of social administration dealing more with the customs and less with the history of Asante. Ward's *History of Ghana*,[45] for many years the standard school text, is little more than an abridgment of Claridge, the author lacking access to many new sources of information.

Thus, in 1960, 140 years after Dupuis' consularship to Kumase and more than 60 years after the Asante mission to England, no real systematic analysis of the government of Asante had been essayed. The situation, however, was not to stay unaltered for long. The new scholarship initiated largely by the extensive research of Ivor Wilks was to stimulate specialized studies of Asante; first, Wilks' own publications on trade, religion, and government in Asante[46] and, second, Fynn's work dealing with the rise and consolidation of Asante power up to the nineteenth century.[47] More recent Ph.D. dissertations and other publications have added great depth to analyses of the structure and functions of the Kumase-based bureaucracy of Asante.

Of particular importance are the works of McCaskie, Owusu-Mensa, Lewin, Aidoo and Wilks (1975). McCaskie (1974)[48] examines the circumstances which led to the establishment of a royal paramountcy in the reign of Asantehene Kwaku Dua Panin and discusses its implications. In a work designed to analyze the structure of government and the distinctive features of Asante political life, McCaskie identifies the processes and instruments by which this Asantehene achieved the royal centralization of power.

The first major work relating to the subject of Asante diplomacy was essayed by Kofi Owusu-Mensa in 1974.[49] In a biographical study the author examined the diplomatic and missionary career of Owusu Ansa, Sr. Following a primarily chronological approach, Owusu-Mensa sketched his subject from his hostage and student years through his missionary days to his later years as an Asante negotiator.

A more important contribution to Asante Studies is Lewin's dissertation, "The Structure of Political Conflict in Asante 1875-1900."[50] Identifying the last quarter of the nineteenth century as a distinct phase in Asante history, Lewin examines the political, institutional, and socioeconomic changes that occurred in that period and gave it its transforming character. The author examines Asante's reaction to the external influences of British intrusions and the internal stimuli of constitutional conflict, and reconstructs the Asante political system within the perspectives of the restructuring of the power of the central government *vis-à-vis* the "confederate" states; the emergence of new economic interests (groups and entrepreneurs); the increasing use of violence as a tool in the settlement of political issues; and the intensification of social upheaval.

Some of these themes are echoed in Aidoo's work analyzing the sources and nature of conflict and the change that resulted from those conflicts from 1867 to 1901.[51] The author discusses the dynamics of Asante's social, economic, and political life, emphasizing the rise of new social and economic groups like the *akonkofo* (commercial entrepreneurs) and *nkwankwaa* (youngmen and commoners).

The most comprehensive single work on Asante, however, is Wilks' 1975 publication, *Asante in the Nineteenth Century: The Structure and Evolution of a Political Order.* In a collection of essays, Wilks provides an in-depth analysis of the structure of the central government of Asante, analyzes its conduct of domestic, provincial, and foreign affairs, and discusses a number of important related issues.

These works have immensely added to the gradual accumulation of information on Asante and have greatly aided our understanding of the subject. They provide frames of reference for any ongoing and future study of nineteenth-century Asante, including the present work, and the writer gratefully acknowledges their contributions. Yet insofar as historians have given attention to analyses of the structure and functions of the Asante central government, a serious gap exists in our knowledge and understanding of the workings of the personnel, instruments, and mechanisms of diplomatic communication. Owusu-Mensa' work unfortunately does not discuss Asante's diplomatic mechanisms, nor does it attempt to place Owusu Ansa's activities within the wider background of Asante diplomatic procedures of which they must have been a part. Owing to their concern for the broader issues of central government, McCaskie (1974,1995), Lewin (1974), Aidoo (1975), and Wilks (1974,1993) gave inadequate attention to analyses of issues and procedures relating to diplomatic conduct, representation, and communication. In this sense, then, this work studies a largely uninvestigated aspect of Asante foreign policy.

A Note on Sources

The principal sources for this study include unpublished documentary material, published works, newspapers and field interviews. Of particular importance to the study are the British Parliamentary Papers and Original Correspondence in the CO. 96 series. However, in many instances where the information cited is available in both the CO. and PP. series, reference is made to the more accessible Parliamentary Papers, as can be found in the Irish University Press editions.

A considerable portion of the information base of this study, particularly in the first four chapters, is derived from orally transmitted sources. The field interviews cited were conducted in the summers of 1976, 1977, and 1980. In addition, a specific survey of 40 *nhenkwaa* was undertaken in May-June 1980.) General information based on the writer's knowledge of Asante society, however, is not footnoted.

CHAPTER 2

Diplomacy and Diplomats

Nhenkwaa

Any discussion of the groups of people from whom the Asantehene draws his corps of envoys must begin with the *nhenkwaa* establishment.[1] Nhenkwaa (sing. *ahenkwaa*) is a compound word derived from the Twi *ohene* (pl. *ahene*) king or chief, and *akoa* (pl. *nkoa*), servant. An *ahenkwaa*, therefore, may be regarded as a servant of a king. All principal Akan chiefs are served by *nhenkwaa* who attend, wait upon, and assist them in their daily domestic and public roles and functions. By virtue of the power and wealth which the Asante nation has garnered since the seventeenth century and the resultant lofty status the occupant of the *Sika Dwa* (Golden Stool) has attained, the Asantehene has tended to command a large body of *nhenkwaa,* numbering several thousand. As Asante over the centuries developed an elaborate administrative machinery centered at *ahemfie* (the Asantehene's residence), the *nhenkwaa* assumed correspondingly increasing roles and functions that extended beyond those of personal household servants to state functionaries. They became the instrument through which the Asantehene's will found expression or execution, and it is precisely in their role as agents of contact between *ahemfie* and the outside world that the *nhenkwaa* must be viewed as persons belonging to the Asante corps of envoys.

In function, then, the *nhenkwaa* are individuals who perform a host of tasks for the Asantehene, including being dispatched on errands and missions. Territorially, contemporary practice suggests a definite pattern in the areas of activity within the diplomatic field of *nhenkwaa* vis-à-vis other groups of envoys: for the most part *nhenkwaa* are sent on "missions" within the city of Kumase and to the district *amanhene* (paramount chiefs) living in an area roughly within a thirty-mile radius from the capital, whereas the *akyeame, afenasoafo,* and *nseniefo* are generally employed on embassies to more distant towns and states. Yet, it should not be thought that this distinction between the spheres of activity of *nhenkwaa* as opposed to other classes of Asante diplomats is or has ever been absolute. Throughout the nineteenth century individual *nhenkwaa* achieved prominence as envoys in the conduct of missions with distant powers like the European nations whose representatives occupied locations along the coastal areas. The example of

Kwaku Bosommuru Dwira is a case in point. An *ahenkwaa* of the *abenase fekuo* (wardrobe department), Kwaku Dwira became one of the senior diplomats of the administrations of Asantehenes Kofi Kakari and Mensa Bonsu, acquiring specialization in British affairs and, for periods of time in the 1870s and 1880s, serving in that capacity as Asante resident ambassador in Cape Coast.[2] At the same time it must be pointed out that individual *nhenkwaa* continue to this day to be engaged in diplomatic assignments that take them outside Asante. Forty percent of the forty *nhenkwaa* surveyed in 1980 had seen diplomatic activity in distant places like New Dwaben, Akwapem, Akyem, Ga, and Bono.

Theoretically, any *ahenkwaa*, by virtue of his status as a servant, may be employed in any task or mission as seen fit by the Asantehene. Thus, of the *nhenkwaa* who participated in the survey, those who had been engaged in missions came from a variety of *nfekuo* (bureaus), including *nkonwasoafo* (stool carriers), *nsumankwaafo* (physician/spiritual caretakers), *afotosanfo* (treasury officials), *nkaneasoafo* (lamp bearers), *abenasefo* (wardrobe officials), *somesisifo* (waist holders), *patomfo* (caretakers of drinks) and *mponponsufo* (bearers of the *Mponponsu* sword). In practice, however, two broad criteria influence the choice of individual *nhenkwaa* as envoys. The first consideration relates to the individual skills, of the *ahenkwaa*—competence, trust, diplomatic skills, and overall suitability, and may be regarded as the open-ended criterion. The second is determined by whether a host's stool is regarded as a *benkum* (left) or *nifa* (right) stool in relationship to the *Sika Dwa*, and may be viewed as the restrictive criterion. Hence, among the *amanhene*, for example, the *Bosommuru* sword, which is always placed to the left of the Asantehene when he sits in session, is sent to the Bantamahene (and the Asantehemaa) while the *Mponponsu,* the sword to the right, is used on missions to the Asafohene, Mamponhene, and Dwabenhene. Although the proper expression used is to say that the sword is sent to a particular *omanhene* or *obirempon*, neither the *Mponponsu* itself nor the *Bosommuru* is actually used in travel; an *mponponsuni* or a *bosommuruni*, signifying the office of the sword, goes on the mission.[3] It cannot be ruled out, however, that other considerations such as patronage and reward for past services or favors were factors in the appointment of envoys.

It has been suggested that a large proportion of the Asantehene's *nhenkwaa* may have been recruited from people of servile origins.[4] While this statement might have had some validity in the early years of the Asantehene's household establishment, there is hardly any support or evidence for a persistence of this view today. Indeed, the suggestion of slave origins in any *ahenkwaa* was decidedly rejected by informants to whom the question was put in field interviews. As one thirty-six-year-old *ahenkwaa* who was born at *ahemfie* and had spent all his life there explained, owing to the closeness of the *ahenkwaa* to the person of the Asantehene and the wealth with which the *ahenkwaa* comes into contact in his daily activities, outsiders are unsuitable as *nhenkwaa*.[5]

Three main developments have accounted for the gradual accumulation, at *ahemfie* and elsewhere in their private homes, of people who collectively constitute the Asantehene's body of personal attendants. War captives have in the past provided one source of recruitment. The Asantehene could claim the services of any war captive or his descendants as *ahenkwaa*. Secondly, a number of individuals have become *nhenkwaa* through a system of voluntary association. A practice rooted in friendship, an individual may voluntarily offer himself or his son to the Asantehene as an *ahenkwaa*. Thirdly, if he so desires, an Asantehene is entitled to the services of children born to the stools he has created. It may be said, additionally, that in theory the Asantehene has the jurisdictional right to claim any Asante as *ahenkwaa*. Furthermore, a person may be selected as an *ahenkwaa* as a way of rewarding the individual's father or family for some favor, service, or assistance rendered in the past.[6]

A factor that has facilitated the recruitment of *nhenkwaa* is its hereditary character. Sons of *nhenkwaa* commonly follow in their fathers' footsteps, for many the Gyaase stools are *mma dwa,* that is, stools of patrifiliation.[7] Of the forty *nhenkwaa* who participated in the survey, only four (that is, ten percent) have non-*ahenkwaa* parentage. In contrast, the study indicated not only a strong tendency for the sons of *nhenkwaa* to become *nhenkwaa* too, but also to serve in the particular *fekuo* of their fathers. This trend is clearly borne out in Table 1. In a number of cases the *ahenkwaa* status goes beyond two generations. Yaw Kobi, an *atumtuni* (gun bearer), for instance, is a fourth generation *ahenkwaa*.

Though all coming under the generic name of *nhenkwaa*, the Asantehene's establishment of household attendants is a complex organization that is marked by sharp differentiations of function and role within separate constituent departments known as *nfekuo*. Some of the principal *nhenkwaa nfekuo* have been referred to above. In addition to these may be added the *atumtufo* (gun bearers), *safiesofo* (holders/keepers of drinks), *adumfo* (executioners) and *abrafo* (constabulary). Among the remaining *nhenkwaa nfekuo* of primary significance to the well-being of the Asantehene is the *soodo (sodo)*. The *soodo* (department of cooks) exhibits elements of a complex organization that have become characteristic of the entire *nhenkwaa* institution. Serving under the Soodohene are subgroups of *boodeedwafo* (cutters of plaintain), *fufuwofo* (pounders of fufu), *nfohoofo* (roasters of meat), *mansufo* (providers of drinking water), and *akwanmofo* (suppliers of chewing stick).[8]

Table 1 : The Hereditary Element of Nhenkwaa

Name of Ahenkwaa	Age	Rank of Ahenkwaa	Highest Rank of Father
Kofi Tuo	60	Fotosani	Fotosani
Kwabena Sarkodie	58	Akonwasoani	Akonwasoani
Kwabena Asare	65	Mponponsuni	Mponponsuni
Osei Tutu Asabere	27	Nsumankwaani	Nsumankwaaahene
Moses Anokye	22	Abenaseni	Deboosohene
Kwasi Afari	29	Kaneasoni	Kaneasohene
Kwabena Boaten	52	Fotosani	Fotosani
Opanin Amponsa	62	Kaneasoni	Kaneasohene
Yaw Baafi	36	Fotosani	Sanaahene
Kwabena Oti	65	Kaneasoni	Kaneasohene
Kwame Mensa	40	Patomni	Patomhene
Kofi Afoakwa	42	Somesisini	Somesisini
Kofi Ababio	35	Afenasoani	Mponponsuhene
Kofi Owusu	18	Abenaseni	Abenasehene

Abenase

In 1819 Bowdich made a perceptive allusion to the existence of an official state wardrobe, to which the envoy had access. "When the King sends an ambassador," he observed, "he enriches the splendour of his suite and attire as much as possible" and sometimes "provides [it] entirely." However, as Bowdich noted, this "is all surrendered on the return and forms a sort of state wardrobe."[9] This reference, no doubt, was to the *abenase fekuo,* which has overall responsibility for the Asantehene's clothing and dressing.

The *abenase* stool has a long history, dating to the time of Asantehene Osei Tutu, who is said to have created it after the Denkyira war of 1701.[10] The *fekuo* was reorganized by Asantehene Osei Tutu Kwame after the Fante campaigns of 1806-1807. Fante war prisoners who were taken captive to Kumase became the masons for the construction of separate quarters for the exclusive residence and use of *abenasefo.* To this day the *abenase* has remained one of the principal stools of service (*esom dwa*) of the Asantehene.

Overall supervision of the *abenase* rests with the Deboosohene, who oversees two major divisional heads: the Abenasehene and the Saanahene. The Abenasehene has care of all the principal items of clothing of the Asantehene, including *mpaboa* (sandals), *abotire* (head band) and *danta* (loin cloth); he also has charge over the *nkaneasofo* (lamp bearers) and *mmowerebubufo* (nail cutters). Other *nhenkwaa* coming under the general purview of the Abenasehene are the Asantehene's kente weavers and the people responsible for dressing the *Kete Kese* (the King's bed). In all essentials, then, the Abenasehene may be regarded as head of the Asantehene's wardrobe.[11]

Figure 1 : The Structure of the Abenase

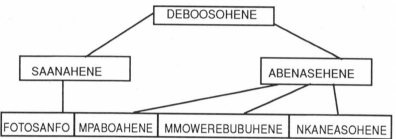

Also coming under the Deboosohene is the Saanahene. This official is responsible for the collection and disbursement of certain types of revenues that accrue to the Asantehene, particularly those derived from court cases, that is, the Asantehene's share of legal fines, fees and *aseda* (thanks-offering). He is also in charge of accounts pertaining to the Akwasidae and Wukudae. In these respects, the Saanahene may be recognized as the Asantehene's Treasurer or Accountant. Working under him are the *afotosanfo*, treasury officials, who use gold-weights to measure gold-dust intended for purchases or donations.[12]

An *ahenkwaa's* life is one of unending service. In return for his hard work and dedication he receives free housing at *ahemfie*. In the past he also received free meals, although today he bears most of the burden of feeding himself. Members of the *nhenkwaa* establishment who are engaged in diplomatic activity regularly derive indirect benefits, primarily by way of gifts, from participation in missions. Gifts given to envoys by their hosts are meant for themselves unless the Asantehene is specifically mentioned as the intended beneficiary. Those *nhenkwaa* who are involved in legal processes such as the summoning of accused persons and witnesses, and participation in the *asemnie* (hearing), often derive fringe benefits in the form of *mmataho* (commissions and fees). These two forms of compensation are no doubt irregular. A more regular support system for *nhenkwaa* is the monthly allowance that is paid to each member through the Treasury of the Kumasi Traditional Council. It is difficult to assess what the average value of an *ahenkwaa* stipend was in the nineteenth century. Suggested figures variously range from l0s:6d, that is, presumably *asuansa,* to £2:7s. In the 1980s, the monthly allowance averages between £10 and £20.[13] It is clear that whereas £20 was enough to support a whole family for a month in the nineteenth century and indeed throughout the greater part of the first half of the twentieth century, the equivalent of ¢40 was woefully inadequate for even a single person in the 1980s. As a result, the majority of *nhenkwaa* now are only partially supported by the Asantehene and have to earn incomes from other sources.

The Asantehene's *nhenkwaa,* as a group, manifest behavior characteristics of unity in diversity. Their unity lies in their corporate identity as servants and in their commonalty of interest as sustainers of the Asante royal establishment; their service and dedication to the occupant of the *Sika Dwa* bind them all together as a single entity. Yet, within this single unit can be identified individual divisions that constitute separate departments. The distinct household as well as governmental duties required of *nhenkwaa* in the care and maintenance of the Asantehene and his administrative system have over time brought about role specialization to such a degree that members of the same *fekuo* not only live in the same quarters but also work and tend to move together. The payment of monthly allowances and the distribution of their share of gifts given to the Asantehene are all done along *nfekuo* lines.

Though the majority of the *nhenkwaa* who were interviewed expressed the opinion that they generally felt that they were sufficiently empowered for the missions they had undertaken, they nevertheless recognized that their activities had on the whole been marked by restrained initiative. Only six of the forty who participated in the survey— and these were all heads or deputy heads of department (*nfekuo*)— indicated that they were at liberty to exercise unlimited power and initiative during their missions. For the most part, *nhenkwaa* portray limited initiative and a want of independence of outlook, as indeed might be expected of a group that is considerably dependent.

Dependence, however, should not be equated with an absence of a sense of pride or a feeling of importance in one's self. Responses to a question which asked the *nhenkwaa* to estimate the importance of their work to the Asantehene's administration left no doubt as to their sentiments on the subject:

How important to Otumfuo's administration do you consider your work as *ahenkwaa*?

Very important	60%
Important	40%

No one rated his work as either "not that important" or "unimportant."

Not only do the *nhenkwaa* entertain a sense of self importance; they are also convinced that they derive a great deal of prestige from their status and activities. Thus, a question on the extent of prestige they enjoy from their work evinced answers that were identical to those on their self-pride:

How much prestige do you derive from your work as *ahenkwaa*?

Very much	40%
Much	60%

A "fair amount of prestige," "little prestige," or "none" drew no response.

If *nhenkwaa* today enjoy such airs of importance at a time when the combined effect of the diminution in the importance of chiefly authority brought about by the emergence of the nation state of Ghana on the one hand, and their need to supplement their meager monthly stipends with incomes derived elsewhere, on the other, has tended to undercut their dependence on the Asantehene, it might be presumed that the *ahenkwaa* feeling of self-pride must have been much more considerable in the nineteenth century. Such indeed was the case, as can be ascertained from one interesting incident which involved Ramseyer and Kühne during their stay in Kumase in the 1870s. According to their own record of the event, the two Basel missionaries were in the midst of a meal preparation when they turned to an *ahenkwaa* who was sitting by to ask for his help in pounding fufu. In talking to the young ahenkwaa, who is unidentified, Ramseyer assumed that he was doing the youngster a favor because he was not involved in any activity at the time and was therefore presumed to have been idle and bored. To the apparent surprise of the two Europeans, the *ahenkwaa* was offended and sharply retorted: "I am an Ashantee, one of the King's slaves (*nhenkwaa*). I have never done such a thing." When, a little later, Ramseyer's wife offered him soap to wash his clothes, the gesture similarly did not go down well with the *ahenkwaa*, who considered the offer as "unbecoming his dignity. "[14] In their view of this incident at least, the Ramseyers and Kühne did not appear to have been in tune with *nhenkwaa* perceptions and attitudes, despite the fact they were in the Asante capital on that occasion for nearly four years; an *ahenkwaa* of the Asantehene, albeit a servant, was held in much higher public esteem than the ordinary citizen. T.B. Freeman, in contrast, showed a more accurate perception of the *ahenkwaa* "mentality" when he made the following observation of an *ahenkwaa* of the *afenasoafo fekuo:*

> The court-messenger in Ashanti bounds along the streets of Kumase with his gold-handled sword of office, or with the golden plate emblazoned on his breast, or the heavy gold manila on his wrist, desirous that all should know he is an important personage, and that his master is indeed the King.[15]

For his loyalty and dedicated service the *ahenkwaa* is eligible for other forms of reward beyond the intangible realm of prestige. A trusted *ahenkwaa* may be given a niece of the Asantehene in marriage.[16] A highly regarded form of recognition is for the Asantehene to attend the funeral of an *ahenkwaa*, his servant.[17] Perhaps the most aspired-to form of honor that the Asantehene can bestow on an *ahenkwaa* is elevation to a stool headship. When Otumfuo Opoku Ware II elevated Antwi Buasiako to the status of *okyeame* on 9 May 1977, thereby increasing the number of the *akyeame* to fourteen, it was certainly in recognition of his years of meritorious service to the *Sika Dwa*.[18]

For most of the people who live at *ahemfie*, *ahenkwaa* is a lifelong status. Many of those interviewed indicated that they had spent practically all their lives at Manhyia (the Asantehene's palace). The participants in the survey ranged in age from 18 to 70 years, while their average age was 42.8 years, a figure which suggests that *nhenkwaa* remain in their position to a mature age. Yet, avenues for advancement are limited. Most *nhenkwaa* begin at the level of *ahenkwaa kuma* (junior *ahenkwaa*), are advanced to a full *ahenkwaa* status after a few years, and remain there for the rest of their lives. Few are advanced to "*fekuohene*," simply because the number of such departmental headships is small in comparison to the total number of *nhenkwaa* within each *fekuo*. Only 6 of the 40 *nhenkwaa* who were surveyed had been promoted, and only once, although their average age was over 40 years.

Notwithstanding the limited opportunities for advancement and the meager incomes that most *nhenkwaa* face, it must be pointed out that a general mood of satisfaction with their position exists within the *nhenkwaa* ranks (although this feeling is stronger among the older *nhenkwaa* than with the younger ones, who may not necessarily like their position). It is an expression of pride in membership of the *ahenkwaa* institution that individuals who begin life as *nhenkwaa* but later resign to pursue careers in public life sometimes take up their respective *nhenkwaa* positions during festivals and other traditional ceremonies.[19] Despite the attractions of more lucrative careers outside the royal household today, the *ahenkwaa* establishment remains an institution of largely voluntary service. The continued existence of the *nhenkwaa* lies in their indispensability to the survival of the Asante royal institution, of which the maintenance of external diplomatic communication is only a part. *Nhenkwaa* attitudes, both today and in the nineteenth century, provide us with valuable insights into the outlook and perceptions of a group of people, many of whom served in diplomatic capacities. It is worthy of note that the nineteenth-century attitudes are interestingly reflected in the *nhenkwaa* of today.

Asomfo

The Asomfohene exercises control over a large body of "public servants" who, together with the *nhenkwaa* living at *aborosanase*, that is, the storey-building section of the Asantehene's palace, carry the major burden of the Asantehene's day-to-day administration. In broad terms the *asomfo* group must be viewed as encompassing the "attendants who live at *ahemfie* and the people who live elsewhere but serve the Asantehene everyday or regularly."[20] By definition, *asomfo* are people whose duty it is to render service (*esom*). Beyond the *nhenkwaa* living at *ahemfie* who are theoretically on duty twenty-four hours a day, seven days a week, each *asomfo* functionary or category of *asomfo* has a specific day of service (*esom da*) every week. On such "service days" the functionary is required to report at *ahemfie* whether or not there is actual need for his services, and he may not leave *ahemfie* before 5 p.m. Thus, the Asomfohene has to be present at *ahemfie* every Tuesday, which is his *esom da*. On a typical *esom da*, the Asomfohene must be in attendance when the Asantehene pours libation and performs purification rites on behalf of the Asante nation. This over, the Asomfohene in turn takes his sword home to purify it, but the sword is returned to *ahemfie* at about 4 p.m.[21]

The exact size of the *asomfo* establishment is unknown, although Kwaku Kankam, the Asomfohene, in 1980 claimed authority over several thousand men. The *asomfo* constitute an essential component of the functionaries who provide not only the basics of the Asante central administration but also the effective links of communication with the outside world.

The *asomfo* stool is an old one, having been created by Asantehene Osei Tutu prior to the Denkyira War,[22] that is, presumably towards the close of the seventeenth century. That the *asomfo* stool history recorded by Joseph Agyeman-Duah lists only eight Asomfohene for a period of about 300 years might at first sight raise two questions: one, the possibility of omission, and two, the long duration of Asomfohene occupancies. Taken that the *asomfo* stool is indeed 300 years old, it is to be presumed that the Asomfohene remain on the stool for an average of nearly 38 years. Interestingly, however, the Agyeman-Duah *asomfo* stool chronology is corroborated by Asomfohene Kwaku Kankam II, who found nothing unusual about 38-year regnal periods. Indeed, the Asomfohene remarked that he had been told by the stool elders that his predecessors were blessed with longevity and that the incumbency of Asomfohene Kofi Nkwantabisa, for example, was a very long one. He also cited the example of Asomfohene Kwabena Safo, who took office during the reign of Asantehene Opoku Ware I and remained on the stool till the administration of Asantehene Osei Tutu Kwame. The incumbent Asomfohene, Kwaku Kankam II, had himself been on the stool for 37 years already by 1980![23]

Afenasoafo and Nseniefo

If a single group of functionaries is to be recognized as that of the Asante official envoy *par excellence*, it is the *afenasoafo* (sword bearers). From early in the nineteenth century the Asantehenes made progressively increasing use of the *afenasoafo* as officials specializing in the conveyance of dispatches and messages, as opposed to the old practice involving the engagement of traders and others whose functions did not normally involve diplomatic activity.[24] It was this trend towards role specialization that made the *afenasoani* Asante's basic category of diplomats. Thus besides their main function as transmitters of messages, the *afenasoafo* came to assume more intricate diplomatic roles, including negotiating for peace and leading trade delegations.

At home the *afenasoafo* were the main diplomatic channels of communication between the Asantehene and visiting envoys. Throughout Dupuis' stay in Kumase in 1820, for example, he was summoned to attend audiences with the Asantehene by *afenasoafo*. During receptions for foreign guests, the "royal messengers stood behind the sovereign, shouldering by the blades large crooked sabres, the emblems of their offices, and displaying the reversed hilts, cased in thin gold shething."[25] The *afenasoafo* apparently held their swords in a reversed position so as to render the golden hilts conspicuous.

Next to the *afenasoafo*, the *nseniefo* (heralds) were the most important agents of communication in the nineteenth century. Very rarely, perhaps never, did a mission lack the presence of a member of either the *afenasoafo*, or the *nseniefo*, or most likely both. This practice has survived to the present day, as *afenasoafo* and *nseniefo* continue to provide the essential components of Asante's corps of envoys.

As criers, the principal function of the *nseniefo* has been the maintenance of order at meetings of the Asantemanhyiamu, the council of state, and whenever the Asantehene sits in court. Order is maintained through their constant shouts of "*tie*" (listen). It was this activity which Bowdich observed in 1817 and described as the "common exclamations" of "Tehoo! Tehing! Odidee! Be silent! Be quiet! Pray hear!" that were "incessantly uttered" by the *nseniefo*.[27] Half a century later, Bonnat reported a similar scene in which "the court criers, a kind of usher responsible for keeping silence," stood behind the Asantehene together with other functionaries. "It is these who, at intervals, utter the cry tie! tie! tie!, which is to say Listen! listen! listen!"[28] The main function of the *nseniefo*, then, is the maintenance of silence and order. In the exact words of Nseniehene Kwasi Addai III, his men "can silence anybody." He himself likened his main role to that of a "Police Superintendent" and "Director of Information."[29]

Another aspect of the Nseniehene's role, as information director, is the dissemination of decrees. Within Greater Asante, the *nseniefo* are charged with the responsibility of publicizing all new decrees and regulations, after the legislative processes involving the Inner Council and the Asantemanhyiamu have been conducted. The Nseniehene, as proclaimer of decrees, orders the *dawurubofo* (gong-gong beaters) to announce the new regulation.[30] In the case of new legislative instruments like the promulgation of the Bowdich Treaty of 1817, the *nseniefo* traveled to all principal towns and villages to assemble the people by gong-gongs or horns and announce the decree. It was the practice on such occasions for all who heard it to reply by a special cry according to the circumstances.[31] Bowdich, who closely observed the judicial process, noted that after the counselors had announced the new treaty to the Inner Council and the Asantemanhyiamu, "Kwadwo Appani (Kwadwo Ampan), the chief crier, proclaimed it to the people, who shouted their thanks."[32]

The Nseniehene exercises other information control responsibilities. News of the death of an Asantehene cannot be released until the Nseniehene, accompanied by the Asomfohene, have gone round to announce it. In the same vein the Nseniehene is the primary official responsible for formally announcing a new Asantehene, after the selection processes have been completed. When, for example, the Asantehemaa's choice of a new Asantehene to succeed Osei Agyeman Prempe II fell upon Nana Poku in 1971, it was a mission composed of the Nseniehene, the Akyeamehene and the Asomfohene that went round the states to announce it.[33] As a senior state functionary, the Nseniehene has other important responsibilities, notably relating to the installation of new chiefs and during major festivals. It is the Nseniehene who pours white clay—a symbol of victory or acceptance—on the Asantehene during his installation, or on other chiefs during the swearing of the oath of allegiance to the Asantehene. It is also he who tastes the drink first before the Asantehene drinks during Adae ceremonies. During periods of travel embargo in the nineteenth century, the Nseniehene and the Asomfohene were jointly charged with responsibility for blocking the roads. In such situations the two controlled travel out of Asante.[34]

Although *nseniefo* were members of most embassies in the nineteenth century (see Chapter 4 below) and continue to feature prominently in a number of Asante missions today, the Nseniehene's actual participation in missions is limited. He is very seldom appointed to embassies; those rare occasions of participation are invariably limited to major missions either to districts or states outside Kumase, or to welcome visiting dignitaries into the capital; and the Nseniehene normally does not go on missions unless they include the Akyeamehene. Nseniehene, Kwasi Addai III, could recall participating in only a few recent missions.[35]

The *nsenie* stool is one of the oldest in Asante, having been created in the pre-Osei Tutu era during Oti Akenten's time. The first *nsenie* incumbent was Kra Kose ne Boako, a name which clearly depicts the fundamental role of *nseniefo* as envoys (*kra kose*).[36] In broad terms the Nseniehene falls under the Gyaase establishment, although he has direct access to the Asantehene (without having to pass through the Gyaasehene). As the occupant of an *esom dwa* (stool of service) the Nseniehene is obligated to attend the Asantehene on specific days of service (*esom da*), which in this case are Mondays and Thursdays, the two days when the Asantehene normally holds court sessions. He is also enjoined to be present at Akwasidae, Fofie, and indeed at all state festivals and public durbars when the Asantehene sits in session.[37]

The exact size of the *nsenie* establishment is not known, but their number is presently large and must have been even larger in the nineteenth century. It is generally believed that the *nsenie fekuo* numbered

at least 1,000 in the nineteenth century.[38] In the 1810s Bowdich estimated that upwards of one hundred of their number were always in
attendance during Asantemanhyiamu sessions.[39] Today, the
Nseniehene continues to head a large establishment whose subheads
include the Dawurubofohene, Nkyetiahene, Abontendomhene,
Esenkwadwomhene, Brosankohene, and Mmammahene.[40]

In the nineteenth century the *nseniefo* also featured prominently
in the reception of visiting dignitaries in Kumase. While the delegations that welcomed visiting diplomats were headed by the Nseniehene,
the Akyeamehene, and the Asomfohene, it was the rank and file of the
nsenie fekuo that swelled up their numbers. Ramseyer and Kühne,
who, though captives, were impressed by the diplomatic welcome they
received in Kumase in 1869, did not fail to comment on the participation of the *nseniefo* in the ceremony: when the Asantehene rose to
return the greetings of his guests, he was heralded by some eighty
individuals, each wearing a cap of monkey skin, adorned by a golden
plate.[41] Their striking appearance caught the attention of most visitors.
Bowdich easily recognized the *nseniefo* by the monkey skin cap they
wore.[42] Hutton was equally struck by their "singular appearance, wearing monkey-skin caps, with a gold plate in front, and long tails hanging
down their backs."[43] Information received from orally transmitted sources
indicates that it was not unusual for a hostile host to cut off an *nsenieni's*
finger as a declaration of war or rebellion. The Nseniehene, Kwadwo
Ampan, is said to have lost four fingers. In some cases the *nseniefo*
were killed altogether by a host as a sign of revolt. Considering the
dangers inherent, on the one hand, in conducting a mission to a state
which was known to be rebellious or whose loyalty was suspect, and
on the other, in announcing sometimes unpopular decrees in distant
districts, the life of an *nsenieni* must have been fraught with uncertainties. But as Nseniehene Kwasi Addai III viewed the situation, these are
some of the hazards of the profession, for after all an *nsenieni's nsabrane*
(appellation) in those days was 'ko ma yenku wo,"that is, "go and be
killed."[44]

The primary functions of the *nseniefo*, then, lay in the maintenance of order, the publication of law, and the dissemination of official
information. It was through the performance of these judicial and legislative tasks that the *nseniefo* acquired the experience and expertise
that qualified them for diplomatic assignments in the reception of official guests and in the conduct of embassies to the provinces and to the
representatives of foreign governments.

Akyeame

The *akyeame* represented a category of senior officials who were some-times called upon to undertake diplomatic tasks as an extension of their domestic functions. The word *okyeame* has been variously trans-lated as "linguist," "spokesman," "interpreter," and "secretary," each of which is an inadequate rendition of the position and role of this official. Attention was drawn as early as 1903 to the inadequacies of the term "linguist" for *okyeame*. "He is not a person skilled in the tongues of men," wrote Casely Hayford, about the *akyeame* in Akan society. "He was called a linguist first by a half-educated native interpreter, tasked to explain his position to the white man, and as 'linguist' he has been known ever since in the language of law and politics on the Gold Coast."[45] Although admittedly the *okyeame* exhibits a great deal of lan-guage competency and skills—often making "use freely of parables to illustrate points in his speech" and indulging in epigrams—the realiza-tion that he is not a linguist as such led Casely Hayford to suggest the term "spokesman." Yet, while the word "spokesman" evidently encom-passes a broader spectrum of the role of the *okyeame* than does "lin-guist," this term is nevertheless narrow. Indeed, Casely Hayford him-self realized this limitation and added: "He is more than a spokesman...he is one of the main props in the Native State System."[46]

The legal mind of this early commentator of Gold Coast tradi-tional political systems led him to essay an enlightened discussion of the *akyeame*:

> He is a sort of confidential officer, who is always about the person of the King or Chief, and is his mouthpiece in every public function, as well as in judicial proceedings. The Lin-guist is generally the repository, or if you like, a walking en-cyclopedia, of all traditional knowledge and information in connection with the stool under which he serves. He is sup-posed to be acquainted with the etiquette of the court, and, in case of a new succession, it will be his duty to instruct the new monarch in the functions of the Crown.[47]

Concluding, Casely Hayford considered "the members of the linguistic body about the most enlightened men of the kingdom" of Asante, where "the art of 'linguistic' oratory is at its best."[48] The *akyeame* indeed are the principal advisors to kings. Their vast store of knowledge and inti-mate relationship with kings make them specially suited as individuals who can provide the best counseling to their monarchs. In view of the inappropriateness of the terms "linguist" and "spokesman," the word "counselor" is a more accurate description of the *okyeame*.

Among the manifold functions performed by the *akyeame* was one of assisting the Asantehene in judicial cases. They served as a "jury," and in the discharge of this duty they followed a judicial process not unlike present-day practices. The *akyeame* examined defendants, retired in a body to consider their judgment, and recommended their verdict to the Asantehene. Although the decision was announced as the Asantehene's, it was doubtlessly based on the *akyeame's* recommendation.[49] Though the *akyeame* were not councilors as such, several of them frequently held membership seats on the Inner Council, which operated as a regular decision-making and judicial body. "As a reward for valuable services," Casely Hayford noted, an *okyeame* "may occasionally be promoted to the King's Council , in which capacity he will practically be the ruling voice warranted by his great experience."[50] Thus, several *akyeame* attended the Council session that met on 22 May 1817 to review Asante-British relations during Bowdich's visit to Kumase. Gyakye *okyeame* Kwadwo Adusel Kyakya and Akankade *okyeame* Kwasi Kankam were definitely members in the 1810s. Similarly, Okyeame Boakye Tenten of the Boakye Yam Panin stool, Okyeame Kwaku Poku Agyeman of the Domakwai, Okyeame Yaw Nantwi of the Akankade, and Okyeame Kwasi Apea of the Butuakwa all held seats on the Asantemanhyiamu under Asantehene Kofi Kakari's administration in the 1870s.[51]

It is not known whether the Asante bureaucracy in the nineteenth century developed to the point that the *akyeame* could be regarded as constituting a cabinet. Although they carried the major executive burden of the administration, the evidence that they operated as a body meeting regularly to take major national decisions (hence a cabinet) is weak. Even so, visitors who possessed a keen insight into the workings of the Asante bureaucracy were not reluctant to draw the comparison, impliedly at least, between the body of *akyeame* and a cabinet in the European tradition. If the *akyeame* collectively were not the exact equivalent of a modern cabinet, each of the principal counselors, as head of a distinct administrative department, was not seen to fall short of a "minister." Thus, at various times, Asante Agyei was viewed as a "foreign minister," Adusei Kyakya as a "confidential minister," Gyaasewahene Opoku Frefre, who had "care of all the tribute, which are deposited," as the equivalent of a Chancellor of the Exchequer, and Akyeamehene Kwaku Poku Agyeman as "minister of foreign affairs."[52]

It was also a common practice for an *okyeame* to be attached to an army. In such situations he would carry responsibility for directing negotiations and exacting taxes, after the conclusion of the campaign, to cover the expenses of the war. Commenting on this military function of the counselor, Bowdich noted:

> No Ashantee army ever proceeds on a campaign without one of them [the *akyeame*] being attached to it, and if the King is present, three or four, to settle the tributes, to make the great laws [treaties], and to try and condemn enemies or rebels at the moment of their falling into their power.[53]

In an earlier observation, Bowdich had stated:

> One of the King's linguists always accompanies an army of any consequence, to whom all the politics of the war are entrusted, and whose talent and intelligence in negotiating, are expected to mature the fruits of the military genius of the general, and to reimburse the expense of the war by heavy fines and contributions.[54]

The *akyeamehene* was the principal diplomatic channel between visiting diplomats and the Asantehene. This was certainly the case with Kwame Poku Agyeman, Domakwaihene, and Akyeamehene during the Kwaku Dua Panin administration. Thus, Okyeame Poku Agyeman was entirely responsible for the visits of Reverend Freeman to Kumase (1839-41). Accompanied by "a large train of attendants with gold-handled swords and canes richly ornamented with gold," the Akyeamehene welcomed the Wesleyan Minister into the city.[55] Throughout Freeman's stay, he was "under the watchful care" of Okyeame Poku Agyeman who, as chief of protocol, conducted and coordinated all activities in connection with the visits and supervised the movements of the official guest.[56] The Akyeamehene was responsible for Freeman's accommodation, arranged and supervised tours of the city for him, served as the principal channel of official communication between the guest and his host, and was in attendance at interviews between the two.[57] At the conclusion of the visits, Okyeame Poku Agyeman also directed the departure ceremonies and delivered the Asantehene's parting gifts. Freeman admitted enjoying "many advantages from being placed by the King under his care," including advice on matters of conduct acceptable in court circles. For playing a role comparable to a modern chief of the president's staff, counselor Poku Agyeman was the only person in the administration who was allowed to visit the Asantehene anytime he pleased.[58] Akyeamehene Kwame Poku Agyeman, as counselor in charge of foreign affairs, exercised protocol responsibilities with respect to all foreign guests.

Akyeamehene Kwame Poku Agyeman's role as chief of protocol was not by any means unique or isolated. Kwaku Poku Agyeman, the

Domakwaihene during Asantehene Kofi Kakari's administration, played a comparable role. As Akyeamehene and a senior member of the Council, "Nsuase" Poku took a leading role in foreign policy decisions of the day and was indeed regarded by at least Ramseyer and Kühne as Minister of Foreign Affairs.[59] Similarly, Osei Tutu Kwame's Domakwaihene, Kwadwo Adusei Kyakya, performed identical functions for visiting envoys in the 1810s and early 1820s. Thus, British Consul Hutton sought audiences with the Asantehene through Adusei Kyakya. By gifts and other means Hutton sought to influence Adusei Kyakya, who, as a minister in charge of foreign affairs, was closest to the Asantehene.[60]

Territorially, each town, district, or region in metropolitan as well as Greater Asante was represented in the capital by an *okyeame* who was responsible for reporting on the state of his areas to the Council.[61] This is the system to which Bowdich had drawn attention in 1819:

> Every subject state was placed under the immediate care of some Ashantee chief generally resident in the capital, who seldom visited it but to receive the tribute from the native ruler, for whose conduct he was in a reasonable degree responsible.[62]

Bowdich cited as examples that Gyaasewahene Opoku Frefre had the care of Akwamu; Adumhene Adum Ata of Nsuta, to be identified as Longero, an area within the bend of the Black Volta; and Adontenhene Owusu Nkwantabisa of Daboya (Gonja). This system of representation has continued to the present day. Thus, at the time of the survey, Baafour Akoto, the occupant of the Butuakwa stool and one of fourteen Asante *akyeame*,[63] exercised responsibility for Dwaben, Kokofu, Nkoranza, Agona, Adonten, Ankobea, and Yendi;[64] Akyeamehene, Nsuase Poku, had authority over Kumawu, Asumegya, Adanse, and the Benkum towns, while Boakye Yam Panin *okyeame*, Boakye Tenten, was responsible for Bekwae and Tekyiman.[65] The exercise of this responsibility took two forms: first, the *okyeame* usually headed major delegations to his areas; and second, the town or district sought audience with the Asantehene through the counselor responsible for the area. In many cases the latter arrangement could be seen as amounting to what in legal terms was known as an *adamfo* relationship, which Rattray viewed in a patron-client perspective:

> Because of the fact that they are not resident in the capital town, certain persons required representation. Further, the institution of 'adamfo' was given rise to by 'the demands of Court etiquette'. The 'adamfo' acted as an intermediary. In

certain respects the 'adamfo' can be looked upon as a 'patron' or 'friend at Court'.[66]

In addition, certain *akyeame* stools carried responsibility for specific foreign states or powers. Thus, the Butuakwa stool was directly responsible for Fante and the British, while responsibility for Elmina and the Dutch rested with the Boakye Yam Kuma stool.

The principles underlying *akyeame* representation point to questions both of jurisdiction and specialization; the counselor's responsibility for his town and districts derived as much from his stool rights as from the accumulated expertise acquired through the exercise of control over the areas. These considerations then provided the rationalization for the appointment of individual *akyeame* as resident commissioners and ambassadors to their areas. Thus, the appointments as resident ambassadors of Okyeame Kwame Butuakwa for Fante in the 1810s and of Kwadwo Akyampon for Elmina in the 1820s, for example, can both be explained by the fact that their respective stools of Butuakwa and Boakye Yam Kuma, of which they were incumbents, carried responsibility for those areas. An important diplomatic function of the *akyeame* therefore was that "they were also sent, in times of peace, as envoys and ambassadors." [67]

The *afenasoafo, nseniefo,* and *akyeame* were the regular—though by no means the only— officials engaged in diplomatic service. At a time and in a society where diplomatic service was yet to be regarded as an exclusive career for most office-holders, the Asantehene employed all and sundry in diplomatic roles as determined by the needs of the situation and the skills of the individual. Thus, at various times some *ahenemma* (princes), members of the royal family, and all ranges of *asomfo*, including *akradwarefo* (soul washers), were called upon to undertake diplomatic tasks. A discussion of embassies involving some members of these groups will be undertaken in Chapter Four.

Classification of Ambassadors

Two main categories of diplomats could be identified: the career ambassador and the *ad hoc* ambassador. By definition the career ambassador devoted the greater part of his life to diplomatic service as Asante's representative, who either resided in a province with accreditation to the area and/or a foreign power, or was appointed to a number of individual missions. This class of diplomats could be subdivided into three: the ambassador-at-large (an example of which was John Owusu Ansa, Sr.), the roving ambassador (such as Owusu Done), and the resident ambassador (an example being Kwame Butuakwa). The *ad hoc* ambassador represented the official who, without being a career diplomat, was appointed to a specific mission. His appointment terminated with the conclusion of the mission. If he was a regular domestic office-holder, he would revert to his former position at the end of his diplomatic assignment. While all career ambassadors were invariably Asantes, appointment as an *ad hoc* ambassador was not contingent upon Asante citizenship. Although space limitations would not permit an analysis of all Asante diplomats who fell under these categories, aspects of the diplomatic careers of examples from each group will be examined so as to bring out their distinguishing characteristics.

The Ambassador-at-large. The ambassador-at-large was Asante's highest ranking diplomat. With or without specific mandates, he was expected to represent all the interests of his nation with foreign governments. Like the resident ambassador, he was generally based at one center, although, unlike the former, the ambassador-at-large's jurisdiction extended to wherever Asante concerns were at stake. His functions were therefore without rigid limits, except for specific missions he was called upon to undertake. From his residence, the ambassador-at-large was automatically an *ex officio* member of all delegations sent to foreign governments that were based in his area. In this sense, then, his position was not unlike that of a present-day permanent representative of a government in a foreign capital. Optimally, the ambassador-at-large's role was that of the official propagandist, advertiser, and interpreter of his government's policies to foreign administrations.

John Owusu Ansa, Sr., was the best known example of the Asante ambassador-at-large.[68] Based for the most part at his Cape Coast residence, he was the principal channel of diplomatic communication between Asante and the British and Dutch administrators at Cape Coast and Elmina, respectively. He provided the vital liaison role either directly on his own or indirectly, by attaching himself to visiting Asante missions. Throughout the 1870s and early 1880s, Owusu Ansa played the utility role of the senior diplomat who housed and counseled visiting Asante ambassadors, including Kofi Afrifa, Kotirko, Kwame Asabi Antwi, and Boakye Tenten. Thus, an 1881 mission to Cape Coast, which was led by Asabi Antwi and was dispatched to extradite the refugee Owusu Taseamandi (see Chapter 4), lodged at his house. He frequently joined visiting envoys to interviews with the British and Dutch administrators at Cape Coast and Elmina, often acting as spokesman. British Administrator Salmon confirmed in a communication to Governor-in-Chief Hennessy in 1872: "Mr. Ansah always accompanied the envoys and seemed to act as their chief advisor."[69]

In 1881 Owusu Ansa did formally write to Governor Griffith for authorization from the British "to act in the capacity of resident ambassador at Cape Coast through whom all messages should be delivered to your Excellency, and forwarded to the King of Ashanti."[70] In doing so, he was seeking formal recognition from the British for a role he had evidently been playing for years, and with authorization from Asante. Indeed, Owusu Ansa had been acting as an intermediary between Asante and the British, particularly on questions relating to war and peace, as far back as the 1850s. In 1853, for instance, he was directly involved in the Asante-British diplomatic negotiations that resulted in the withdrawal of the Asante forces that had invaded the coast. Writing to London in 1854, Reverend Freeman accordingly recognized the importance of Owusu Ansa's mediation role in 1853 and gave him due credit for the normalization of Asante-British relations.[71] During the periods of tense relations that centered around the detention of European captives Ramseyer, Kühne, and Bonnat in Kumase (1869–1873) and the alleged declaration of war by Asante (1881), Owusu Ansa's mediation efforts once again came into play. Commenting on Asante's final success in averting war in 1881, he disclosed: "I advised the King to send a man of the first importance, and particularly named Prince Buaki [Boakye], to negotiate and sue for peace." Considering the very delicate and exacting nature of the discussions which he, in conjunction with Okyeame Boakye Tenten, conducted with Governor Samuel Rowe in 1881, Owusu Ansa's own profession of satisfaction with his role in "the very favourable and successful termination of the negotiations" between the two sides must have seemed somewhat restrained.[72]

As ambassador-at-large Owusu Ansa performed numerous other tasks, often displaying a large measure of personal initiative. He directed discussions in 1871 on Asante's position on the Anglo-Dutch exchange of forts at Elmina; placed an order for the purchase of ammunitions (300 sniders) from England to aid him in his reorganization of the Asante army; negotiated and pleaded for the release of Akyampon Yaw, the Asante resident ambassador for Elmina and Dutch affairs who was twice arrested by Dutch officials, in 1871 and 1872; and generally interceded on behalf of Asante traders who fell into trouble.[73] When, in 1882, rumors circulated about an alleged sacrifice of 200 girls in Kumase, Owusu Ansa became the *fidei defensor* who upheld the government's cause, image, and position, and disclaimed the reports as shameful lies.[74]

The Roving Ambassador. Also enjoying the rank of a senior diplomat, the roving ambassador's mission was however such that its conduct necessitated considerable travel to several areas. He was therefore of a status and role identical to those of a Traveling Commissioner. Unlike the ambassador-at-large, the roving ambassador was initially charged with a specific mandate, although he was generally given considerable jurisdictional power over all matters that, within reasonable judgment, affected the interests of Asante, and he was permitted to travel to other locations as necessitated by the objectives of the mission. In consequence, it was within his discretion to make on-the-spot decisions or to refer matters to the capital.

Among the nineteenth-century diplomats of note in this category was *oheneba* Owusu Dome, a son of Asantehene Osei Kwame. From the ominous beginnings of early banishment, Owusu Dome rose to become Asante's roving ambassador in Fante and his government's prime negotiator with the British in the early 1820s. Prior to his entry upon the diplomatic scene in 1820, Owusu Dome had been well acquainted with the Asante administrative systems, having held office within the *atenefo fekuo* (torchbearers department).[75]

The background to the embassy which Owusu Dome led to the British administration in January 1820 lay in the inadequacies of the Bowdich Treaty of 1817 as a working basis for an Asante-British understanding. According to the Asantehene's copy which was retained in Kumase, conditions existed which both enjoined the British administrators to eliminate rebellious conduct on the part of the coastal inhabitants and imposed fines on all individuals and groups for failure to carry out their obligations. On the strength of this understanding, Owusu Dome was commissioned with the full powers commensurate with the status of a roving ambassador—he was empowered to negotiate and resolve the whole dispute—and authorized to demand fines.[76] The appointment of the Owusu Dome mission itself followed a full year of fruitless diplomatic efforts by which the Asantehene had sought to impress upon British administrators the necessity of complying with existing agreements.

Accompanied by a numerous retinue which included 500 armed men and a party of about 1,000 attendants and bearers, Owusu Dome made a gallant entry into Cape Coast in early January 1820. His staff included Okyeame Ammo Panin and two Muslims who may have been attached to the embassy to perform functions related to record keeping and spiritual protection. At the embassy's first meeting with Governor J. Hope-Smith and the elders and *ahene* (chiefs) of Cape Coast on 7 January, the ambassador outlined his mission before the castle officials, carefully retracing the whole history of the dispute. In a long speech said to have lasted two hours, Owusu Dome, through the medium of Okyeame Ammo Panin who acted as spokesman, laid chiefly hold on the stipulations of the Asante-British Treaty of 1817, accusing the British of failure to carry out their obligations as demanded by its terms. Armed with the full powers with which he had been vested, Owusu Dome then proceeded to impose fines of 1,600 ounces of gold each on the British administration and the town of Cape Coast.[77]

At a subsequent meeting on 9 January, Owusu Dome repeated the fine demand and hinted that non-compliance with this condition might possibly provoke war. Joseph Dupuis, who had shortly before arrived on the scene as a direct representative of the British government (rather than the Royal Africa Company which then controlled the British settlements on the coast), was impressed with the careful diplomacy of the Asante envoy. However, the intransigence of British officials would have led to an impasse, but for the timely intervention of Dupuis, who offered to proceed to Kumase and personally settle the matter. In the event, Owusu Dome remained in Cape Coast to await further developments and instructions from headquarters. But as a direct representative of the Asantehene, he assured consul-designate Dupuis of his safety and that of other members of his party while in Asante, emphasizing that the persons of ambassadors were at all times held inviolable in Asante.[78]

On Dupuis' return to Cape Coast he was accompanied by an Asante embassy which had been instructed to proceed to England with gifts for the British crown, a universal practice that was in unison with African tradition among friendly countries.[79] However, the envoys who were to have accompanied Dupuis were denied passage in the boat that was to have taken them to England, and the castle in other ways failed to cooperate with the Asante embassy. In the circumstances, Owusu Dome remained in Cape Coast on Dupuis' assurance that he would arrange for the Asante envoys to leave, once he arrived in England.

While the Asante delegation was waiting in Cape Coast with the Asantehene's sanction, Owusu Dome's position and functions quickly assumed the additional dimension of a resident ambassador. The Dutch administration at Elmina certainly saw him in this light, and as an ambassador who carried jurisdiction "for the settlement of whatever problems" that might arise.[80] Indeed, Owusu Dome was apparently empowered to secure the services of Elmina, if need arose, in the event of an armed conflict. Giving critical appraisals of the political climate of the area to Kumase, he may have had wind of the change that was being contemplated about the official assumption of control of the settlements and might have apprised his government of this move. The Asante ambassador bore the issue of eight months' waiting "with admirable patience and forbearance even without a murmur."[81]

Meanwhile, a local Fante dispute that was to further test Owusu Dome's diplomatic abilities was erupting; it involved Opentri, a man who acted in the capacity of the Asantehene's *osafohene* (captain) for Abora Dunkwa, and Tando, a resident of the outlying area of Cape Coast. As Asante resident with jurisdiction over the area, Owusu Dome was authorized by the Asantehene to investigate the matter and hold a court of inquiry. In early February 1820, while the investigations were in progress, Opentri executed a runaway slave of his at Mouri. When the British administration heard of this development, it quickly dispatched to Mouri a detachment of ninety soldiers and eight officers who surprised and killed Opentri. Because the British were aware that Opentri's conduct was already under investigation, their action in taking the matter into their own hands and in killing Opentri met with Owusu Dome's disapproval. He pointed out to the British Governor that if he had any reasons to be displeased with Opentri's actions, he should have raised the objection with the Asantehene through him. He also dispatched an express messenger to Kumase to report the incident and to request instructions. At the same time, in line with his authority as roving ambassador, he went to Elmina to explain the circumstances surrounding Opentri's death and to alert the people to stand by in case their assistance was needed in the eventuality of an outbreak of war.[82] As no satisfactory resolution of the dispute was in sight, Owusu Dome, following directives from the central government and within his jurisdiction as roving ambassador, retired from Cape Coast and established his headquarters at Manso on the Cape Coast-Kumase route in March 1821. Concurrent with this move, he ordered a cessation of trade. Reindorf who wrote towards the close of the century and derived a great deal of his information from orally transmitted sources, recalled that at this time "trade was entirely stopped."[83] Although the matter was not fully settled, Owusu Dome was soon afterwards recalled to the capital.

Showing remarkable maturity for his youthful age—he was a man "apparently between the ages of thirty and thirty-five" at the time of Dupuis' visit [84]—Owusu Dome employed skillful diplomacy in averting open warfare in situations which were fraught with grave conflicts. Evidently operating under provocations, he bore the castle's affronts to his person with remarkable tolerance and restraint at a time when a less tactful person might have resorted to open hostility. It is a credit to Owusu Dome's versatility and skills that he responded admirably to unexpected changes in the local situation which led him to perform the role of a roving ambassador and establish administrative bases at

Cape Coast and subsequently at Manso.

In space and time, the role of the roving ambassador and the office of the resident ambassador might in some instances overlap. The major distinction between the two lay in the discretionary powers which the former possessed to establish bases at locations that seemed appropriate for the execution of his mission, in contrast to the latter who was posted to a single location. This was an important distinction in territorial terms between the appointment, for example, of Owusu Dome, and those of men like Kofi Afrifa and Kwame Bosommuru Dwira, who served as resident ambassadors at Cape Coast in the 1870s.

The Resident Ambassador. The resident ambassador was the local diplomatic representative of the Asantehene. He was usually permitted a great deal of jurisdictional powers, leverage, and local initiative. Within discretion, his scope included all the interests of Asante. He was permitted to establish a local office, staffed by subordinate officers working under him.

The office of the resident ambassador was a historical outgrowth of Asante's policy of provincial administration. The character of Asante's provincial administration initially virtually left previous chiefs in their positions, as long as they submitted to the Asantehene's authority. This was a situation that was strewn with inherent dangers, and it was the need to counteract this weakness that partly led to the creation of the office of the resident commissioner as a check on the activities of provincial chiefs and also as an on-the-spot direct representative of the central government. Brodie Cruickshank, whose long years of residence and administrative experience in the Gold Coast provided him with a deep understanding of traditional political structures, thus commented on Asante's provincial policy of administration, which gave birth to the resident commissioner:

> It was no part of the Ashantee policy, however, to alter the government of the conquered country. The chiefs of the different tribes remained in possession of what power the conqueror thought fit to leave them, with the style and rank of a captain of the king; and in that capacity they acted as so many lieutenants, governing the country in the king's name, at the same time that they continued to receive the allegiance and service of their own vassals and slaves.

> But the king was not content to leave the government entirely in the hands of the native chiefs, who might possibly in the course of time rally the prostrate energies of the country and combine to throw off his yoke. In consequence of this

suspicion, which ever haunts the minds of usurpers, he appointed pro-consuls of the Ashantee race, men of trust and confidence, to reside with the fallen chiefs, to notify to them the royal will, to exercise a general superintendence over them, and especially to guard against and to spy out any conspiracies that might be formed to recover their independence.[85]

Thus it came about that administrative machineries developed under which resident commissioners or representatives were set up with responsibility for such areas as Elmina, Akuapem, and English, Danish, and Dutch Accra in the early nineteenth century.

As an agent of provincial administration, the resident commissioner was charged with responsibility for ensuring the continued subordination of his province to the Asantehene's authority, towards which end he was authorized to set up a court of justice for trying cases of insubordination, revolt, and other forms of misconduct. Above all, it was the resident commissioner's responsibility to levy various forms of local taxes as imposed by the central government of Kumase and to facilitate the trading activities of both private Asantes and *batafo* (official traders).

As might be expected of the provincial "organ of his government," the resident commissioner was hardly a popular local figure, though he was nevertheless expected to maintain law and order. During the protracted Asante-Gyaman war of 1819 the Asante resident in Fante protested against the falsity of rumors of a Gyaman victory, which were then being imprudently spread by the local coastal peoples, who were encouraged, perhaps, by the castle. Throughout the long campaign the resident was looked upon disfavorably as a "spy or inspector" over the actions of the coastal peoples and the castle.[86]

The resident ambassador was brought into being by a combination of two situations: first, a natural outgrowth of the office of the resident commissioner, as fashioned by Asante's perception of his role, and second, changes that occurred in the structure of Asante in the course of the nineteenth century. As has been pointed out above, the resident commissioner was essentially an agent of provincial administration. However, Asante's perception of this official as a representative of the central government in a distant location drew no distinction between internal affairs and matters that belonged to the foreign realm; the resident commissioner represented his government's interests both in the provinces and with foreign government officials in the area. Thus, the resident commissioner in Fante traditionally carried responsibility for British affairs. In this respect, therefore, it was not unusual in the early decades of the nineteenth century for single individuals to perform the dual roles of resident commissioner and resident ambassador, and the career of Kwame Butuakwa is illustrative of this duality.

In the course of the nineteenth century the resident representatives of Asante in the southern provinces became progressively more of pure resident ambassadors and less of provincial administrators. This development took place as the treaties of 1831 and 1874 required Asante to relinquish authority over most of the southern provinces, including Fante. Thus, in contrast to Kwame Butuakwa, Kofi Afrifa and Bosommuru Dwira held in the 1870s and 1880s resident ambassadorships whose "foreign" character was more pronounced. Even so, in line with the Asante context of the resident ambassador as being fundamentally a representative of his government, Kofi Afrifa and Bosommuru Dwira carried responsibility for the conduct of Asantes living in or visiting Fante, in addition to serving as Asante's appointed representatives with mandates for British affairs. While it is true that the intensification of diplomatic activity and the increasingly long duration of *ad hoc* embassies partly emphasized the need for an on-the-spot representative of the Asantehene, the creation of the resident ambassador had other benefits besides. It allowed for continuity and made possible the retention of quality personnel at the same post.

The diplomatic career of Kwame Butuakwa is illustrative of the role of the resident representative in serving as both an official with accreditation to a foreign power—in this case the British—and in the performance of tasks related to provincial administration. A grandson of Asantehene Opoku Ware, Kwame Butuakwa's insights into the workings of the Asante bureaucracy were gained during his early years, variously as an *okradwareni* (pl. *akradwarefo*: "washer of the King's soul"), *fotosani* (pl. *fotosanfo*: treasury official), and as a *batani* (pl. *batafo*: state trader).[87] It was during his trading ventures to Cape Coast particularly that he acquired the familiarity with the coastal areas to which he was later to be posted. The early decades of the nineteenth century were a time of severely strained relations between Asante on the one hand, and Fante and its British allies on the other, and it was precisely incidents that were associated with law enforcement problems in Fante that both made as well as marred, to an extent, the career of Kwame Butuakwa, one of Asante's foremost resident ambassadors.

Kwame Butuakwa based his residence and administration at Abora Dunkwa. An Asante envoy "deputed by the king to the Fantees," Dupuis recalled, resided at Abora,[88] apparently made necessary after the invasions of 1807, 1811, and 1817. This observation is corroborated by oral evidence:

With war and trading, it became necessary for Asante to have a representative on the coast. As more and more Asantes trading along the coast found it necessary to live in Fante in order to carry on their business, the need for a representative arose. Kwame Butuakwa was himself a trader. As *ohene's* representative, he was a kind of loose representative who sought the interests of Asantes and supervised their movements.[89]

Kwame Butuakwa did not evidently establish himself as Asante's resident ambassador until 1816. Directing a well developed administrative system, he was assisted by a staff of subordinate officials who included Amon Bata and Apenten Nto.[90]

Rising quickly through the ranks of the *fotosanfo* and *batafo*, Kwame Butuakwa distinguished himself in his first major diplomatic assignment: the mission to Gyaman around 1811. The incidents which occasioned this mission were centered around the illegal replication of the *Sika Dwa* (the Golden Stool) by Gyamanhene Adinkra, an action which, in its blatant violation of the Asante constitution, was tantamount to rebellion. Oral accounts of the mission reveal as much fascination with, as competence in, the conduct of Kwame Butuakwa—the urgency with which the envoy treated his mission, "starving all the way"; the combination of persuasive skills and forthrightness employed in addressing the Gyaman councilors, who were told: "you and your head cannot sit on the same stool"; and the seeming ease with which he effected the surrender of the stool.[91] Apparently in recognition of his efforts, Asantehene Osei Tutu Kwame rewarded Kwame Butuakwa with gifts which included three peredwans of gold dust and a male and female "slave."

It is known that in his pre-resident ambassador career Kwame Butuakwa undertook other missions, principally to the coastal areas of Fante, Elmina, and Komenda, and possibly as far away as Keta. That he was involved during this period in official roles on behalf of the Asantehene—negotiating with Dutch, British, and Danish administrators for the release of Asante prisoners and disciplining local residents such as the king of Great Komenda for misconduct—would suggest that Kwame Butuakwa's appointment to the resident ambassadorship might well have pre-dated 1816. Indeed, one version of his career, which was orally transmitted to the writer, clearly pointed out that he was given official responsibility for Fante affairs well before the Gyaman mission of 1811.[92] When Asante-British relations grew more tense in

1822–23 and clearly drifted towards open hostility, Kwame Butuakwa wisely moved his administrative base further north, relocating himself at Manso on the main road leading to Kumase. Shortly before the outbreak of open war in 1823, he was recalled to Kumase.

Kwame Butuakwa's resident ambassadorship (1816–1823) was an eventful period. He discharged his duties in a decisive, fearless, and forthright way, sometimes at the cost of being blunt. His approach several times landed him in open friction with the English and Dutch officials. In 1816 Dutch Governor Daendels had him publicly flogged in retaliation for his action in seizing a number of Dutch slaves. A year later the resident ambassador was accused by the British of interfering with their official communications to the Asantehene. On this count at least, he was clearly without blame, as he was enforcing, rather than impeding, central government directives for the proper conveyance of dispatches by official carriers.[93] Shortly thereafter, Kwame Butuakwa was embroiled in another controversy; this time the British accused him of collaborating with Samuel Kato Brew in exporting slaves to the West Indies and South America.[94] The charges were hardly substantiated, and though the Asantehene appeared to have viewed the matter seriously, his attitude was ostensibly intended to placate the British with whom he was still optimistic of maintaining peaceful relations. A final incident, and one which may have greatly contributed to a definite rupture in Asante-British relations involved Kwame Butuakwa in 1822. A Fante sergeant[95] in the service of the Royal Africa Company, who had been disrespectful to the Asantehene, was seized at Agyaa and delivered to Kwame Butuakwa, in whose hands the policeman remained for some four or five months before being executed. The course of events indicated that in carrying out the capital punishment, the resident ambassador was actually the reluctant executor of an unpopular Council decision, thereby committing his reputation to suffer as a result. On British Governor Sir Charles MacCarthy's return to the Gold Coast from Sierra Leone, he determined to surprise Kwame Butuakwa at Abora Dunkwa. News of British designs apparently leaked, and the British forces were turned back with heavy losses.[96]

Meanwhile, following Kwame Butuakwa's recall to the capital in 1823, Asantehene Osei Tutu Kwame lost no time in giving him military, judicial, and diplomatic appointments. Coming in the wake of the controversial incidents in Fante, the Asantehene's action, *ipso facto,* both exonerated Kwame Butuakwa and assured him of the King's confidence. Together with Owusu Kra, he was immediately appointed to the headship of a contingent to suppress a rebellion in the southwest—in Twifo, Denkyira, and Wassa.[97] On his return he was honored by being appointed *okyeame* for the new Butuakwa stool created by Osei Tutu Kwame. He participated in the 1826 Asante battle against the British at Katamanso, upon the conclusion of which he was appointed to the headship of the Asante delegation to negotiate for peace with the British in 1827. Kwame Butuakwa continued to combine the role of an *okyeame* with that of a diplomat in the l830s, when he led a mission to Akyem Abuakwa to seek the return of the Dwaben who had left Asante to settle there.[98]

Kwame Butuakwa pursued a diplomatic career with dedication and considerable distinction. Evidently committed to the peaceful resolution of conflicts through diplomatic approaches, his marginal role in Asante's military campaigns against the southern provinces and their British allies in 1824 and 1826 might have emanated from a deliberate expression of disapproval of military instruments as opposed to diplomatic channels. Holding appointments during the difficult times of strained relations with the British and the southern provinces, he faithfully served the interests of the central government, even to the detriment of his own popularity. His action in executing a Fante sergeant earned him a reputation for atrocity in the Fante press.[99] His memory in Asante oral accounts, however, rests on a double reputation: firstly, as the resident ambassador *par excellence,* and secondly, as *"kotwebrefo,"*that is, the initiator of troubles" (in Fante and Gyaman).[100] His local administration, which was manned by a staff of junior officials and functionaries, became a model for the nineteenth century.

Evolution of the Ambassador and the Resident Ambassador

The ambassador, and more so the resident ambassador, was called into being by communications problems (distance) and the needs created by the increasing frequency of governmental efficiency. For the maintenance of effective extra-Kumase links with both foreign powers and the far-flung provinces, an effective channel of communication was essential. The ambassador was therefore a function of effective administration not only for law enforcement but also for the speedy transmission of information. Indeed, Wilks has postulated that there was an inverse relationship between the message-delay factor and the efficacy of control of the provinces.[101]

It has been pointed out that distances between Kumase and the outlying provinces, including the coastal centers of Accra, Cape Coast, and Elmina, were seen in relation to how many days' journeying it took one to get to those points from the metropolitan center of Kumase or vice versa. Thus, Accra was considered to be a 15-day journey from

Kumase, Cape Coast 12, Elmina 13, and Bonduku 11.[102] Ecological conditions naturally made traveling faster in the savanna area than in the forest region. In the early nineteenth century the average distance covered in a day in the forest area was estimated at between 15 and 16 miles, making allowance for up to 5 or 6 miles for the winding nature of the roads. These figures which were based on information which Bowdich and Dupuis obtained in Kumase, are conservative. They did not take recognition of unavoidable delays that were often caused by rain and poor traveling conditions. Moreover, certain days of the month were considered "bad," that is, unpropitious for traveling.[103] Thus, a journey from Kumase to Cape Coast, for example, usually took much longer than twelve days. It is evident that where a situation arose in the provinces that required continuous on-the-spot attention or frequent reference to Kumase for instructions or decisions, the system of sending messengers to and fro would be woefully unsatisfactory. Thus, as the functional need for more permanent representation became progressively pronounced, the office of the resident commissioner or resident ambassador evolved.

Concurrently, rules regulating who should be charged with responsibility for carrying official messages to and from the Asantehene and their conduct *en route* came into being. The practice of relying on traders for the transmission of information (as had been the case in the eighteenth century) was slowly discouraged in favor of "special messengers." Thus, Huydecoper noted in 1816 that "express messengers" were being sent with dispatches to Elmina instead of ivory traders.[104] Resident ambassadors were apparently given responsibility for enforcing this regulation. Kwame Butuakwa, in particular, acquired a reputation for the strict enforcement of this directive:

> Quamina, the Ashantee captain at *Abrah*, has refused to allow any letters to pass that place which may be given in charge to Ashantee traders, on the plea that by so doing he would incur the displeasure of the King; who, he says, expects that especial messengers will be engaged here to proceed with all letters to the capital. Not long ago a trader who had received a letter was detained by him at *Abrah*, and the letter returned.[105]

In thereby carrying out central government instructions regarding the transmission of official dispatches, Kwame Butuakwa aroused the dislike of Governor Hope-Smith, who misconstrued his action as an undue interference with his communication to the Asantehene. Nonetheless, it is in such developments that one should look for the increasing specialization that led to the evolution of the ambassador. It was the combined effect of the need for effective communication with foreign powers on the one hand, and the growing emphasis on the use of specialized personnel for the dispatch of messages on the other, that brought about the emergence of the ambassador.

Ranking of Ambassadors

Though all envoys were agents of the Asantehene's external relations, a ranking was observable among Asante ambassadors. Two major categories were identifiable: first, the high-powered envoy who could negotiate, and second, the message-bearer, pure and simple, who lacked the authority to negotiate, that is, a "living letter." It has been pointed out above that officeholders who were given diplomatic appointments carried their status with them at home. The rank of such a diplomatic appointee could therefore be identified by his symbol of office, whether as an *okyeame*, an *afenasoani*, or an *nsenieni*. "The rank of the chiefs (*akyeame*)," Ramseyer and Kühne observed, "can be seen by the different insignia or emblems of their dignity, which always follow them." [106] In the case of the senior *akyeame*, each had his appellations (praisenames) which could be sounded on a drum or horn. Thus, Ramseyer and Kühne again noted that "all the principal captains have their special strains or mottos for their horns and drums," that of Okyeame Boakye Tenten being *"Nnonkofo didi yen atem ene sen?"* (Why should slaves insult us?). [107]

The size of an ambassador's train was invariably in consonance with his rank. Hence, an ambassador of high status or rank was usually accompanied by a large following. Thus, when news of Owusu Dome's approach to Cape Coast reached the coastal officials in early 1820, the ambassador's "large retinue" gave a sure indication of his "high rank. "[108] Indeed, news of its large size of 1,200 men inadvertently created in castle circles a picture of an army.

In conformity with diplomatic conventions everywhere, the rank of an Asante envoy in large measure determined the kind of reception he was accorded by his recipients. For this reason European administrators to whom Asante envoys were sent often endeavored to determine their rank in advance so that they could be given an appropriate reception. Thus, in connection with an Asante mission to discuss peace terms following the 1807 invasion of Fante, British Governor Colonel Torrane advised Henry Meredith: "You must let me know, of what consequence the messengers are, that I may treat them accordingly; and this it will be advisable to acquaint me of before their arrival."[109] In general, the *akyeame* were of a rank superior to that of the *afenasoafo*, whose was in turn higher than that of the *nseniefo*.

Eligibility for Ambassadorship

High in the order of criteria for the selection of an envoy to lead a mission were the diplomat's individual skills and his familiarity with and knowledge of the area being sent to.[110] These apart, the appointee's position with the Asante bureaucracy and his previous performance in positions of responsibility were equally important considerations. An examination of the biographies of Asante envoys suggests that they were, as elsewhere, men of social standing and successful pre-diplomatic careers: either as councilors, civil servants, generals and counselors, or as successful *Gyaase* (household) functionaries (such as *batafo, afenasoafo, nseniefo, fotosanfo,* etc.). A few illustrations will be cited here.

Owusu Koko Kuma, who in the 1870s handled a number of delicate missions of trust as confidential envoy to the British, saw early training as a *batani*. He also combined the office of councilor with military experience, receiving training during the military reorganization of Asantehene Mensa Bonsu. He is also credited with the command of 300 troops who were stationed in Kintampo to check smuggling in the northwest in 1880–81.[111] Akyampon Yaw, who headed the regional administration at Elmina (1872–74) as resident ambassador for Elmina, the southwest, and for Dutch affairs, was Boakye Yam Kuma's counselor. Of perhaps even greater significance to his diplomatic career was the fact that he was a proven general. Akyampon Yaw commanded the Sehwi contingent of the army which invaded the south-western provinces in 1872–73.[112] Earlier, he had made his military mark when he was given responsibility for the pacification of the southwest during the 1868–69 campaign to restore order in the protectorate. It was through these campaigns that he acquired the sound knowledge of the southwest that qualified him as the Asante resident ambassador at Elmina. Akyampon Yaw also appears to have served in the *saana*, the Asantehene's household treasury.[113] Gyakye Nantwi's claim to a diplomatic career lay in part in his administrative experience as a *gyaasewani* (officer of the Exchequer) and in part in military distinction. He held positions of command during the campaigns for the reoccupation of the eastern provinces in 1868–69 and 1872–73. Later in the 1870s, Gyakye Nantwi became a prime channel for diplomatic negotiations with the British (1868–70), in which regard he is best remembered for leading an important mission in 1876 to explain to British administrators that what they criticized as "human sacrifice" was in reality capital punishment executed under due process of law.[114] Gyakye Nantwi's early acquaintances with the bureaucratic process were made through the *Gyaase,* the Asantehene's household organization.

Whatever claim to eligibility as an ambassador Akyampon Yaw, Owusu Koko Kuma, and Gyakye Nantwi acquired through the successful conduct of military campaigns, the Owusu Ansas—John Sr. and Jr., and Albert—derived from the role of civil servants. Their English education and the benefit of a long attachment to the British gave them a familiarity with and insights into British modes of conduct, which made them especially qualified as negotiators with the British. Boakye Tenten's pre-diplomatic reputation, however, stemmed from his years of experience as a member of the Asantehene's council and as Boakye Yam Panin counselor. The success of his Salaga resident ambassadorship in the 1870s certainly increased his claim as a diplomat and pointed favorably to his appointment to head the all-important mission to the British administration in 1881.

Royal links and associations were an asset to, though not a precondition of, diplomatic appointment. Boakye Tenten was husband to Asantehemaa (queen-mother) Afua Kobi and therefore stepfather to Asantehene Kofi Kakari. Akyampon Yaw was described as "chief barber" to Asantehene Kwaku Dua, uncle to Asantehene Kofi Kakari and "chief over his household."[115] Owusu Koko Kuma, who was *oheneba* Owusu Ansa Sr.'s nephew, was a man "the king regarded as his grandson."[16] Royal associations were equally important in the rise of Kwaku Bosommuru Dwira as an ambassador of trust and confidence in the 1870s and early 1880s. Described as a chamberlain and private councilor to Asantehene Kofi Kakari, *abenaseni* Kwaku Bosommuru Dwira "possessed great influence" in the Asantemanhyiamu and over the Asantehene.[117] Furthermore, he may well have been a son of Asantehene Osei Yaw Akoto.[118]

It cannot be doubted, too, that other factors like politics, patronage and competition sometimes influenced diplomatic appointments. The Council's selection of Okyeame Boakye Tenten to head the 1881 embassy to the British, for example, was considerably determined by the political necessities of the time which called for a leader who was unmistakably committed to the peace cause. The same political considerations loomed large in the decision to entrust Okyeame Kofi Bene with the leadership of the mission of 1881 which preceded Boakye Tenten's. In contrast, Owusu Ansa Jr.'s appointment as one of the leaders of the 1894 mission to England was the result of his individual skills of literacy, as much as his successful exploitation of the benefits of competition. On the other hand, the rise of *esen* "Akoa Ye Na" through the diplomatic ranks appeared to have stemmed from the application of the principle of reward for meritorious service.

Skills

As Asante civil society became increasingly complex in the course of the nineteenth century, so did merit and talent rather than birth become the criteria for both appointment and advancement in the domestic as well as foreign fields. Contemporaneously, the specialized character that certain offices were beginning to assume brought into play the need for and an emphasis on specialized skills. Job openings created by an expanding administrative machinery in turn produced an influx of job seekers into the capital of Kumase. Two parallel developments provided avenues for placement and orientation-training for the position aspired to. Firstly, by attaching himself to an office-holder's *dampan* (bureau),[119] a young aspiring job-seeker could prepare himself for ultimate succession either through observation or through buying himself into the incumbent's favor by the performance of menial jobs for him. Secondly, a son of an officeholder, by accompanying his father to work, carrying his staff, umbrella, or other marks of office, and again serving his "master," similarly prepared himself for the future. In either case there was a development equivalent to orientation-training or apprenticeship.

The patrilineal character of many of the stools under the *Gyaase* provided sons with avenues for understudying, making it possible for them to acquire training suitable for eventual succession. Emphasizing the importance of this opportunity for training, Okyeame Baafour Akoto observed:

> The *afenasoafo* office, for example, is passed on by patrifiliation. The aspirant follows his father to court. Therefore a person cannot go to court if his father is not an *ahenkwaa*.[120]

In the same way "every Nseniehene's son is taught right from birth about message delivery and other skills including even how to wear his cloth."[121]

The form and mode of instruction, therefore, were largely informal. "The Asante envoys, as *nhenkwaa*, pick up necessary skills at *ahemfie*," confirmed Barima Owusu Ansa in an interview in 1976. "They learn by observation and imitation. As young men they carry stools to court and learn *mpaninsem* at court.[122] This is known as *'ahemfie adesua'* (court learning), which is schooling in itself." [123] The training continues throughout the period the *ahenkwaa* is in office, enabling him to extend his knowledge to cover a broad spectrum of subjects. Thus, the *okyeame*, for instance,

> comes by his knowledge from his very early acquaintance with Court functions, history, and tradition, continuing his education or training throughout the greater portion of his life, and often extending the field of his inquiries till his knowledge embraces the political history of the whole State, as well as of sister States. When he speaks, therefore, he does so as one having authority, and is listened to with the greatest respect.[124]

Asante functionaries as well as aspiring office-holders for the most part acquired their training by observing court proceedings, for "the elders teach you if you are humble."[125]

But once an opening fell, it was qualification and the diligent application of the aspirant to the opportunities available rather than birth that insured first, the acquisition of the post, and second, advancement at that position. Emphasizing the importance of merit as a criterion for office acquisition and personal advancement on the job, an anonymous writer of "The African Times" noted in 1883 that "the Ashantees acknowledge the advantage of encouraging every virtue, the direction of which is to advance the interest of the country, by enlisting among the nobility any person who distinguishes himself in the patriotic display of every such virtue."[126]

No matter the qualities demonstrated in the prediplomatic career, a diplomat was expected to possess special skills. That Asante Agyei, a diplomat of the 1810s and 1820s, became increasingly recognized as having "the best head for hard palavers,"[127] and distinguished himself in consequence of this reputation, underscores the fact that forensic abilities were an asset. Without doubt European visitors to the country were struck by the high level of oratorical skills in the society at large. The people of the Gold Coast, commented one nineteenth-century observer, "have a great turn for oratory; and on occasions, where they are obliged to display their eloquence to the utmost extent, their expressions are accompanied with much feeling and energy." [128] The Asantes in particular were "remarkable for the powers of oratory." [129] A detailed appraisal of oratorical skills in Asantes in general and in their *akyeame* envoys in particular has been essayed by Casely Hayford:

> The art of 'linguistic' oratory is at its best in Ashanti where, coupled with acuteness of a high order, it makes the mem-

bers of the linguistic body about the most enlightened men of the kingdom. Boatsin [Kwaku Boaten], the Linguist of the King of Ashanti, being once pressed with questions about the indemnity in a 'palaver' between the Governor and some Ashanti ambassadors, calmly said: *'Se yeri bo inkoro, na se yansa ma yeri dzi kaa asem dzia, inke ma ka bi. Na iyi die waba itumi asem;'* meaning, "If this were a regular 'palaver,' and we were discussing matters with wisdom, I could hold my own. But this is a matter of might."[130]

Like Owusu Dome in 1820, ambassadors were expected to be capable of delivering their messages "in an able speech,"[131] and of recapitulating the history of the subject, if so empowered, in accurate detail. Envoys, in short, had to demonstrate proven skills in oratory.

In addition, retentive memory was indispensable. In a country where an absence of a written tradition created an emphasis on the oral preservation of records and events, "every person is careful to commit to memory, at an early age, the laws and various customs. The natives are very particular in that respect; especially the panyins, or elders, who may be considered the oracles of the laws. This accounts in some measure for the strong memories of the people here: in proceedings of a complicated nature, they are seldom lost in confusion or error; they relate circumstances with perspicuity."[132] Of particular importance to the diplomats who operated in an age and in a society that relied heavily on oral diplomacy, retentive memory was a prerequisite. Administrator Salmon attested to this when he recognized that ambassador Kotirko "substantiated word for word what the King writes."[133]

Besides the general training which young aspiring office-holders acquired through understudying, specific skills were demanded of each particular diplomatic position. A sound knowledge of central government policies, an understanding of local politics, and the ability to maintain effective links of communication between the area and headquarters were required of the resident ambassador. The *okyeame* "comes of a stock used to public speaking functions,"[134] and must be conversant with legal questions and procedures. Generally, he must be "an intelligent, bright, and witty individual."[135] The *afenasoafo* were required to have demonstrated the ability to verbally transmit messages accurately, and the *nseniefo* skills in the publication of government decrees and other directives. Both of these ranks of office-holders had to receive instruction in *nkontaabu*, a form of accounting.[136]

In general, envoys were expected to portray truthfulness, fearlessness, and dedication. Using ambassador Tando of the 1810s as a model, Dutch Governor-General Daendels adjudged him to possess what he considered to be three qualities so necessary in a negotiator: "intelligence, judgment and patience."[137] Indeed, Asante monarchs expected their envoys as well as those of other countries to be patient. Showing exasperation at the impatience of Henry Vroom who was sent as a British emissary to Kumase in 1894, Asantehene Agyeman Prempe exclaimed: "A man on political business must have a patient spirit." [138] In all respects Asante envoys were not found to be wanting in the skills associated with diplomacy. British Governor Pine in 1864 described an *afenasoani* envoy of apparently lower rank, who had been captured in the Akyem Swedru area during a campaign to reoccupy the southern provinces, following their invasion by Asante in the previous year, as being "singularly intelligent."[139] Blackenbury, indeed, considered Asante ambassadors to be "well-bred." [140]

Advancement

The quick rise in Asante of Asante Agyei and the equally impressive advancement, through the diplomatic ranks, of Kotirko, both of whom were of non-Asante origins, provided strong evidence that avenues for upward mobility existed, even for foreigners, as long as they possessed the necessary skills. Agyei was of Akwamu origins; Kotirko, an Adanseni by birth, was later to return to his Adanse home to serve the secessionist Adansehene against the Asantehene. A commoner by birth, Agyei saw early life as a salt carrier on the Volta river. He must have struck Akwamuhene Akoto as a dedicated and zealous young man, for he was soon invited to become a member of the Akwamuhene's palace guard. It was a journey to Kumase around 1805 in the company of his king that provided Agyei with the opportunity for entering the service of Asantehene Osei Tutu Kwame. The occasion for the visit was a summons to the Akwamuhene by the Asantehene to answer charges of wrongful behavior. An assembled Asantemanhyiamu was astounded but impressed by the oratorical and judicial skills of Agyei, who harangued the council for upwards of three hours in defense of his master. Arguing that the prosecution witnesses had misrepresented the case in Osei Tutu Kwame's favor, Agyei brought forward convincing evidence against the Asantehene.[141]

The outcome of the trial itself was of less consequence than the conduct of Agyei, who was now taken into the service of the Asantehene in recognition of his abilities. Beginning at the common entry point for all *nhenkwaa* recruits, Asante Agyei, as he now came to be called, worked his way to the very top through sheer employment of his remarkable skills. He rose from a junior *okyeame* position to that of a senior counselor, advancing, "by his splendid talents, and his firmness in the cause of truth, till he was raised to be the linguist for all foreign palavers, the highest office he could hold which was not hereditary."[142] In that capacity, he undertook several diplomatic missions on behalf of Asantehene Osei Tutu Kwame. In 1815, despite his youthful age, he was attached as *okyeame* responsible for the war negotiations to *osahene* (Ankobeahene) Amankwa Abunyewa's army to suppress an Akyem revolt. Having acquitted himself in an exemplary fashion in this connection, Asante Agyei was quickly appointed to a mission to demand the Fantes who had taken advantage of the 1816 eruption to escape to Asen in the hope of eluding the Asantehene's vigilance. After four months of long negotiation, the Asante ambassador was successful and returned with a number of Fantes to stand trial in Kumase.[143]

Asante Agyei is known to have been involved in other major diplomatic tasks, including missions to Gyaman and Accra before his premature death in about 1823. It has been established that his career is illustrative of the fact that merit rather than birth had become the criterion for advancement in the Asante administration by the first quarter of the nineteenth century. An equally significant aspect of the career lies in the area of the Asantehene's willingness to recognize and amply reward meritorious service, for Asante Agyei received gifts of a house, gold dust, and servants, in addition to quick promotions from Osei Tutu Kwame, in appreciation of his exceptional performance.[144]

Mandate

The mandate or "procuration" specified the areas of authority of the envoy. Owusu Dome's embassy of 1820 and that of Boakye Tenten in 1881, among others, indicate that there was a direct correlation between the powers entrusted to an envoy and his status, and vice versa. Hence, envoys of higher status were permitted more initiative and greater latitude than lesser envoys. The former could conclude agreements on terms already specifically accepted by the Asantehene, in which case they did not have to refer the case to Kumase.

The exercise of reasonable discretion in consonance with the mission of a senior envoy was usually permissible. During a mission to the British administration in Accra in 1891 by ambassador Nseniehene Kofi Apea, for example, Governor Griffith took the opportunity to discuss the issue of Asante arms purchases. In tune with the exercise of initiative that Kofi Apea had been permitted, the ambassador allayed the Governor's fears by assuring him that the purchases were "not for any hostile purposes, but for hunting and trading."[145] The conduct of the Owusu Taseamandi extradition mission provides another illustration. The mission was led by a son of the late diplomat, Akuma Afenasoafohene Amankwa Akuma, and was originally dispatched in early 1881 to seek the return of the refugee, Owusu Taseamandi, from Asen. When, however, the envoys were informed in Asen Edubease by the local chief that Owusu Tasemandi had escaped further south to Cape Coast, the mission decided without reference to Kumase to pursue the Gyaman prince to the coast.[146] Once in Cape Coast, the decision was taken, again without reference to the Asantehene, to seek the intercession of senior resident envoys Asabi Antwi and Kwaku Bosommuru Dwira, who were better informed about affairs on the coast, on how best to approach the British administration with the extradition question.[147]

Whatever the nature of his authority, the *raison d'etre* of the Asante envoy was to provide a channel of communication. Hence, he was in most cases empowered to negotiate at best, rather than to conclude. Thus, even when a most senior diplomat of the caliber of Asabi Antwi was empowered by the Asantehene to negotiate on his behalf with Sir Garnet Wolseley in February 1874, there were limitations on the extent of his contractual powers. Asabi Antwi discussed peace terms with the British general at Fomena, objected to the value of the indemnity being demanded of Asante, made an initial payment, and took issue with the British proposal that Asante renounce claims to Adanse. However, he was not authorized to conclude the agreement and therefore had to carry the draft peace treaty to Kumase for the Council's approval.[148] Similarly, Owusu Dome's high stature notwithstanding, he was expected to act within the bounds of his mandate. That Owusu Dome in 1820 carried the authority to negotiate (in contrast to the restricted powers of the three envoys that preceded him on the Komenda issue in 1819) , cannot be doubted; he was given "full powers to negotiate and settle the dispute." [149] But that his authority was nonetheless not without restraint came in evidence when, in response to the Governor's demand that he renounce Asante's imposition of a fine on the castle, he declared that it was "impossible for him to abrogate what the king had decreed." [150]

In contrast to the superior mandates of senior diplomats, envoys of lesser status, whose roles did not amount to much beyond message-bearers or letter-carriers, were hardly given any initiative. They might not in any way alter the form or substance of a message. As Owusu Ansa Sr. pointed out in 1881 to British Governor Griffith in the heat of the controversy over whether or not senior diplomat Asabi Antwi, as head of a mission to demand the extradition of Owusu Taseamandi, implicitly through the use of the Golden Axe, or explicitly through actual statements, threatened war on the coast, "no Ashanti taking the King's message would dare to add to or take from it."[151] In general no effort was made to conceal an envoy's limited status.

In all cases, however, with the exception of the ambassador-at-large and the resident ambassador, the envoy was appointed for a specific mission, that is, a specific subject. Matters outside the scope of his subject were outside his jurisdiction. He was however expected to report on such matters. Even where the matter was within his mandate but had undergone substantial changes before his arrival on the scene, the envoy was expected to send to Kumase to report the changed circumstance. The Asantehene might then revise the envoy's mandate.

Irrespective of his status or rank, very rarely did an envoy of Asante possess *plena potestas* in an absolute sense such as could be seen from John Owusu Ansa Jr.'s letter of appointment to the headship of the 1894–95 mission to London (see p. 125). Owusu Ansa was given "full power as ambassador extraordinary and minister plenipotentiary" to "negotiate and conclude all such treaties" as related to "diverse matters" affecting Asante.[152] Thus empowered, he was equipped with full authority to undertake all forms of negotiation, and to take any action he considered necessary for the promotion of those interests. Earlier, his father, the senior Owusu Ansa, had enjoyed similar powers. The exercise of *plena potestas* by Owusu Ansa Sr., emanated from two sources: firstly, specific mandates from the Asantehene-in-Council, and secondly, a personal conviction that he could offer his services in whatever capacity they would be useful in striving for an Asante-British understanding.

Owusu Ansa's exercise of his mandate as ambassador-at-large has been discussed above. A rare action which he took unilaterally, and one which ordinarily required the Asantemanhyiamu's authorization, is worthy of comment, insofar as it was indicative of his wide powers. Ramseyer and Kühne's detailed account of the incident is cited:

> While living in Cape Coast, he [Owusu Ansa] had been repeatedly solicited to intercede for the Ashantee traders, when they got into difficulties with the Fantees. Now that he was away, there would be no one who understood English, and had, at the same time, the good of the Ashantees at heart. He therefore, conjointly with Kotiko and Afrifa, the representatives of Ashantee, thought it best for communication to cease so that during his absence, no inextricable complications might occur. The monarch, and nearly all the council, agreed with the rules which had been adopted.[153]

Credentials and Symbols

Credentials have always been an integral part of diplomatic practice everywhere, Asante not excepted. Particularly for a society that utilized the trappings of oral diplomacy to a considerable extent, great importance was attached to the proper use and recognition of symbolic credentials. The progressive acceptance of the written form of diplomacy and written credentials in the nineteenth century therefore did not in any way diminish Asante's dependence on diplomatic paraphernalia.

A wide variety of symbols including swords (*afena,* pl. *mfena*), shields (*afenakyem,* pl. *mfenakyem*), axes (*akuma,* pl. *nkuma*), and staffs (*poma,* pl. *mpoma*) were used by envoys as emblems on official missions. These objects, which were invariably their symbols of office, then became their badges of credence on missions, entitling them to diplomatic recognition from their hosts and free passage as passports. In time, the symbol of office of the *afenasoani,* "the gold-hilted sword," came to be associated indubitably with the Asantehene's envoy. The sword was made up of three parts: the blade, which was usually of steel; the hilt, which was made of wood but often covered with gold; and the sheath or scabbard, which encased the sword. This latter part was usually made of the skins of animals like leopards, and on top of it could be commonly found the *abosode,* a gold casting of a symbolic object. While an *afenasoani* normally carried this type of emblem on embassies, he could alternatively be given a special type of sword, if the object of the mission was to convey a special message. It was the symbolic meaning attached to the *abosode* that often indicated the purpose for which a particular sword was employed. Swords used on missions belonged to the category known as *asomfomfena,* which distinguished them from ceremonial swords such as *keteanomfena* (swords used in ceremonies connected with the purification of the king's soul or those associated with black stools), *abrafomena* (bayonets used by the *abrafo,* the constabulary), *sepo* (knives used by executioners), and other special swords.[154]

Although the Asomfohene is reputed to possess or exercise control over some two dozen *asomfomfena,* Asomfohene Kwaku Kankam indicated in 1980 that only some nine of them were important or had been used in recent memory. He listed these as Gyapatire, Abobonnua, Worasatire, Nsonoma, Bonomu Ankama, Akyekyede, Gyapatia, Suntire, and Akuma. [155] Each of the *asomfomfena* is distinguished by its use, significance, and, in some cases, its custodian. There are restrictions on the use of most of these swords. Some can normally be used only for "missions" to specific districts or states. Thus, the Nsonoma, which is so called because its *abosode* is an image of the star, is traditionally used by delegations to powerful states like Akyem, Kumawu, and Kokofu.[156] Abobonnua, which is named after a powerful forest animal, is borne by envoys sent to the Adansehene, while the Bonomu Ankama is sent to Bono, and Worasatire to Banna. The Gyapatia, Gyagyatire and Suntire are considered personal swords of the Asomfohene and are not sent out except when the Asomfohene himself goes on the mission.[157] The origins of the Gyagyatire and Worosatire are both associated with traditions relating to Asante conquests in the eighteenth century. [158]

Among the most revered of the Asante swords is the Golden Axe. Asante tradition clearly indicates that the significance of the Golden Axe is that it evidences the determination and ability to cut through thick and thin to the accomplishment of the object of the mission. [159] Traditional practice also suggests that the Akuma is usually used as a last resort. A regular sword would first be used to summon a chief or offender. If he fails to respond to the call, then the Akyekyede might be sent. The significance of the Akyekyede, which is so called because its *abosode* is an image of a tortoise, lies in its intended message, that "we will catch up with you even if we walk as slowly as a tortoise." It is only after the offending party has failed to answer the second call that the Akuma is used. As the Asomfohene emphasized, "if a sword is sent and no response is heard, then the axe is sent." [160]

The white flag, though traditionally a symbol of victory in Akan society, was used in wartime to identify the approach of an envoy with a message of peace or with peaceful intent. Thus, during the approach to Kumase of British forces under Sir Garnet Wolseley in January 1874, the British general suggested to Asantehene Kofi Kakari, who was anxious to sue for peace, that his envoys "carry a white flag plainly displayed at the end of a staff, in order that they may be known...to be friendly messengers."[161] In response, ambassador Owusu Koko Kuma, who was authorized by the Asantehene to negotiate with the British general and have "everything properly arranged," accordingly left Kumase on January 9 with a white flag in hand.[162] There is evidence to suggest that the use of the white flag as a symbol of truce pre-dated this incident. During the Asante invasion of Fante in 1807, for example, British officials in a beleaguered Anomabo castle had lowered a white flag over its walls in surrender. The Asante forces who were fully acquainted with the rules of war and peace, on this occasion showed full recognition of the meaning of the symbol by observing it as a flag of truce.[163]

The practice of sending envoys carrying jawbones of defeated enemies to friendly states was generally considered as a "courteous and highly complimentary" act. Jawbones signified victory, and the recipient states were expected to join in the celebration of success in war. Contrary to this expectation, however, Asante jawbone-carrying envoys were grossly insulted and assaulted in Komenda and Cape Coast in 1819.

It is impracticable to discuss all the symbols used in connection with diplomatic practice. In addition to those mentioned above, which had universal recognition in the Gold Coast, it might be further stated that "any kind of leaf placed between the lips is a symbol of silence. An ambassador returning from a foreign court and having a leaf in the mouth, shows his inability to express the message he brought." In such circumstances, the king was expected to declare that in reporting any insulting message the envoy was not to be held responsible, after which he delivered his message freely.[165]

From early in the century the Asante government sought enforcement of measures to ensure that only individuals carrying the appropriate symbols — swords, shields, and staffs — were recognized as official envoys by foreign government representatives and treated as such. Instances of impersonation were apparently rare, for as early as 1817, at a time when the standardization of diplomatic procedures was yet to be firmly implanted, Governor Hope-Smith observed that he was not aware of any Asantes who had introduced themselves except "as were duly authorized by the King." However, to forestall incidents of false representation, he indicated that in future "none will be attended to unless they bear his cane."[166]

Representation

The Asante ambassador was a direct representative of the Asantehene, whether or not he could negotiate and conclude. His action entered into a direct relationship with his host. The notion of representation to the full extent of a contractual relationship was therefore not alien to Asante diplomatic practice. This was borne out, for example, in Asantehene Mensa Bonsu's response to diplomat Asabi Antwi's alleged declaration of war to the British administration in Cape Coast in 1881. Okyeame Boakye Tenten was instructed in a follow-up mission to repudiate Asabi Antwi's action because it lacked authorization. However, because Asabi Antwi was "the servant of the King, and the King was bound by the acts of his servant," the Asantehene expressed his regret for the mistake through ambassador Boakye Tenten.[167] Asabi Antwi was not reprimanded because of the principle of delegation of power; an Asantehene is responsible for the actions of those he delegates.[168]

The ambassador was the mirror through which the external image of the Asantehene was reflected. It was for this reason that the Asantehene attempted to project the ambassador's image through the provision of a wardrobe.[169] The envoy was therefore expected to receive the honor due to his sender, and an insult to him was similarly considered as an insult to his master. However, "if you do good to the envoy, you do good to the King."[170]

Functions of Ambassadors

The earlier discussion of the role and position of the ambassador-at-large, the roving ambassador, and the resident ambassador provides a useful, though inconclusive, indication of the range of functions performed by Asante ambassadors. Like diplomats everywhere, Asante envoys performed a variety of functions, both overtly and covertly, as demanded by the foreign policy concerns and the security and peace-maintenance needs of their country in relation to its neighbors. These functions included negotiating, concluding, ratifying, and proroguing treaties; negotiating, offering, and accepting security or protection; seeking, offering, and courting the friendship or support of foreign states or governments; and settling disputes, suppressing rebellions, and issuing protests. Others of prominence were quasi-judicial functions like demanding fines and ordering the extradition of criminals, and intelligence duties such as espionage or obtaining "legitimate" information. Also of note were publicity (propaganda) and ceremonial roles, commercial duties, and all types of peripheral functions. Oftentimes envoys performed interrelated roles, as diplomatic and peace-maintenance functions were invariably inseparable. The four embassies sent to Cape Coast and Komenda in 1819–1820 following the incidents connected with the spread of rumors about an Asante defeat at the hands of Gyaman, for instance, were a function essentially of provincial administration, which were given rise to by the need to suppress rebellious behavior in Fante.

It was customary for a new Asantehene to send goodwill missions to each ally, friendly or tributary state, to inform it of the death of his predecessor and his own accession to the *Sika Dwa*. Asantehene

Kofi Kakari followed this tradition and dispatched a mission to, among others, Elmina, whose king reciprocated by sending one of his chiefs, Ando, to Kumase to convey his condolence and assist at the funeral obsequies of the late Asantehene.[171] Two goodwill missions were sent to Cape Coast in January and February 1875. The first announced the enthronement of Mensa Bonsu as Asantehene in place of his dethroned brother Kofi Kakari, repeated the Asantehene's wish for peace, and complained about assaults on Asante traders by Dwaben. Expressing the new Asantehene's good intentions towards the British administration, the embassy declared that the Asantehene "desires to be on the same friendly terms with the Governor as those which existed between the old king and Governor Maclean and that his wish is for peace, trade and open roads." [172] The second, which confirmed the enstoolment of Mensa Bonsu, was reported to have been led by "one of the Ambassadors who came down to Cape Coast to sign the Treaty [of Fomena] in March last," in all probability, Asabi Antwi.[173]

Some missions were known to have been motivated by educational goals. The Osei Broni mission of March 1877 had a second objective, besides seeking the intercession of the Cape Coast merchants in the restoration of peaceful Asante-British relations. It was instructed to approach the Reverend J. Fletcher with a request for the re-establishment of schools in Kumase.[174]

In certain cases envoys were employed to perform military-related functions. Envoys were employed to send messages relating to the conduct of campaigns to generals during wars; were used to convey news of results of wars to Kumase as well as from Kumase to neighboring states and governments; and were attached to armies to direct peace negotiations on the conclusion of campaigns. Envoys also undertook other military functions like arranging for the purchase of arms, perhaps the most publicized example being the case involving the purchase of sniders by Owusu Ansa, Sr. Before his return to England in 1874, Owusu Ansa had received a letter from a French agent offering to supply sniders to Asante. This intelligence was communicated to the Asantehene by the Asante ambassadors in Cape Coast (Asabi Antwi and Kwaku Bosommuru Dwira). During his return to Kumase in 1875, Owusu Ansa did not apparently encourage Asantehene Mensa Bonsu when the subject came up for discussion. Eventually, during his last visit to Kumase in 1878, when Owusu Ansa realized that the Asantehene was in earnest about ordering sniders and would purchase them anyway, he gave the order for 300 sniders to an English firm. The sniders were received a year later, sent to the royal magazine at the Asantehene's village, and became part of the weapons used by the

Asantehene's bodyguard under Kwame Firempon, the Atutuohene.[175]

As might be expected of most government representatives in diplomatic careers, Asante envoys were found in intelligence-gathering roles as well. The need to maintain both an efficient administrative system in the extensive and sprawling Asante empire and effective communication links between it and foreign powers required the operation of a complicated intelligence system, whose efficacy did not fail to attract the notice of foreign government officials. "There is a wonderful network of communication between the natives," commented one British administrator, "which enables them to pick up information and to work quietly towards the attainment of any desired object."[176] This was a system in which envoys played a vital role in providing the Asante administration with information concerning foreign governments, provincial officials, and subject peoples as well. So intricate was the intelligence system that diplomats and other senior office-holders were themselves closely observed by young men employed for the purpose:

> The King of Ashante maintains such an efficient system of espionage, that it is difficult for his subjects to speak or act in any manner derogatory to his authority without his being made acquainted with his offence. He employs a number of clever boys, trained for the purpose, who are placed as spies upon the conduct of the great men, and convey to the king a report of all they see and hear.[177]

In another interesting incident, the Asantehene's envoys who had been sent to *osahene* (general) Acting Anantehene Apea Nyanyo during the Fante campaign of 1807 were to spy upon the Asante general and later provide evidence for the prosecution during his trial. The envoys, it was subsequently learned, had been "concealed in a distant part of the frontier" to watch on Apea Nyanyo's actions.[178]

Numerous other instances survive of Asante ambassadors being involved in intelligence functions either on express authorizations from the government or on their own initiative. It is known that while ambassador Owusu Dome was waiting in Cape Coast in 1820 in the hope of receiving instructions from Joseph Dupuis for an Asante embassy to proceed to England, he conveyed intelligence information to Kumase about the projected change from company to official control of the settlements.[179] When, in 1880, H. T. Ussher sent presents to Mensa Bonsu on his assumption of the governorship, the Asantehene "availed himself of the opportunity to send messengers down to the coast, ostensibly to thank Governor Ussher for his presents, but really to ascertain secretly the views and position of the British Government with regard to Adanse. These messengers, after being received at Accra, returned to Cape Coast, and remained there collecting information and watching events, explaining their delay in returning to their country by a number of frivolous excuses."[180]

There can be no doubt that among the important duties performed by ambassadors Kofi Afrifa, Kwaku Bosommuru Dwira, and Asabi Antwi during their extended stay in Cape Coast during the 1870s and 1880s was an information-gathering function, and though the British administration claimed that they were "regarded with great suspicion by all residents" there, the Asante government viewed their role as essential nevertheless. British suspicions were apparently confirmed when, within days of his arrival at Elmina in January 1881, the refugee, Owusu Taseamandi, was able to observe and report to them that:

> the Asanti ambassadors at Cape Coast are waiting there to watch the motions of the Government. They go about and listen to what is going on and being said, and then send their news to the King.[181]

Although the Asante government recruited from the ranks of a varied spectrum of functionaries for diplomatic personnel, the *afenasoafo* and the *nseniefo* invariably came to be recognized as providing the essentials of the body of envoys, most of whom undertook diplomatic appointments as an extension of their domestic roles. As elsewhere, Asante envoys were marked by distinctions of rank and status and diversity of functions, but all had to demonstrate relevant skills for appointment and promotion. Akin to diplomatic procedures everywhere, recognized symbols came into being, which Asante envoys both carried as proper credentials and received the due recognition for them. The functions performed by envoys encompassed a broad range of issues, seemingly an indication of the increasing demands that the foreign policy concerns were placing on the administration and the specialized character that diplomatic appointments were assuming.

CHAPTER 3

The Conduct of Embassies

This chapter seeks to examine the organization of embassies from the point they were commissioned to the time of their return. The principal approach employed is to analyze the conduct of embassies along a set of issues commonly associated with the operation of an ambassador and his management of a mission. The important considerations are to assess, firstly, the extent to which established patterns of behavior and modes of conduct can be said to have existed for Asante ambassadors, and secondly, the degree to which these trends may have been identical with, or at variance with, those relating to diplomatic practice elsewhere. To promote an understanding of the operation of these features that characterized Asante diplomacy, the trends herein identified are supported wherever possible with illustrative cases from embassies that were sent out and which provided the background for the development of those procedures. Where useful, an extrapolation of, and comparison with, contemporary procedures will be made. It will become apparent that some of the current procedures go back into the nineteenth century.

The Foreign Policy Decision-Making Process

All major foreign policy issues, including questions relating to war and peace, important diplomatic appointments, and the commissioning of major embassies were decided upon and executed by the King-in-Council. The counselors, it would appear, enjoyed a substantive voice in foreign policy decisions in contrast to their relatively limited influence over domestic policy. Bowdich, Dupuis, Ramseyer, Kühne, and others who had the benefit of observing the decision-making process in Kumase left clear descriptions of the operation of this system. Thus, Bowdich noted of the role of the *akyeame* (counselors):

> The constitution requires or admits an interference of the Aristocracy in all foreign politics, extending even to a veto on the King's decision; but they watch rather than share the domestic administration, generally influencing it by their opinion, but never appearing to control it from authority; and their opinions on civil questions, are submitted with a deference, directly in contrast to their bold declarations on subjects of war and tribute, which amount to injunction.[1]

The justification for such a constitutional arrangement, it seemed, lay in the safeguarding of the national interest: "the interference of the Aristocracy in all foreign politics, makes the nation more formidable to its enemies, who feel they cannot provoke with impunity, where there are so many guardians of the military glory." [2]

The right of the counselors to participate in foreign policy decisions was therefore both dictated by national considerations and written into the constitution. It was in the exercise of this right, for example, that the preliminaries and final drafts of the Bowdich and Dupuis Treaties of 1817 and 1820 were discussed and debated upon at length. It was the operation of the same constitutional tenet that permitted the cautious and long deliberations that centered on the detention of Ramseyer, Kühne, and Bonnat from 1869 to 1873. [3]

The Appointment and Commissioning of Envoys

The selection and appointment of envoys followed well established procedures. It was the King-in-Council that served as the commissioning body for most important and high-powered embassies. In the case of the less-powered missions, the Asomfohene appeared to have had a more direct involvement. Outlining the Asomfohene's role from contemporary practice, the incumbent in 1980 explained that the Asantehene usually sends for the Asomfohene, who reports with his men. Then, the Asomfohene appoints the envoy suitable for the mission. [4] Often, the appointed envoy is accompanied by the Nseniehene's men. Where the mission is concerned with an important matter of state, a meeting of all the *akyeame* may be convened to discuss the appointment of envoys and other issues relating to the conduct of the mission. The *okyeame* who has responsibility for the area to which the mission is being sent may collaborate with the Asomfohene in the selection of the *afenasoafo* (swordbearers). [5]

Surviving evidence strongly indicates that, in the nineteenth-century at least, a commissioning ceremony was performed to mark the formal appointment of the envoy. The envoy was instructed *viva voce*, his mandate specifying what was to be said, done, and how. He was sworn to oath. Bowdich had the opportunity of observing that envoys who were to carry Asantehene Osei Tutu Kwame's letters to Cape Coast in 1817 "were impressively sworn; they received their instructions in a speech from the linguist of nearly two hours." [6] Further light on the ceremonies marking the formal commissioning of ambassadors is shed by the appointment of Kwasi Apente in 1823. The available evidence on this diplomat's identity appears to link him to Apenten Nto, who served under resident ambassador Kwame Butuakwa at Abora Dunkwa.[7] Shortly after the Abora Dunkwa encounter involving British forces and Kwame Butuakwa, Asantehene Osei Tutu Kwame dispatched Kwasi Apente at the head of a mission to Accra to gather intelligence information about British Governor Sir Charles MacCarthy's movements and to ascertain which side the Ga were likely to support, in the event of an Asante-British war.[8] Kwasi Apente was commissioned and sworn on oath in Kumase before his departure. As part of the ceremony, his lips were "wounded" by the sword of the heir apparent Osei Yaw Akoto; that is, he bit tightly on the sword, with which he swore to fight the British thus:

> No nation will dare to invade Kumase, unless we rather make
> war against that nation. Whoever attempts to burn Kumase,
> shall quench the fire with his own.[9]

From Mrs. Lee's vivid description of the Inner Council can be recreated a similar scene of the swearing-in of *afenasoafo:*

> ...in the center ... is one of the ministers, or linguists, making
> a messenger swear to be true to his duty, before he starts,
> the oath he enforces by biting a sword.[10]

This was obviously the same scene which Bowdich had witnessed in 1817, Mrs. Lee, Bowdich's wife, having derived her information from the extensive notes of her husband. In his description of this ceremony at which Akyeamehene Kwadwo Adusei Kyakya performed the commissioning rites of four envoys, Bowdich noted: "The chief, Adoosey, is swearing a royal messenger ... by putting a gold handled sword between his teeth, whilst Agay [Asante Agyei] delivers the charge, and exhorts him to be resolute."[11]

   In the swearing-in ceremony of special envoys, the oath of draught was usually administered. The envoy was required to take in a special "medicine," by which he undertook to report the message word for word as it had been delivered to him. Where such an oath was given, the death penalty might be invoked for perverting messages.[12] Among the earliest detailed relevant accounts of this oath is that of Dupuis, who noted that it "is administered in all cases where the monarch's interests are concerned...that they might divulge nothing prejudicial to their sovereign, during their sojourn at the settlements."[13] In line with the format for new appointments, envoys were also made to take other oaths ("fetich") and formalities which emphasized the importance attached to the mission.[14]

   Commissioning instructions detailing duties and limitations were strictly defined by a whole set of oral directives akin to those given to a chief on his enstoolment and were publicly recited before the appointee.[15] The commissioning instructions of two *afenasoafo* who were sent to Anantahene Apea Dankwa in May 1816, for example, clearly left no room for ambiguity or doubt as to what the Asantehene expected of his envoys with regard to his orders:

> You must go to the camp and tell Appia that I have not ordered him to make any attack on Commany but only sent him to look for Codjo Coema, Saffroccie and Krala who have offended me, and so he must not do anything against Commany at the request of the Elminas: and that a King's orders must be obeyed, but by no means the orders of his subjects.... [16]

Unless their mandates gave them personal initiative, Asante envoys generally found their orders indeed preemptory. Such certainly was the case with envoy Adu Borade, who arrived in Cape Coast in 1819 with the Asantehene's copy of the Bowdich Treaty to convince Governor Hope-Smith that he was bound by the terms of the treaty to intervene in the Komenda dispute. The envoy declared that his orders were preemptory and that he was instructed to leave behind the copy of the dishonored treaty unless the Governor undertook to do justice to the Asantehene.[17] Dutch Governor-General Daendels' observation about the behavior of Asante envoys sent to him in April 1816 confirmed this view about the limited mandates of most envoys of lower rank: "To speak with them about anything except their mission is useless. They appear ignorant or dare not answer.... These messengers of the Ashantees have not the power to say yes or no."[18] What is evidenced by these comments is not so much the limited authority of envoys when they were so commissioned, as the remarkable way in which they carried out their orders, diplomatically sidestepping issues that lay outside their mandates.

To receive the oath of an appointee, the Asantehene held up his two fingers, a sign, traditionally, of approbation. Most commissioning ceremonies took place during the Odwira festival, at which time the Asantemanhyiamu (Council) usually met to discuss affairs of state in the domestic as well as the foreign domains. In most cases the commissioning of an envoy was accompanied by much ceremony and solemnity.

There is evidence to indicate that the practice of *akyeame* participation in foreign policy decisions has survived to the present day. The major policy making relating to external affairs, the visits of foreign dignitaries, the appointment of high-powered embassies, and the like, all take place at meetings of the Asantehene, the *akyeame,* and other important functionaries. The right of the counselors to be a part of the decision-making process, however, should not be confused with the Asantehene's authority to make decisions on everyday affairs and implement them by himself. Persons contacted in field interviews who had participated in diplomatic activity repeatedly cited instances when the Asantehene called for them and simply sent them out on missions without any meeting of the Council. Indeed, the Asantehene's authority would be circumscribed and his administration impeded, if he were to seek the Council's consent or approval before undertaking every action.

While the foreign policy decision-making processes have continued in essentials to the present day, it is to be noted that some changes have occurred over time. The modern political structure of Ghana has brought about a reduction in the political power and responsibilities of traditional authorities, which in turn has resulted in a general diminution of traditional diplomatic activity. But although Asante no longer communicates with foreign powers on the basis of a sovereign power, diplomatic activity with other local authorities within Ghana and with the national government continues. All forty functionaries who were surveyed in 1980 indicated that they had participated in diplomatic activity, and as many as twenty-eight, that is, seventy percent, had actually led independent missions. The mean number of missions undertaken by each envoy was in fact nearly twenty for a group whose average age was slightly over 42 years.

The study produced a number of other interesting results which shed more light on the nature and extent of present-day diplomatic activity and provide a frame of reference for comparisons with nineteenth-century procedures. Although the ages of the envoys at the time of their first mission ranged from 7 to 49, the average age at first mission was 23.6 years. Though it might be reasonably presumed that the average figure was lower in the nineteenth century, in view of the fact that the size of embassies was generally larger and most embassies were accompanied by large trains of people who included young attendants, it might also be assumed that the participant who saw his first involvement in an embassy at the age of seven did so in the capacity of an attendant. Two participants in the study did not acquire their first experience in missions until the age of forty-nine. This is an unusually late age, but part of the explanation presumably lies in the fact that they grew up during the period of the exile of Osei Agyeman Prempe I, when of course there was no Asantehene in Kumase. The average time lapse between the first mission and the first independent mission was 4.8 years, which suggests that envoys prove themselves worthy of being entrusted with sole responsibility for a mission or its leadership in less than five years.

Other comparisons between diplomatic practice today and that of the nineteenth century are worthy of mention. No commissioning ceremonies are performed today for most small-scale missions. The field data indicate that for such missions the Asantehene sends out the envoys without any ritual or ceremony. For the most important or larger missions where commissioning ceremonies are performed, the *afenasoani* is given a sword and the *nsenieni* (herald) a hat, but the rite of the biting of the sword, which Bowdich so vividly described in 1819, no longer takes place. The envoy's instructions are still given by the Asantehene through the appropriate *okyeame*. [19]

As in the nineteenth century the majority of envoys belong to the rank and file, whose functions for the most part amount to no more than delivering messages or summoning individuals. Even so, seventy percent of the envoys who took part in the study expressed the opinion that they were commissioned with adequate powers for the missions they had undertaken, no matter how low their status was.

Composition of Embassies

There was a correlation between the composition of an embassy and its importance. Missions entrusted with affairs affecting the sovereignty of Asante tended to be representative of the whole nation. Thus, the Asabi Antwi mission, which was dispatched to Cape Coast with a signed copy of the Treaty of Fomena for ratification in 1874, comprised representatives of "every state—Dwaben, Kokofu, Bekwae, Nsuta, Mampon, etc."[20] The Boakye Tenten Mission in 1881, whose responsibility was to assure the British administration of Asantehene Mensa Bonsu's peaceful disposition, similarly included representatives of the *amanto,* that is, the districts of Bekwae, Kokofu, Mampon, and Nsuta, which, along with Kumawu, Dwaben, and Kumase, constituted the core of metropolitan Asante."[21] In 1880 Asantehene Agyeman Prempe appointed an important embassy to discuss and attempt to settle with the British administration the issue of Asante's relationship with the provinces of Mampon, Kwahu, and Adanse, which were slowly being absorbed into the British protectorate. Announcing the dispatch of this mission, whose leadership was entrusted to Kofi Apea, the Asantehene notified the British administrator at Accra that the embassy included representatives "from every Chief in the kingdom of Ashanti." [22]

The grandeur or pomp associated with embassies was also in direct relationship to the rank of the leader. By tradition, senior ambassadors of superior rank and status conducted themselves in grand style on official business. Of the entry of Owusu Dome into Cape Coast in January 1820, Dupuis, who was as much impressed by the event as the Merchant Company's officials, reported: "the ambassador entered the place with a degree of military splendour unknown there since the conquest of Fante by the King: and according to prevailing courtesy, the town chiefs headed by Aggry [Aggrey] were drawn up to receive their unwelcome visitors."[23] Tando, an ambassador of the early decades of the nineteenth century, who acquired a reputation (or notoriety) for his handling of Wassa affairs, was used to visiting Cape Coast "in great pomp. "[24] In addition, each *okyeame* had in consonance with his rank his "insignia or emblems of dignity," which were carried by his retinue behind him. [25]

Size of Embassies

Ceremonial pomp being the *sine qua non* of Asante diplomacy, every effort was made to impress recipient governments with the size of embassies, which was in itself an index to the embassies' importance. Very large embassies were therefore not unusual, particularly when the subject in question affected the image, reputation, or sovereignty of the Asante nation.

Following the conclusion of the Dupuis Treaty in 1820, an Asante embassy arrived in Cape Coast for the settlement of outstanding disputes with the British. The embassy of seven was to be joined in Cape Coast by *oheneba* (prince) Owusu Dome, with plans for proceeding to England. Besides Owusu Dome, the leader, the only senior member was Okyeame Anno Panin, the six others being described as "subordinate" officers. However, the delegation was followed by a large retinue which seemed to have picked up additional men along the way to Cape Coast. The traveling suite had an "advanced guard"; there were "five hundred armed men, besides servants and bearers in a considerable number."[26] The entire train of Owusu Dome, "at the lowest estimate, was about twelve hundred."[27] The size of the 1820 mission was by no means atypical of important embassies. Also characteristic of such large embassies was the false impression its size sometimes created in British administration circles of an army.

When Asabihene Kwame Antwi arrived in Cape Coast on 12 March 1874 for the ratification of the Treaty of Fomena, the size of his embassy gave a sure indication of the importance of his mission, which touched upon the independence of Asante. He headed a large party which, with followers, numbered 300 men.[28] In December 1880 Asabi

Antwi again led a large embassy to the British. Accompanied by "a very numerous suite," he called on the British Civil Commissioner at Cape Coast, Edmund Watt, to express Asantehene Mensa Bonsu's gratitude for complimentary gifts lately received from Governor Ussher.[29] The mission also gave notice to the British administration of the impending funeral activities for the late Dwabenhemaa Akosua Afrakuma. Although no figures are available for the size of Asabi Antwi's train on this occasion, "a very numerous suite" might be interpreted as amounting to several tens, if not hundreds, of people. A month later, when a joint embassy of Asante and Dwaben was dispatched to Accra to celebrate the funerals of Dwabenhemaa Afrakuma and ambassador Gyakye Nantwi, who had died in Accra in 1880, the large size of the party caused an "unprecedented alarm, almost approaching to a scare."[30] Before meeting his untimely death in Accra, the size of an embassy which ambassador Gyakye Nantwi had headed to discuss questions relating to the delicate issue of reforms in capital punishment with the British administration had caused so much consternation that a British official, Sir Sanford Freeling, had had to intervene before it could cross the Pra River.[31]

In April 1890 a high-level embassy under the headship of Nseniehene Kofi Apea left Kumase to discuss questions regarding the secession of Dwaben, Adanse, Kokofu, and Bekwae with the British administration on the Gold Coast. The size of the embassy was so large that the Asantehene found it necessary to write to the British administrator to request a change in the venue of the meeting from Accra to Elmina, to reduce the expenses to be incurred in supporting the party: "As I find that the number of them with their servants will be about a thousand, their expenses will be too much on us, so I beg to ask your kind favour in order to meet them at Elmina Castle to have the palaver settled there, and that during their stay at Elmina they could easily obtain enough provisions...." Indeed, Kofi Apea's personal retinue alone numbered 150 persons.[32]

The sizes of embassies and other official delegations today are no longer as large as they were in the nineteenth century; contemporary political conditions make official parties of the size of several hundreds unnecessary and impracticable. The results of the survey of 40 functionaries confirmed that most embassies today are small parties.

Table 2:   Average Size of Embassies

Size of Embassies	Percentage of Envoys Participating
1 – 3 persons	65
4 – 6 persons	30
7 – 10 persons	5
Over 10 persons	0

Though the Asantehene today may not find the political need to employ as much pomp and pageantry as in the nineteenth century in his diplomatic representation, ceremonial display continues to be an indispensable component of all Asante official functions.

Reception and Formal Audience

It appears from an examination of the major missions for which a "full" record was kept that the audience followed a standard format:

  i.   the introduction of the leading members of the embassy
  ii.   the felicitation or exchange of greetings
  iii.   a recapitulation, during which the history of the mission or the recent relations between Asante and the recipient state were retraced
  iv.   the message
  v.   the reply
  vi.   the leave-taking

A message- or letter-bearing envoy of lower rank might not be authorized to "recapitulate," and might only deliver his message. For high-powered missions empowered to negotiate, it was customary for only the greetings or felicitations to be delivered at the first meeting. A second meeting would then be arranged at which the negotiations would take place. Thus, although Governor Daendels reported that an embassy of "a numerous deputation" arrived at Elmina on 13 April 1816, the message—one of assurances of Asante friendship—was not communicated until two days later.[33] Similarly, Governor Samuel Rowe received the Boakye Tenten mission of 1881 at Praso on 16 February, when "the usual complimentary speeches were made and returned. After these the Prince Buaki [Boakye] asked if I would appoint when he would deliver the message."[34] Until the next day when the official message was delivered, the conversation centered on the weather and, in the words of Governor Rowe, subjects that "had no reference to the point in the dispute."[35] The amusing and otiose exchange between the two, therefore, must not be seen as altogether accidental; it was a carefully orchestrated move to postpone the message-delivery, which, by Asante custom, was not normally given at the first meeting.

In most cases the leaders of missions personally delivered the message. In some instances, however, and particularly in some of the bigger missions, a specially qualified "spokesman" besides the leader was attached to the embassy as its "*okyeame*" to deliver the message. Such a person had the gift and training for presenting the case in "more eloquent language."[36] Hence, at the meeting of the Asante delegation and the Governor's party on 18 February 1881, for example, Okyeame Kofi Bene delivered the message, although John Owusu Ansa Sr., the senior ambassador, was present. When the Kofi Apea mission met John R. Holmes, the District Commissioner at Cape Coast in July 1890, it was Yaw Boaten who, as "spokesman" for the delegation, gave the message.[37] In a similar fashion, Boakye Yam Panin *okyeame* Kwaku Fokuo was attached to the London mission of 1894–95 as "spokesman," although the appointed leaders were Kyidomhene Kwame Boaten and John Owusu Ansa, Jr. For this reason it was Kwaku Fokuo who announced to Governor Griffith the purpose and circumstances that had led to the appointment of the embassy.[38] Where both the Asomfohene and the Nseniehene were members of an embassy, the former delivered the message. If the Akyeamehene was in the delegation, he gave the message.[39]

The message-delivery itself also took a specific form. The envoy spoke in the Asantehene's name. Thus, most sentences started with: "The King, my master has instructed me to..."; or "the King sent me to..."; or "I am further to say that..."[40] During missions, the *okyeame's* staff was held by a carrier, although it was the practice for him to hold it when he was delivering the message.[41]

According to the prevailing Akan custom, embassies first reported to the host king's *okyeame*, through whom they also sought interviews and addressed the recipient. Customarily, the delivery of gifts usually preceded the message. Drinking to the health of the sender and recipient sovereigns was also a commonplace practice.[42]

Audience Denial

As might be expected in diplomatic practice at a time when, without the benefit of the communications systems that technology has placed at the disposal of the modern foreign service, pre-arranged meetings could not often be scheduled, instances of audience denial did occur. Such incidents were a slur on the image of both the ambassador and his sender and did not make for the improved relations which Asante continuously sought with its neighbors. Even worse in their impact on foreign relations were the occasions of deliberate audience denial which Asante suffered.

On 12 January 1874 ambassador Owusu Koko Kuma arrived at the British camp at Prasu with both written and oral messages for Sir Garnet Wolseley. Heading a party of fifteen which included the released German missionary J. Kühne, Owusu Koko Kuma was authorized to reassure the British General of Asantehene Kofi Kakari's desire for peace. Towards the achievement of the embassy's primary objective which was to dissuade Garnet Wolseley from advancing on Kumase, the Asante ambassador had been entrusted with responsibility for resolving all differences with the British. To his great dismay and disappointment, however, Owusu Koko Kuma was denied an interview with Major-General Wolseley, although he apparently succeeded in holding discussions with some of the lesser British officers.[43] On Owusu Koko's return the Asantehene expressed regret over Wolseley's refusal to grant an audience to his envoy,[44] the incident failing to assure Asante of the sincerity of the British administration in its professed intentions of peace.

Two instances of audience denial occurred in connection with Asante embassies appointed to treat with the British Government in London in 1820 and 1895, respectively. Though the circumstances differed in detail and nature, both incidents were blatantly enforced in terms of British refusals to grant audiences, and were identical in their violations of diplomatic etiquette and equally shattering in their effect on the faith Asante reposed in the British Government as an honest pursuer of peace. Following the conclusion of the visit to Kumase of Joseph Dupuis as British Consul and Agent in 1820, he was accompanied by an Asante embassy which bore presents from Asantehene Osei Tutu Kwame to King George III of England. However, in Cape Coast the ambassadors were refused passage on a waiting boat by Sir George Collier, the officer commanding the British West Africa Squadron.[45]

By 1895, three quarters of a century after aborting the first attempt by an official Asante delegation to meet with the British sovereign, the British administration had seen a great volume of diplomatic activity from Asante, undeniably as evidence of Asante's determination to reach a satisfactory working relationship. But British attitude towards receiving an Asante embassy in London had apparently not changed.

Even though the 1894–95 embassy was duly appointed by the governing Asantemanhyiamu body of Asante and its members were commissioned orally as well as in writing with proper authorization, Administrator Griffith, acting upon instructions from his government in London, forbade the delegation from proceeding to England. The embassy challenged the validity of Griffith's prohibition, questioning whether "Her Majesty's Government has ever exercised the right of forbidding visitors from any part of the world into their country, or whether the Government has acquired any special rights of this nature over the Kingdom" of Asante.[46] Convinced that the mission would be a failure if the envoys did not meet with the British Government in London, the delegation set sail nonetheless for England, having in the meantime sought legal assistance in their attempts to approach their would-be hosts. In England, the embassy of Kwame Boaten and John Owusu Ansa, Jr., employed every legitimate diplomatic and legal avenue at its disposal to seek an audience with the British Crown—all to no avail.[47]

British justification for refusing to meet with a delegation with peaceful intent from a country to which they had long accorded diplomatic recognition and with which they had had a history of active diplomatic relations was based on frivolous and highly contestable grounds — accusations that the head of Asante, Agyeman Prempe I, was King of Kumase rather than of Asante; that his government practiced human sacrifice; and that the leader of the embassy, John Owusu Ansa, Jr., and his brother Albert were not Asante nationals because their father John Owusu Ansa, Sr., received British training and held appointments with the British administration at Cape Coast. An unstated but clearly more overriding justification in British thinking may well have arisen from a shift in British colonial policy, which was evidently being contemplated at the time of the Asante mission: the British decision to seek the forceful elimination of Asante (rather than the peaceful resolution of differences) must have made any policy that called for the reception of an embassy wholly untenable.[48]

Duration of Embassies

"He who goes out on legitimate business ought not to remain out too long," declared Asantehene Osei Tutu Kwame to visiting Dutch envoy W. Huydecoper in 1816, in a discussion of the conduct of people on diplomatic assignments. This is true above all else, the Asantehene emphasized, in matters of importance such as Asante's relations with its southern neighbors.[49] Speed, both in the travel of embassies and in the transmission of dispatches, was an important factor in external communications. As such, when the Asantehene sent out a mission, he expected the task to be accomplished in the shortest time possible.

It has been pointed out above that in the nineteenth century there were accepted time durations for travel between the metropolitan capital of Kumase and the regional centers; that the time periods represented estimations under ideal conditions; and that therefore most embassies traveled slower than the optimum time durations.[50] To avoid unnecessary delays, time limitations were often imposed on embassies and letter carriers for the completion of their missions. The duration of the Gyaman mission of 1878 was fixed at one month. [51] In another instance, Asantehene Kofi Kakari advised Major-General Wolseley, to whom he was dispatching a mission under the leadership of Esen Kwaku in 1874, not to delay with his response, explaining: "I beg to say that I have given them only fourteen days to perform their journey in and out," that is, to Praso and back.[52]

Technological advances have naturally made travel faster today than in the nineteenth century, and most embassies therefore are of much shorter durations now. Of the envoys who were surveyed, 75 percent indicated that their missions were completed on the average in less than one week, while 25 percent said that their embassies on the whole lasted one to two weeks. There was no mention of embassies which lasted beyond two weeks.

Traveling Pace

Since most embassies traveled over, rather than below, the ideal time durations set for the major distances, the government found it necessary to institute measures for the speedy conveyance of dispatches when the need for urgency arose. Envoys or letter carriers operating under conditions by which they were classified as "express messengers" or "quick runners" provided Asante's response to the problem. Thus, the Dutch administration at Elmina reckoned that under post-haste conditions the distance to Kumase could be covered in three days of seven hours travel each to Asen and another four similar days' journey to the Asante capital.[53] Hence, an "express messenger" who left Kumase with a message and various dispatches, the latest of which was dated 25 June 1816, arrived at Elmina on 11 July, having completed the distance in only 16 days although the envoy passed through Wassa to convey W. Huydecoper's compliments and to discuss proposals for the construction of a road through Wassa with the local chief.[54]

There were occasions, however, when speed was sacrificed for a solemn, deliberate pace. This was generally characteristic of large embassies when such a calculated, slow pace was utilized to emphasize the importance and solemnity of the mission. Contemporary reports concerning Owusu Dome's embassy to Cape Coast in 1820 indicated that the ambassador moved at such a slow pace that "his approach had been so long a theme of conversation on the coast."[55] Typical of large embassies, the "advance guard" of Owusu Dome's traveling suite announced his approach long before his arrival. Ambassador Tando was known to have visited Cape Coast in the grandest of styles, "never going the shortest distance, but in his taffeta hammock, covered with gorgeous umbrella, and surrounded by flatterers, who even wiped the ground before he trod on it."[56] The Owusu Taseamandi extradition mission of 1881 was small in size, but being "a solemn mission," news of its approach indicated that the envoys were "delaying in a stately way" along the coast between Elmina and Cape Coast.[57] The extradition subject itself, touching on national security, was regarded as a "serious palaver," and the solemnity and gravity of the mission were augmented by the use of the Golden Axe.

Inviolability of Ambassadors

The most comprehensive single picture of diplomatic inviolability in Asante is contained in Joseph Dupuis' commentary on the subject. Immunities were generally not guaranteed, Dupuis observed, except:

> the character of ambassador, whose person should be held inviolate, that of king's merchant or trader which is equally sacred, hunters of elephants in the king's name, and on his account; and lastly, men of rank, or others whose influence or interest at court is powerful enough to gain for them a travelling protection by the use of the king's name, and recommendation to other sovereigns and princes. These, and only such characters, are passports for the subjects of Ashantee, by which they may travel in security....[58]

To this list should be added, generally, men on all types of official business carrying swords, shields, axes, canes, and other symbols of office. Though these objects were not in themselves passports as Bowdich contended, they gave the bearers considerable immunities because they evidenced the royal or official origin of their missions.

Several Asante oaths could also be used to secure immunities. On his arrest by Dutch Governor Nagtglas in 1871, for example, the resident ambassador for Elmina, Akyampon Yaw, secured his freedom for thirty days by "swearing the great oath of the king to return to Kumase."[59] The oaths generally refer to calamitous events or disasters in the history of Asante. By the Memeneda Akromanti, for example, Asantes recall to mind the grievous misfortune which befell their nation one Saturday when their king Osei Tutu died in a war against the Akyem. If a person who was adjured by such an oath refused to obey, the inference was that he did not care about how much Asantes suffered on that occasion. By the deduction that he who is not for me is against me, the conclusion was drawn that whoever treated such an oath with contempt or disdain was an enemy of Asante.[60]

Diplomatic inviolability and its general recognition were related to political stability, which ultimately guaranteed a level of personal security for even non-diplomats. In the Gold Coast at large and Asante in particular, respect for state sovereignty facilitated the observance of immunities for government representatives. Indeed, Asante always considered all envoys to be "sacred either in peace or in war." Such an assurance was given to the British administration at Cape Coast for the safety of Joseph Dupuis, W. Hutton, and other members of their party in going to Kumase.[61] In assuring the Governor and his council that there was no cause for them to be apprehensive about the safety of the Dupuis mission because the persons of envoys were held inviolate in Asante, Owusu Dome reminded them that "that the king thinks highly of his ambassadors, there can be no doubt, from the manner in which he punished the Assins and Fantees for having killed two of his messengers in 1806."[62]

Perversions of Inviolability

In general, European administrators on the Gold Coast were not unmindful of the fact that envoys were "sacred" and were entitled to pass unmolested anywhere,[63] although this awareness did not nonetheless preclude perversions of inviolability. Numerous instances of violations of the rights of Asante envoys to the security of their persons and properties occurred in the nineteenth century, perhaps not unexpected altogether in that age. The offending parties were both European administrators and local subject and independent states.

Among the best known cases of violations of inviolability were the instances that marred Asante's relations with Asen and Fante in the late eighteenth and early nineteenth centuries and culminated in the Asante invasion of those areas in 1806–1807. The crisis originated as a local Asen feud over jurisdictional matters between Asen Apemanimhene Amo Adae on the one hand, and Kwaku Aputae and Kwadwo Tibu, who jointly exercised authority over Asen Atandanso, on the other. The handling of this dispute by Asantehene Osei Kwame and his successor Osei Tutu Kwame underscored their government's determination to restore order to its dependent provinces. In a succession of events, Aputae and Tibu showed not only their unwillingness to cooperate with Amo Adae, in whose favor the Asantehene's verdict in the case went, but also their flagrant disregard of universal diplomatic norms regarding the inviolability of ambassadors. Asante envoys who were dispatched to Kwaku Aputae and Kwadwo Tibu were massacred by the Asen leaders, who "tauntingly suspended their mutilated bodies upon trees" by the feet or arms. [64] When further attempts initiated by Asantehene Osei Kwame to resolve the Asen conflict were rejected by Aputai and Tibu with decisive disrespect, Asante forces under the command of Anantahene Apea Dankwa and Gyaasewahene Opoku Frefre entered Asen in 1798. Faced with imminent defeat, the Asen rebels escaped southwards to Asikuma and then to Abora. In his anxiety to seek a peaceful solution wherever possible, the Asantehene sent envoys with presents to the king of Abora, attempting to reopen negotiations. The gifts were accepted, but the Council of Abora refused to cooperate. As a result the Asante army was ordered to advance on Fante, and although the latter was decisively routed, Kwaku Aputae and Kwadwo Tibu eluded capture.[65]

Soon after his accession to the *Sika Dwa* (Golden Stool), Osei Tutu Kwame turned his attention to Asen and Fante affairs. As part of his efforts to resume negotiations, he dispatched in 1805 an embassy to Abora, headed by Esom Adu, tentatively to be identified as Dadiesoba *okyeame* and Adontenhene Kwaaten Pete's nephew.[66] The embassy was instructed to request from the Fante free passage for the Asante army in pursuit of the Asen rebel leaders, who had meanwhile taken refuge on the coast. Once again, the Asante envoys were brutally tortured: "their bodies were cut open and stuffed with a preparation of salt and malaqueta pepper."[67] The Asen rebellion of the late eighteenth and early nineteenth centuries, which was exacerbated by repeated violations of immunities for diplomats, directly led to the Asante invasion of Fante in 1806 and, for the timely surrender of British administrators at Anomabo Castle, would have resulted in an Asante-British war owing to British protection for the Asen rebels.

The campaign of 1818–19 to suppress a Gyaman rebellion had an unexpected effect on Asante's relations with the British and Fante in the form of a patent disregard for diplomatic inviolability by the local residents. As the campaign became prolonged, the Fante encouraged the spread of rumors originating in Kumase regarding disasters said to have befallen the Asante army and began to break into rejoicings of a Gyaman victory and tauntings of Asante residents. When the war was finally over, the Asantehene sent envoys to Fante and Komenda with jawbones as "trophies of success." At Komenda the envoys were treated with insult and assault, and were "turned out of the town in contemptuous defiance and ridicule," one of them, Esen Koso, losing his gold cap, the sign of his office, in the affray. They proceeded to Cape Coast to seek redress, in accordance with existing agreements, from Governor Hope-Smith, who showed no inclination to assume interest or responsibility.

Yet another major incident involving perversions of inviolability belongs to this period. Shortly after his return to the Gold Coast from Sierra Leone as head of the British settlements in 1823, Sir Charles MacCarthy resolved to resort to war to clear British differences with Asante. Towards the prosecution of his designs, he proclaimed martial law in Accra. During this time the renowned ambassador, Asante Agyei, was in Accra on official business. In contravention of diplomatic immunities, he was arrested and imprisoned in James Fort. The Ga chiefs interceded on Asante Agyei's behalf, in consequence of which he was released. On his return to Kumase, the Asante envoy is said to have advised hundreds of traders he met on their way to the coast to return.[69]

Unprovoked attacks on Asante envoys traveling through the southern provinces continued throughout the century. In 1865 the British administration formally acknowledged that such conduct on the part of the Asen, Wassa, Denkyira, and other people was improper and conceded that the government may even have condoned such behavior. Reporting to his home government in September of that year, Governor Edward Conran noted that the recent silence on the part of Asante (since 1863) was:

> attributable to the dangerous and improper policy hitherto pursued by the people of the Protectorate residing on its border (Denkera, Wassa and Assin in particular) who conceive it to be their duty towards this Government to behead and ill-treat such unfortunate harmless Ashantees as may show their faces amongst them, possibly messengers of peace on their way to the Governor... whilst in some instances these Assins have even sent to the Governor here Ashantee jawbones as trophies and a sure indication of another immediate invasion.... Such men as happen to escape run back to Coomassie telling their King and Chiefs (naturally enough) how they have been treated by this Government for permitting such a state of things to exist among a tribe in our Protectorate instead of our endeavouring to... cultivate a proper understanding.

Conran cited as an example the "cruel behaviour in sending back to Coomassie, with an insulting message, the head of one of the King's Messengers" who was sent on a mission to Akyem Kotokuhene Agyeman in 1862 and continued:

> Conduct [was] repeated, I am sorry to say, in August 1863 by the Assins who flogged messengers passing through their country en route to Coomassie from this coast, having come down from the King to the Governor with a message, men I myself saw here....Conduct [was] for the third time followed by the old Queen of Assin [Amma Dankoaa], whose people in April last in a large company entered the Ashante country capturing a chief named Appintah, his grandchild and thirteen others.... [70]

To curtail such improper conduct, Governor Conran recommended the stationing at such locations along the Kumase-Cape Coast route as Manso, Yankomase, and Praso, of "special messengers" who could read, write, and speak Twi and Fante, and who could be his representatives in maintaining order and protecting people passing up and down the major roads. George Blankson, the Fante who on several occasions served as British emissary to the Asante government, was earmarked as one of such law enforcement commissioners. Nothing is known of the outcome of these measures, which seems to suggest that they might not have been followed through, and in consequence, perversions of inviolability persisted.

Among the senior Asante ambassadors of the nineteenth century who suffered the indignation of breaches of inviolability was Akyampon Yaw. As resident ambassador for the southwestern provinces and for Dutch affairs, Akyampon Yaw's posting to Elmina coincided with the period of secret negotiations between the Dutch and British administrations for the transfer of the former's settlements to the latter. The British refused to proceed with the negotiations as long as Dutch title to Elmina was in doubt. The dubiousness of Dutch claims to Elmina seemed to have been reinforced by the presence of Akyampon Yaw, who, as the Asante government's resident, represented Asante's title to the place. To emphasize their view of the case, the British therefore insisted upon the removal from Elmina of the Asante resident ambassador. On 14 April 1871 the Dutch authorities accordingly arrested Akyampon Yaw and threatened to suspend the payment of the "notes" to the Asantehene until he withdrew his claim to Elmina.[71] On swearing the Asantehene's oath to return to Kumase in thirty days, Akyampon Yaw was released. However, the British government was not prepared to have anything to do with the transfer of forts while the

Asante resident ambassador remained in Elmina. Writing to the Earl of Kimberley on 8 February 1872, Arthur Kennedy insisted that the Dutch authorities be called upon to remove Akyampon Yaw to the west as a "preliminary" to any further steps in the transfer.[72] In October Akyampon Yaw, his two sons Yaw Kodua and Kofi Boakye, and other members of his party were recaptured.[73]

When Akyampon Yaw finally left Elmina, the Fante prevented him from taking his stool with him, thereby committing a further violation of diplomatic inviolability. On his return to Kumase, he requested the Asantehene to provide him with some men to accompany him to the coast to recover his stool. In Asen, however, Akyampon Yaw was again intercepted, and he succeeded in making his way to Elmina only because he received reinforcements from Kumase.

Perhaps the most publicized violation of diplomatic inviolability involved John Owusu Ansa, Sr., in Cape Coast in 1873, when his house was plundered, his servants murdered, and his life and those of his family and other envoys living with him threatened. A detailed account of the incident is provided by Brackenbury, who recorded that "on the 16th of March, an outrage of a most cruel and savage character had occurred in the town of Cape Coast. Five Ashantis who were living in the house of Prince Ansah had been seized by a mob, who had dragged them to the beach and cut off their heads."[74] The victims included members of the families of envoys Kotirko, Bosommuru Dwira, and Owusu Koko Kuma. Afarkwa, a servant of John Owusu Ansa, Sr., and a man who had lived on the coast for twenty-two years, was also decapitated. Owusu Ansa sent to ask for protection, and a party of policemen arrived just in time to save him and the rest from being murdered by the Fante mob which was led by Messrs. W. E. Davidson, James Brew, and James Amissah. With difficulty, a pregnant woman, later to be identified as the wife of Kotirko, was rescued through the efforts of the British administration. It became necessary for Owusu Ansa and Kotirko to be temporarily lodged at the castle for their own safety.

Fearing for his life, Owusu Ansa wrote to Administrator Harley to request a more permanent arrangement from the British:

> As the popular feeling among the masses of the people in this town is just now so strong against me that I cannot hope for at least some time to come to live out in the town in peace and safety, I humbly entreat your Excellency kindly to consider whether I can be removed, under the kind auspices of her Majesty's Government, to some other place in the British colonies or Settlements on this Coast. [75]

The younger John Owusu Ansa came close to suffering a breach of diplomatic immunity in January 1885, at a time when he was leading an Asante embassy to England. While the embassy was in Cape Coast, a warrant was issued for the arrest of Owusu Ansa on a charge of being late to court to appear as a witness. Although the arrest could not be effected because Owusu Ansa himself, unaware of the warrant, showed up in court soon afterwards, and the court dismissed the action, the embassy wrote to register its displeasure to the British administration that the warrant was issued out at all: "from the fact that the said Prince being known to your Government as one of the special ambassadors accredited to your Excellency and her Brittanic Majesty... we believe that the law should have been inoperative on his person according to the general usages of international courtesy." [76]

Such incidents of disregard for the safety of ambassadors were considered crimes of the highest order, serious enough to lead possibly to war. It cannot be doubted, for instance, that the Asen and Fante assaults on Asante envoys weighed heavily in Osei Tutu Kwame's decision to march on the coast in 1806. The same trend of thought appeared evident in the Asantehene's explanation of the cause of the Gyaman war to visiting British envoy Joseph Dupuis. Addressing a captive son of Adinkra of Gyaman before Mr. Dupuis in 1820, Osei Tutu Kwame emphasized: Adinkra "killed my sword bearers and sent me an insulting message."[77] Earlier, during the negotiations that preceded the Bowdich Treaty in 1817, Akyeamehene Kwadwo Adusei Kyakya had painstakingly complained about the wrongs the Asantehene suffered at the hands of the Fante, who "scourged his messengers." British administrators must have been pleased that Asantehene Kofi Kakari did not make the perversions of inviolability which Akyampon Yaw suffered a cause of the 1873 Asante invasion of the coast—a cause which would have been plausible in view of the pressure which the British brought upon the Dutch to arrest Akyampon Yaw. [78] Violations of the guarantees of diplomats to the safety of their persons and their properties could also lead to the closure of the great roads. Following the Komenda jawbone incident of 1819 and the death of Opentri, for example, Asantehene Osei Tutu Kwame reluctantly reacted by forbidding his traders to visit the coast. The gravity with which Asante viewed the issue of inviolability lay in considerations of representation: an affront or insult to an ambassador could be equated with the same to his sender.[79]

Remuneration and Sustenance of Ambassadors

Although ambassadors were remunerated in various forms, they received no pay as such. Host governments generally supported ambassadors for the period of their residence in the foreign land through voluntary gifts which were collectively referred to as *ahohosomde*. Such gifts were also intended to help in defraying the expenses of the journey.[80] As a general rule, all gifts received by envoys from their recipients were meant for themselves, except those specifically intended for the Asantehene. On the envoy's return, he was expected to announce, and where possible, show all gifts received to the Asantehene so that the latter might know the generosity of the hosts and appropriately thank them. [81]

By making himself known at every town along the way as an official envoy, he could also enjoy the generosity of the inhabitants through whose territories he passed.[82] Indeed, diplomats were permitted, within reasonable bounds, to support themselves en route. There is evidence, however, of the susceptibility of this right to abuse, and of reports of the excessive grabbing of food, provisions, drinks, and other requisitions in an extortionist manner. Brodie Cruickshank, for example, noted that "a systematic course of oppression and exploitation was practiced by the king's officers."[83]

A significant part of the income of the foreign service personnel was derived from fees and commissions which accrued to them as *nseniefo, afenasoafo,* and *akyeame* in connection with their regular legal functions. The *nseniefo,* for example, received a fee for the publication of decrees. The case of the Nseniehene Kwadwo Ampan, who was entitled to receive between 10 ackies (five-eighths of an ounce of gold) and 20 ackies from the government and the people, respectively, for publicizing decrees in Kumase in the early nineteenth century has been cited.[84] Because many of the officials who served in diplomatic capacities were drawn from the palace functionaries, a large portion of their revenue came from *aseda* and *mmataho*. In general terms *aseda* may be regarded as court fines and fees, and was paid by the innocent party as a way of offering thanks and for "the purpose of securing witnesses to attest to the judgment of the court."[85] *Mmataho* was the commission that accrued to the court functionaries from *aseda*. An *afenasoani* derived 2s out of an *aseda* of £4: 13s, a commission of approximately one-fortieth. That for an *okyeame*, whose proportion was larger than the *afensoani's,* amounted to £6: l2s out of 6 peredwans (£48), that is, about one-eighth.[86] One further source of income existed for members of the *Gyaasewa* (Exchequer) as "commissions" derived from the disbursement of government revenues. Bowdich observed in the l8l0s that the royal weights were one-third heavier than the current weights in the country, and that "all the gold expended in provision being weighed out in the former and laid out in the latter, the difference enrich" the *Gyaasewa* functionaries, whence "the linguists derive the greater part of their income."[87]

One form of financial arrangement for ambassadors was along "contract" basis. The ambassador or leader of a mission was paid a lump sum of money for the expenses of himself and the members of his party. On his return he was expected to render account. The Gyaman mission of 1878 throws illuminating insights into the operation of this arrangement and the financial organization connected with large embassies. From his Cape Coast base Owusu Ansa, Sr., was entrusted with responsibility for organizing a goodwill mission to Bonduku, for the expenses of which he was advanced 80 oz. of gold. In this particular instance Owusu Ansa himself never proceeded beyond Kumase. However, he succeeded in engaging the services of Carl Nielson as head of the mission and J. J. C. Huydecoper as clerk-interpreter. Owusu Ansa also claimed that he engaged various individuals totaling nearly 60, including hammockmen, carriers, and servants. He had the authority to negotiate the salaries of the men he hired. Nielson's salary was fixed at £200 and Huydecoper's at £100. The hammockmen and others were to be paid wages at ls.6d a day.[88]

The mission was attended with failures and disasters. Not long after his arrival in Bonduku, Carl Nielson died. Lacking the proper authority to assume the leadership of the mission, Huydecoper returned to Kumase for a fresh mandate. The Asantehmanhyiamu commissioned him to the leadership of the mission, and accordingly raised his pay from £100 to £144. On Huydecoper's return, the hammockmen had deserted him. The statements of Kwadwo Obimpe and Tamfuben, both hammockmen, though conflicting as to whether Carl Nielson actually did or did not see the Gyamanhene, were in agreement that Huydecoper suspended the pay of the hammockmen the moment Nielson died.[89]

Difficulties continued to bedevil the Gyaman mission and apparently led to Huydecoper's withdrawal from Bonduku to Banda for safety reasons.[90] For Owusu Ansa, a series of legal suits was awaiting him in the "British" court at Cape Coast in 1879. The hammockmen brought forward claims of arrears of pay totaling £537 4s 8d. At the same time, dissatisfied with his commission, Huydecoper accused Owusu Ansa of cheating him and threatened to sue him for £1,004: 8s:10 1/2d, reckoned at about £150 a month. [91] Although we do not know the verdicts in these suits, Owusu Ansa himself reported that in a third case brought forward against him by an envoy sent from Kumase to inquire after Mr. Nielson's death, he was adjudged the loser and was fined.

The financial problems that faced the Gyaman mission were certainly atypical of nineteenth century embassies. However, the contract arrangement on which this and many other missions operated brought to the fore two important characteristics: the autonomy in financial control which ambassadors and leaders of mission enjoyed, and the absence of standardized rates for diplomats. A more common form of financial arrangement however, continues to be the direct, non-contract system by which the envoy is given a sum of money to cover the expenses of his mission. Such payments are made before the commencement of the journey. All envoys who were contacted during the field interviews indicated that the value of the money is variable rather than fixed.

There is reason to believe that diplomatic service as a whole was not well remunerated in the nineteenth century. It can be inferred from Owusu Ansa, Sr.'s complaints about inadequate compensation and difficulty in getting paid after undertaking missions that diplomatic service was not well rewarded financially. Though most envoys found it rewarding to lead missions, it was generally the fringe benefits, including the opportunity to undertake private business in the area being sent to, rather than the actual monetary remuneration that made foreign service financially attractive. However, it is significant to note that evidence of envoys facing financial hardships on missions, or being indebted, or securing loans to defray expenses was rare; that most diplomats were income-earning, full-time, domestic office-holders; and that the majority of the people who served as envoys fell outside the Owusu Ansa, Sr. syndrome. Given these considerations diplomatic service can be said to have been financially competitive. Furthermore, the distinction has to be drawn between being adequately compensated for specific occasions when one is called upon to undertake missions, on the one hand, and receiving remuneration as a permanent functionary as an *afenasoani, okyeame* or *fotosani* (treasury official), on the other. For whereas seventy percent of those who were surveyed in 1980 indicated that they felt that they had been adequately rewarded for their participation in missions, their opinion on the level of financial support they received as permanent functionaries was a different matter altogether.

Successful Completion of Missions

The general practice was for returning envoys to report to the Asantehene sitting in Council. Information derived from orally transmitted sources also suggests that except for the *nhenkwaa* (household servants) who reported directly to the Asantehene on their return from usually low-level missions, it was the normal practice in the nineteenth century for *afenasoafo,* who received their appointment as envoys through the Asomfohene, first to report to the head of the *asomfo* (servants) establishment on their return before they were taken to the Asantehene.[92] Envoys were expected to give detailed accounts of the conduct of their missions and, in particular, deliver accurately the response to the messages they had carried. They were also expected to report on all matters which, though lying outside the immediate purview of their missions, could be considered useful information that needed to be brought to the government's attention. Until the envoy had been formally received by the Asantehene and the Asantemanhyiamu and had rendered an account of his mission, he was forbidden to divulge information relating to his mission. Before then, he was enjoined to refrain from public contact, if he was considered to be the bearer of sensitive political information.

For long a myth has been maintained by some European authors that "an invariable rule of the Ashantees is to behead the man who bears bad tiding."[93] This falls into the general picture painted of the Asantehene of an autocrat unrestrained by law. The truth is that like diplomatic missions in every age and every society, the successful completion of a mission was looked to with joy by all concerned. Asantehene Agyeman Prempe I expressed the sentiments of the governments of Asante when he remarked that "it is an honour to him [the ambassador] in our country's custom to come back when the case is properly settled."[94] Though this observation was made with respect to Kofi Apea's mission of 1890, the Asantehene's statement candidly reflected the importance the government attached to the successful completion of missions. En route in Elmina on an embassy to negotiate the return of Asante refugees with the British administration in Accra, Kofi Apea wrote to District Commissioner J. R. Holmes of Cape Coast in July 1890 to seek his assistance in obtaining an interview with Governor W. B. Griffith. The letter itself revealed the great anxiety of the ambassador to meet personally with the Governor in Accra rather than his regional representative in Cape Coast, for without that his mission would be considered a failure:

> I earnestly pray that I should be permitted to proceed down to Accra to see his Excellency personally before I return to Ashantee, for without my seeing first his Excellency, my return to Ashantee will be sorrowful both to the king and all his subjects.[95]

When no resolution of the issue was in sight and Kofi Apea, determined in his resolve to accomplish the goal of his mission, prolonged his stay in Accra, the Asantehene seemed to have approved of his ambassador's course of action: "I know that Chief Appia's stay on the coast is an expense to you," he wrote to British administrator Griffith in January 1891, "yet still I pray that he may be allowed to wait until the case for which he came for be properly settled before your Excellency;" for, according to Asante tradition, it was a great honor for ambassadors to return home after their missions had been accomplished.[96] Six months later the Asantehene expressed his feeling of great disappointment to the British Governor that Kofi Apea had had to return to Kumase without fulfilling the goals of his mission, having been denied the full cooperation of the British administration:

> I regret to say that my representative Chief Appia's mission to the coast has proved unsatisfactory, his mission has being [sic] of a useless character, and I write this from the ground of my heart, that I have felt it very much: I know that white men like plain and true, so I do not wish to conceal any thing from you, and I write this with a friendly spirit.[97]

Kyidomhene Kwame Boaten, who was to be appointed the traditional head of the 1894–95 embassy to England, led an earlier mission which further exemplified the determination of ambassadors to seek the successful completion of their missions. Kwame Boaten is reported to have first seen the British Governor in Accra on 16 October 1884. He thanked the British administration for sending commissioners Barrow and Kirby to Kumase in an effort to settle the succession dispute and requested that Captain Barrow be sent back to Asante to "look into the establishment of peace." Kwame Boaten refused to return home until such time that a British Commissioner was appointed, and was reported to be still in Accra in August 1886, having intimated that the most immediate goals of his mission would be regarded as unsuccessful if he were to go back without the "white officer."[98]

Ambassador Kwame Boaten remained on the coast for nearly four years. He held another meeting with W. B. Griffith on 13 January 1888, at which he requested that the Governor give him a response to be taken back to Kumase to show that he had properly performed the duties entrusted him. Kwame Boaten finally returned to Kumase on 25 January 1888. His sense of accomplishment on this occasion rested on the fact that he was accompanied to Kumase by Dr. Sullivan, a surgeon in the service of the colonial government, and Assistant Inspector E. A. Barnett.

Okyeame Boaten's concern, which epitomized those of other ambassadors in similar situations, was that he might be considered negligent if he returned home without achieving the main object of his mission. Despite the long duration of his embassy, Administrator Griffith considered that the Asante ambassador fully justified the trust and confidence reposed in him.[99] In what virtually amounted to an endorsement of his conduct, Governor Griffith observed that Kwame Boaten "carried out his mission loyally and faithfully to his country, so far as it was in his power to do this."[100] As long as he was not recalled, it was Kwame Boaten's firm belief that the government intended to abide by his original commission and therefore expected him to seek the successful end of his mission.

Anxiety to conclude missions successfully led some envoys to exercise discretion in undertaking actions beyond what could have been foreseen on the commencement of their missions. When Asante was pushed into a situation where it had to pay an indemnity as the price of peace in 1881, ambassador Boakye Tenten's concern for the successful conclusion of an Asante-British understanding led him to remain in Elmina after his discussions with Governor Samuel Rowe until the third and final installment towards the 2,000 ounces of gold being demanded by the British had been received from Kumase. Until then, he went out of his way to pawn his personal ornaments as security.[101]

Portraying an identical sense of responsibility, ambassador Gyakye Nantwi's zeal and commitment to his 1878 mission to the British caused him to prolong his stay for two years, eventually committing suicide unexpectedly in Accra out of frustration.[102] For one whole year beginning in November 1894, the embassy to England used every means at its disposal, including engaging the services of a counsel, to seek an audience with the British government, for the *raison d'être* of the mission, which was to bring certain representations before the No. 10 Downing Street administration, would be considered as having been unfulfilled if he were to return home without an audience.[103]

Misconduct and Penalties

As might be expected, instances of misconduct were known to have occurred on the part of some diplomatic officials. Corruption was a common form of misconduct, particularly in the early part of the century, when laws regulating the conduct of diplomatic personnel were just beginning to come into force. It is believed, for example, that the Asantehenes were defrauded of a significant proportion of ground rent collected in respect of the castles. Bowdich estimated that out of 62 ounces paid as ground rent on Christiansborg Castle in 1816 and 1817, the envoys sent to collect the tax embezzled 23 ounces, that is, 37 percent.[104] Evidence was also prevalent of suppression and extortion on the part of some resident ambassadors in Fante and Ga, often in the Asantehene's name.[105] Improper behavior took other forms, including presumption, insubordination, and bribery. Other major forms of misconduct were treachery, indiscretion, mismanagement, and exceeding authority.

The incidents of misconduct cited and discussed below are significant for the insights they provide not only into the slowly emerging rules of conduct for envoys but also into the Asante judicial process itself. All reported cases of misconduct were investigated, thoroughly tried, and dealt with in accordance with the prevailing judicial system. Both the prosecution and the defense could avail themselves of witnesses at the trials which were held in public. That the accused official was provided with opportunities for defending himself is evidence of the rein given to the due process of law. Instances were therefore known of envoys being acquitted after it had been proved that they were not guilty of the charges preferred against them.

In 1816 resident ambassador Kwame Butuakwa was recalled to Kumase "to answer for his conduct," an apparent reference to the negotiation of the Fante notes and his refusal to permit letters to be transmitted from Cape Coast to Kumase unless carried by legitimate envoys. Kwame Butuakwa's conduct in the two circumstances was investigated, and he was exonerated on both counts. Though Thomas Bowdich claimed that he interceded on Kwame Butuakwa's behalf, the ambassador was evidently beyond reproach; no wrong-doing could be substantiated in the matter of the notes, while the insistence that only official envoys be entrusted with the care of dispatches was clearly a central government directive that was apparently unknown to the British administration at Cape Coast at the time.[106] Elmina ambassador Akyampon Yaw provides another example of a diplomat who was vindicated after investigations into his conduct in 1872 had failed to corroborate charges of mishandling of Elmina affairs. Thus, rather than facing possible disgrace, Akyampon Yaw was "set up with all due honours," that is, reinstated with a new commission to liberate the southwest with a force of 3,000 men.[107]

An instance involving the conduct of a mission to Cape Coast by Okra Dehye in 1819 illustrates both the high premium placed on proper behavior on the part of envoys and the vigilance of the Asantehene and his government in enforcing rules of conduct. Okra Dehye who arrived in Cape Coast to request the governor's mediation in an incident involving an assault on Asante jawbone-carrying envoys by Komenda, returned with "an uncourteous and unfriendly" response; British Governor Hope Smith is reported to have told Okra Dehye that the Asantehene could come down on Cape Coast "in forty days, or in twenty, or as soon as he thought proper. Asantehene Osei Tutu Kwame, who least expected such an uncomplimentary reply from the Africa Company official, was enraged to a great degree of anger against this officer, whom he accused of falsehood."[108] Okra Dehye was put under arrest, pending an investigation.[109] Upon the dispatch to Cape Coast in June 1819 of another envoy to ascertain whether Okra Dehye had deceived the Asantehene, or Mr. Hope-Smith had actually made those defiant remarks, evidence came to light that the Governor's message might have been distorted by interpreter De Graft, whereupon he was set free.

Cases involving envoys who were tried and found guilty of misconduct shed important light on our understanding of the range of improper behavior and the corresponding penalties. Envoy "Okranameah" was accused of misconduct on suspicions of falsehood in 1819. He reported in Kumase that he had been neglected by his host Mr. Hope-Smith, and that he had been denied a present. A trial was held at Bowdich's instigation, and when the envoy's box was sent for and searched, two engravings were found, which confirmed Okranameah's guilt.[110] Evidence brought forward at the trial left no doubt that the envoy grossly misrepresented to the Asantehene his reception in Cape Coast; that he was treated with "the greatest civility; and that on his departure he himself expressed gratification on the attention he had received." Okranameah was also found guilty on another count of irregularity with respect to goods he had purchased in Cape Coast while on official duties, and was disgraced.[111]

Tando, an ambassador who specialized in southwest Gold Coast affairs, presents an interesting case of misconduct: that of exceeding one's mandate. Tando received a commission in 1816 to investigate and settle an Elmina dispute. Although he was authorized to work out a settlement, the proposals were to have been submitted to the Asantehmanhyiamu for final ratification. After holding discussions in Elmina, Tando, on his own accord, proceeded to Wassa, where he evidently scored a diplomatic victory by conciliating the local king and binding the people to an agreement to be of good behavior. He then returned to Elmina to impose this settlement on an assembly of the kings and elders of Elmina and Komenda, going as far as to announce penalties for violations of the treaty. Following the conclusion of the agreement, Wassa deputies went to Kumase to protest that ambassador Tando had made false representations to them.[112] Irrespective of the merits of the Wassa complaints, there was a general feeling in Kumase about the success of Tando's mission and his ability to produce a concrete agreement. Notwithstanding, Tando was severely reprimanded by the Asantehene; his offense was one of presumption. In a letter to Dutch Governor-General Daendels, Asantehene Osei Tutu Kwame sharply criticized his ambassador for acting *ultra vires:*

> I sent this person to the Wassa to fetch my prisoners of war, and did not sent him for any other matters; so I repudiate all that he has done. [113]

In a separate statement, the Asantehene summed up his disgust at Tando's indiscretion: "No man must dare to do good out of his own head." The issue of Tando's indiscretion has been raised elsewhere by Wilks. [114] The seriousness of Tando's conduct lay in the political implication of the ambassador's action, which, albeit undertaken in good faith, was that he was thought to have reactivated "a palaver which he [the king] and his great men meant to sleep for a long time."[115]

There were some indications at the time that the Asantehene looked to the Dutch Administrator rather than his ambassador for an overall settlement of Wassa disputes. Even so, Tando's action in working out a Wassa settlement without consultation with his government *ipso facto* removed the agreement from the Asantehene's control. Not Tando's position as a senior diplomat, nor his renown as a "trusty servant of his king," nor his reputation for honesty could save him from punishment.[116] He was retired in 1819 from his embassy in Akyem, "stripped of all his property for his presumption and from a noble became a beggar." Thus, the ambassador who used to visit Cape Coast "in great pomp" now had "scarcely a cloth to cover him." [117]

Following the loss of Elmina to the British in 1872, the Asante government set up a Court of Inquiry to investigate the circumstances surrounding the transaction. At the trial, Akyampon Yaw brought forward charges against ambassadors Kofi Afrifa and Kotirko for being accomplices in the controversial "Certificate of Apology" and therefore for surrendering Elmina to the British. Kofi Afrifa was found guilty, a verdict which was given credence to by his infraction of import regulations; Afrifa was known to have brought from the coast goods he failed to declare in Kumase but secretly conveyed to his village for sale. He was flogged, his hands and feet put in the stocks (logs), and his property and wives confiscated as punishment for his falsehood.[118] It might be inferred from Kotirko's sudden departure from Kumase that he might have similarly been disgraced. He left Kumase for Adanse where he resumed his career as a confidential envoy in the service of the Adansehene, Kwaku Nkansa, and is known to have become hostile to the interests of Asante.[119]

Although the subject of misconduct was initially received with some degree of reluctance or reticence by some informants during the field interviews, there were no grounds to lead to the inference that the quality of the responses was impaired. Responses to a question which asked the informants to list the common forms of misconduct in a descending order of incidence produced the following results:

1. Exceeding authority
2. Presumptuousness
3. Indiscretion
4. Bribery or embezzlement
5. Treachery
6. Mismanagement

The evidence indicates that the incidence of misconduct is generally low today.

Given that the majority of the respondents expressed the opinion that they were sufficiently empowered for their missions, the fact that "exceeding authority" topped the list of offenses seemed surprising. However, it should be borne in mind that diplomatic representation involves to a large extent issues of mandate and its exercise. That mismanagement is considered the least common form of offense is a wholesome commentary on the competence of the personnel employed in diplomatic activity; the relatively low incidence of bribery and treachery is a no less healthy reflection on the conduct of people engaged in a service that places a high premium on trust and honesty.

The usual penalty for misconduct in the nineteenth century was loss of office and properties. The gold dust of all disgraced persons became state revenue. Thus, on Acting Anantahene Apea Nyanyo's disgrace in 1817, three jars of gold dust were confiscated from him. [120] Under certain circumstances, it was considered more honorable for a disgraced public officer to take his own life "rather than continue living as an object of ridicule." [121] Such a consideration might have influenced the envoy who is believed to have shot himself on the Pra River on 2 January 1874. The occasion was the dispatch of two envoys to British General Garnet Wolseley with letters and an offer of peace. Sir Garnet Wolseley declined to receive the envoys and ordered that they should be shown the British preparations for war. A Gatling mitrailleuse was fired, which caused one of the envoys to remark to his colleague that every hope of defense was lost. His comrade taunted him with cowardice and threatened to report him to the Asantehene, whereupon he was reported to have shot himself rather than return to face the consequences of his faint-heartedness. [122] Humiliated office-holders could also be expected to go into voluntary exile. The usual penalties for misconduct today include cautioning, reprimanding, fining, disgracing, demotion, and removal from office.

As diplomatic activity grew in response to the need for an adjustment of Asante's relations with its neighbors, so did procedures regulating diplomatic practice and the conduct of envoys on missions become standardized and systematized. Thus, formal procedures developed regarding diplomatic appointments, audiences, travel, conduct, and return—developments which pointed in the direction of increasing specialization and which were undoubtedly in line with diplomatic representation everywhere.

CHAPTER 4

Some Major Embassies

This is a two part chapter; in the first section the involvement of prominent minority groups in diplomatic careers is examined, while in the second, case studies of several major embassies are undertaken. The thrust of the analysis of the major embassies provided here is along lines intended to substantiate the behavior characteristics of embassies identified in the previous chapter, bring to the fore the complex organization of such embassies, and underscore the importance of large embassies in Asante diplomacy.

In the typologies of Asante embassies three major classificatory groups could be identified. In a descending order of importance, these were recognized as follows.

1. Those which comprised an *obirempon*, that is, a divisional chief, a senior *okyeame*, an *afenasoani*, and an *nsenieni*;

2. Those that were headed by a junior *okyeame* but also included an *afenasoani* and an *nsenieni*; and

3. Those that were led by an *afenasoani* or an *nsenieni*.[1]

In all cases a member of the *afenasoafo* and/or *nseniefo* was always present and actually headed the third type of embassies. Sizes ranged from hundreds in the first group to just two or one in the third.

Major embassies that comprised several hundred persons or more characteristically consisted of three parts: an advance party which announced the approach of the embassy and prepared for the main group; the main body which consisted of the leader and his staff, in other words, the core members of the party; and the entourage which rounded up the group. The majority of the members of large embassies was made up of tens or hundreds of carriers, hammockmen, and all ranges of attendants and servants. Ambassadors who commanded large delegations were commonly served by a staff, including interpreters, secretaries or scribes, account-keepers, and spokesmen.

Prominent Minority Groups in Diplomatic Careers

Akradwarefo. In an age and society where achieved status was a mark of great distinction, persons of common and even unfree origins found ample opportunities for personal advancement through proven skills and accomplishments. This can be said of members of the *Gyaase* establishment whose recruitment pattern, initially at least, showed some intake of men of common and unfree extraction. "There is no doubt," Rattray claims, "that the Gyasefo were in olden days recruited from the slave class."[2] Such persons came to be looked upon as stool servants. They performed household functions, many of them minor, such as those associated with the chamberlain in medieval Europe but nonetheless essential and requiring trust because the individuals were attached to the king's person.

That men of such origins not only found their way ultimately into an ambassador's following, but also utilized opportunities available to them to rise to play important roles in the foreign service, is a creditable commentary on the avenues for upward mobility that existed in Asante. In a society which practiced a policy that approximated closely to institutionalized assimilation of slaves, men of unfree origin found ample opportunities for personal advancement and enjoyed liberal privileges and rights. Slaves could "drink *abosom*" (take oath) and serve as competent witnesses in court.[3] Actual cases were known of slaves winning legal suits against chiefs, hence giving rise to the saying "*odonko sene Akanni*," that is, "a slave surpasses a [free] Akan."[4] Slaves could, and many in fact did, amass considerable wealth and power. It was common practice for a master to give his slave a piece of land to cultivate, and "this would belong to the slave as surely as it would in case of a free man."[5] Slave owners frequently gave their daughters in marriage to their confidential slaves. As has been succinctly put, the rights of the Asante slave "seemed in many instances practically the ordinary privileges of any Ashanti free man, with whom in these respects his position did not seem to compare so unfavourably."[6]

The Asante ambassador *par excellence*, it has been pointed out above, was the *afenasoani*, and next to him the *nsenieni*. Yet, it is worthy of note that some members of "minority groups" (outside the *afenasoafo* and *nseniefo nfekuo*), including persons who may even have had servile origins initially, acquired prominence in diplomatic roles. Among such minority groups of note were the *akradwarefo* (washers of the King's soul), some of whom rose through the rank and file to headships of embassies.

The European records of the nineteenth century are replete with references to *akradwarefo* being employed in embassies to the British administration at Cape Coast and later Accra, the Dutch at Elmina, and the Danish in Accra, respectively. The distinctive badge of office of the *okradwareni*—a gold plate which was carried on the breast—made him unmistakably identifiable and entitled him to the honor due him as a royal envoy. Shaped like a crescent, the plate was also adorned with stars and gossamer wings, all of solid gold. It would appear from our sources of the early nineteenth century that the European hosts of *akradwarefo* envoys were pleased and satisfied with their credentials.

The use of *akradwarefo* as envoys seems to have grown out of the time-tested practice of trusted servants or attendants being sent on long trading journeys away from home on behalf of their masters.[7] Bowdich attested to this in his observation that "confidential slaves were everywhere in the service of chiefs."[8] The "male character" of most of the Asante service stools meant that not only could sons succeed fathers but also that they could utilize avenues for orientation-training in the form of understudying. As the Asantehene in the nineteenth century increasingly came to make appointments based on merit rather than ascription, so did men from "minority groups" continue to make their mark in diplomatic appointments.

The European sources of the early decades of the nineteenth century provide ample evidence that the officials who were sent from Kumase as envoys to receive groundrent from the British, Dutch, and Danish authorities on the coast were mostly drawn from *akradwarefo* ranks.[9] Prominent among these men who enjoyed the rank and recognition of ambassador was Fosu Kra. Fosu Kra had a distinguished diplomatic career in which he undertook several assignments to the Dutch at Elmina and the British at Cape Coast, successfully rising through the ranks. Arriving in Elmina towards the end of 1820, Fosu Kra made a payment of one hundred ounces of gold in respect of credit facilities which had been granted by Governor-General Daendels for the purchase of gunpowder and firearms in 1818, after which he remained in Elmina to demand the *kostgeld* (ground-rent) for 1821. At a meeting with the Dutch officials on 17 February 1821, ambassador Fosu Kra, who was evidently empowered to negotiate, refused to accept the *kostgeld* on the grounds that the Asantehene was being overcharged for goods given in lieu of cash payment. Following Dutch accusations that Fosu Kra wanted to have the goods at a lower price so that he could in turn make profit by reselling them at a higher price to the Asantehene, the ambassador fell out of the King's favor and was recalled to the capital.[10]

The composition of the embassy that was appointed to treat with the British Government in London in 1820 gave further evidence of the involvement of prominent "minority groups" in diplomatic roles. The embassy showed a high proportion of *Gyaase* officials, most of whom were undoubtedly from *nfekuo* other than the traditionally envoy-based *afenasoafo*. Besides the Asantehene's Treasurer who was appointed leader, all the six other members of the embassy were described as "subordinate" officers who nonetheless were "men of rank and influence in the government," and possibly *nhenkwaa* as well, for "their offices required their daily attendance about the person of their sovereign." [11] The mission included one of the Asantehene's *akradwarefo* and three "confidential slaves," [12] all as envoys to explain the views and sentiments of Kumase to the King of England. It is a matter of record, however, that the embassy never left Cape Coast as the castle did everything possible to thwart its departure for London.

The increasing specialization that came about in the Asante bureaucracy in the course of the nineteenth century progressively emphasized the position of the *afenasoani* as the official envoy of the Asantehene. Even so, the evidence is conclusive that *akradwarefo* continued to be engaged in some diplomatic assignments and in particular on confidential missions. One such *okradwareni*, who is unidentified by name, accompanied ambassador Owusu Koko Kuma (son of Saamanhene Akyampon Panin) on a mission to the British authorities at Cape Coast in 1872. While the embassy was in Cape Coast, this *okradwareni* was dispatched to convey a confidential message to the Asantehene regarding a proposed visit by Joseph Dawson to Kumase. Though British emissary Dawson was already on his way to Kumase before the *okradwareni* set out, the latter, referred to simply as "Occra," by traveling day and night, passed Joseph Dawson and conveyed intelligence of Dawson's approach to Kumase.[13] Ramseyer and Kühne further attested to the continued role of *akradwarefo* in the foreign service in the 1870s. On their way to Kumase, for example, the two German captives were met at Asokore by an "ambassador" of the Asantehene with presents and a message. This envoy wore a "large round gold plate on his breast," and was evidently more than a mere message-bearer, for he endeavored to comfort Ramseyer and Kühne by kind words and assurances of the friendship of the Asantehene. [14] *Akradwarefo* continued throughout the century not only to be essential components of embassies but also to lead some embassies themselves even as late as the 1880s and 1890s.

We are faced with limitations in our efforts to create complete biographical profiles of nineteenth-century *akradwarefo* envoys. Many appear in our sources in connection with one or at best a few missions, and at times when, in all probability, they might have already reached the height of their careers. Many more are referred to anonymously as the King's "Accra" or "Occra," that is, *Okra*. However, the present state of our knowledge, even inconclusive as it is, leaves no doubt that hundreds of *akradwarefo* came to be employed in Asante's diplomatic service; the investigator is almost overwhelmed by the repeated references to the Asantehene's "Kra" as envoy. The indications are also in the direction of role-specialization in the conduct of confidential diplomatic missions.

Nseniefo. In one sense, *nseniefo* cannot be regarded as belonging to the "minority group" category. After all, *nseniefo* were essential components of most, if not practically all embassies. Yet, it can be said at the same time that *nseniefo* usually only led what has been described above as the third or small-scale type of embassy. In this sense, then, an *nsenieni* being entrusted with the headship of a large, important embassy was outside the typical syndrome, and it is precisely for this reason that individual *nseniefo* who achieved this kind of distinction may be considered as falling into the minority group syndrome. The long diplomatic career of *esen* Kwame "Akoa Ye Na" is a case in point. First entering upon the diplomatic scene in 1881, he was a member of the Okyeame Kofi Bene mission which was sent to Cape Coast in February of that year in an effort to thaw the tension that was building up in Asante-British relations. The mission recapitulated the whole story surrounding Owusu Taseamandi's escape from Kumase and disclaimed official responsibility for Asabi Antwi's alleged declaration of war. This mission marked the beginning of a lasting diplomatic partnership between Afenasoani Akyampon Daban and Esen Kwame "Akoa Ye Na." Quickly rising through the ranks, Esen Kwame next became Asante's choice of an envoy to inform Governor Griffith of Agyeman Prempe's assumption of office as Asantehene. In the message which he delivered in Accra on 6 July 1888, Esen Kwame also registered the Asantehene's protest against the Kokofuhene who, it was claimed, was planning to invade Kumase as evidence of his disapproval of the election of Agyeman Prempe.[15]

Having executed this mission with credit, Esen Kwame subsequently came to be appointed one of the leading members of the Kofi Apea mission of 1890–91. This powerful embassy requested British cooperation in the matter of the return to Asante of Kokofu, Dwaben, and Bekwae, which had lately sought British protection. The embassy was on the whole composed of men of considerable "social and official status." Kofi Apea, the head, was the Nseniehene and also a "man of high rank and position," and the same could be said of Okyeame Yaw Boaten and Afenasoani Akyampon Daban. The other prominent members, it is significant to note, were from the "minority" ranks: Okra Yaw and Okra

Kwasi as representatives of Dwabenhene Yaw Sapon and Ohemaa Boatemmaa, respectively, and Esen "Akoa Ye Na," who had already made his mark in earlier diplomatic appointments.[16]

Six years later, in March 1894, Esen "Akoa Ye Na," now an accomplished career diplomat, reached Accra, accompanied by Kwabena Antwi on a mission charged with two responsibilities: first, to complain about the behavior of Asante refugees who were molesting traders in the area between Praso and the coast through an improper use of the Great Oath, and second, to impress upon the British administrators that it would be courteous to the Asantehene if British officers sent to the areas north of Kumase could pass through the Asante capital.[17] It is a feather in the cap of "Akoa Ye Na" and a testimony to his meritorious service that he was the diplomat chosen for the promulgation in the colony of new, or we might say the enforcement of existing, regulations regarding diplomatic conduct and courtesy. That he had earned the appellation or praisename "Akoa Ye Na," that is, "a [good] servant is rare" by 1881 would seem to suggest that he had by then established a reputation for trustworthiness and diligence.

Nsumankwaafo. The extant evidence indicates that *nsumankwaafo* (spiritual caretakers) also served in some embassies, particularly of the larger type, to take care of the spiritual needs of the leader and the other members. The *nsumankwaafo* must be distinguished from *adunsinfo* ("herbalists") and "Asante Nkramo" (Muslim Holy men), although all three performed related functions. The Nsumankwaahene's major task was to protect the Asantehene whenever he had bad dreams, during the birth of royals, in times of war, and, in general, at all other times.[18] The office was hereditary and the incumbent was distinguished by the peculiar way in which he wore his hair.[19] The Nsumankwaahene served only the needs of the Asantehene and was therefore not expected to accompany embassies. If and when the Asantehene traveled, the Nsumankwaahene was expected to go with him. In wartime the Nsumankwaahene was expected to volunteer to join.[20] However, since every chief had his own *suman* (protective charm) and therefore his *nsumankwaani*, that is, spiritual caretaker, such an individual might be asked by his chief to accompany him on an embassy.

In some instances "Asante Nkramofo" were also included in embassies to protect the members and work for the success of the mission through prayers, amulets and charms. The inclusion, for instance, of Kwaku Sawu, described as "fetishman,"[21] but in all probability an *nsumankwaani,* in the Kwame Antwi mission of 1874, and the attachment, similarly, of Muslims to the Owusu Dome, Owusu Koko Kuma and Boakye Tenten missions of 1820, 1874, and 1881, respectively, are all suggestive of the role played by *nkramofo* and *nsumankwaafo* in Asante diplomatic history.[22]

Women. In an age when diplomatic careers, as indeed other public offices, were dominated by men, at least one career belonging to the female gender stood out clearly as remarkable as any. An *oheneba* (daughter) of Asantehene Osei Kwadwo, Akyaawa, who was also known as Yaa Akyaa, pursued a diplomatic career that was distinguished in its own right and pioneering by the standards of the time, for which reason she acquired the nickname "Yikwan," that is, path-maker.[23]

From an early life that is still shrouded in relative obscurity beyond the known fact of her attachment to the Taa Dwemo Shrine at Akorase, Akyaawa Yikwan entered upon the public scene in August 1826 as a member of the royal entourage of Asantehene Osei Yaw Akoto during his campaign of southeastern Gold Coast. It is to be presumed that Akyaawa's role in this campaign was associated with a religious function stemming from her devotion to the Taa Dwemo *suman* ("fetish"). At the Battle of Katamanso (1826) Akyaawa suffered the misfortune of being taken captive, along with the Asantehene's wife, Akua Pusuwa, and other royals.[24]

Negotiations for a settlement of Asante's relations with the southeastern provinces, on the one hand, and the British and the southwestern states, on the other, began immediately following Asante's defeat at Katamanso. In the peace initiatives and moves which lingered on till 1831, Akyaawa's role was significant, less for her *suman* devotions on behalf of Asanteman during her period of captivity than for her demonstrated diplomatic skills after her release. Asante's initial postwar peace drives were channeled through the intermediary of her southern provinces, notable Adanse. In this direction, the Asantemanhyiamu authorized the Adanse *ahene* (chiefs) to approach the British administration, the peace offer being conveyed through a preliminary Adanse delegation which arrived in Cape Coast in June 1827. The main Asante embassy reached Cape Coast in October, led by a senior *nsenie* officeholder, who may be presumed to have been Asomfohene Kwadwo Apeagyei.[25] A draft treaty was prepared which, *inter alia,* required Asante to entrust to the care of the British two royal princes as hostages and a large quantity of gold as security deposit. As a demonstration of British faith in the peace moves, Governor H. Lumley released a number of Asante war prisoners. Contrary to popular belief, those who were set free at this time did not include Akyaawa, largely because she had been captured in an area over which the Danes claimed jurisdictional rights. The embassy returned to Kumase in February 1828.

Though falling short of a formal acceptance of the draft treaty, Asantehene Osei Yaw Akoto found its general intent satisfactory. However, he failed to ratify it and requested an end to the blockade of Fante and the release of Akyaawa and the other royals still held captive as British gestures of good faith.[26] For the moment, the British refused to negotiate the terms of the treaty, thereby stalling the peace moves

The assumption of control of the settlements by the Committee of Merchants in 1829 was marked by a revival of the spirit of peace. Responding to a suggestion from the British administration, the Asante government dispatched a peace mission to President George Maclean in mid-1830. The headship of the embassy was entrusted to Okyeame Kwakwa, who is traditionally remembered as a diplomat. Other senior members were Akuma Afenasoafohene Amankwa Akuma, *afenasoani* Kofi Nkwantabisa, and Nkonnwasoafohene Kankam Kyekyere. The embassy assured President Maclean of the Asantehene's desire for peace and requested the release of the Asante royals who were still in captivity. From Cape Coast the envoys proceeded to Accra, accompanied by Maclean, who hoped to use his personal influence with the Danish authorities to secure the release of the royals. When, to their surprise, the party learned in Accra that Akyaawa was not among the captives held in the Danish fort, Maclean demonstrated an act of supreme faith in Asante's goodwill by reimbursing a merchant who had earlier purchased Akyaawa in the sum of ten peredwans (£80). This action was itself a testimony to the confidence Maclean reposed in Akyaawa's ability to employ her influence with the Asantehene in working towards an Asante-British peace. Akyaawa returned to Kumase late in the year after passing through Cape Coast.

Akyaawa's release rekindled the peace hopes. Early in 1831 a high-powered mission was commissioned to conclude with the British the protracted peace negotiations. Included in the mission was Okyeame Kwakwa although leadership was entrusted now to Akyaawa, whose four-and-half years' stay on the coast, familiarity with European modes of conduct and close association with President Maclean clearly made her well suited for this position. The embassy arrived in Cape Coast on 8 April, and after a series of negotiating sessions concluded on the 27th of the month a Treaty of Peace and Free Commerce with the British, the document being signed on behalf of the Asante government by *oheneba* Akyaawa and Okyeame Kwakwa. The *ahene* of Fante, Asen, Twifo, Wassa, Denkyira, and other southwestern states also submitted to the treaty. As part of the peace agreement Akyaawa made on behalf of her government a refundable security deposit of 600 ounces of gold to the British, to whose care in addition she delivered two Asante *ahenemma*, Owusu Nkwantabisa and Owusu Ansa, sons of Asantehene Osei Yaw Akoto and Osei Tutu Kwame, respectively.[27] Simultaneously, Akyaawa entered into discussions with the Dutch through the intermediary of the Asante resident ambassador at Elmina, Kwadwo Akyampon. It was essential for the Dutch, perennial allies of Asante, to be assured that the new peace initiatives with the British did not in any way imply an abandonment of Asante's friendship.

Though the treaty was subscribed to by the western *ahene*, no lasting peace in the Gold Coast could be hoped for without the involvement of the southeastern *ahene*. With this in view, George Maclean, along with the Asante ambassadors, proceeded to Accra in May. Maclean and the Asante envoys held discussions with a number of *ahene* and delegates representing, among others, Akyem Abuakwa, Akyem Kotoku, Akuapem, and Akwamu, explaining to them the conditions and terms of the Asante-British peace treaty. Following this, Akyaawa and her associates scored another diplomatic triumph by concluding a separate peace agreement with the Danish administrators at Christiansborg. The chiefs of Akwamu, Ada, Osu, Labadi, Teshi, and other southeastern states were a party to this treaty. With this diplomatic success, the Asante envoys returned to Cape Coast in September, a Ga escort being provided for their safety.[33] Before making the homeward journey Akyaawa returned to Elmina to meet with Dutch Governor F. Last and the Edina *ahene* and elders to express again the friendship and goodwill of Asante towards them. The envoys, together with the freed captives, left Cape Coast on 4 October 1831, arriving in Kumase late that month or in early November. The highly enthusiastic welcome the party received on that occasion and the official gratification subsequently expressed in the personal conduct of the embassy and in its delicate negotiations by its leader Akyaawa, presumably occasioned the justly deserved appellation "Yikwan." On her return to Kumase, Akyaawa is reported to have bought a slave whom she named "Nkranfo ye mmoa," meaning "the Ga are fools" for sparing the life of such a woman as herself.[28]

Thrust into foreign policy issues late in life by her participation in the southeastern campaign of 1826, Akyaawa's diplomatic career was brief but nonetheless outstanding. Though an *oheneba* by birth, her claim to diplomatic appointments rested not on ascription, but solely on her negotiating skills, which were amply demonstrated in her pre-diplomatic captive years. Conducting delicate negotiations with European powers following a period of severely strained relations in the mid-1820s, Akyaawa cautiously assuaged Dutch sentiments while at the same time securing important agreements with the British and the Danes. Although some problems of interpretation were to develop subsequently, the twin peace treaties of 1831, for all their imperfections, ushered in a thirty-year period which was the most pacific of the nineteenth century. This in itself is a highly favorable commentary on the career of Akyaawa Yikwan, whose successful entry into what was then generally considered a male domain was therefore a pioneering event.

Some Major Embassies

The Kankam Embassy of 1858. Despite the popular pacific view commonly held of the 1850s in traditional accounts (based on the false assumption that an absence of a major Asante-British armed conflict could be taken as an indication of peace), it has become increasingly clear that the decade was not without serious issues of conflict between the two powers. Asante's demand for the repatriation of the *sikani* refugee, Kwasi Gyani, was a lingering problem, and so were several other extradition issues. During Governor Winniett's visit to Kumase in 1848 Asantehene Kwaku Dua Panin had apparently secured the renewal of British commitment to the reciprocal obligations of ensuring the return of refugees. In 1853, with recurring refugees issues still unresolved, the Asantehene accused the British administration of failure to undertake its responsibilities with regards to runaways; Winniett "did not fulfill the promise" to assist in the return of the Asen and Denkyira, Kwaku Dua charged, while Stephen Hill had failed to cooperate in Asante's recent attempts to recover its subjects who had taken refuge south of the Pra. [29]

At the same time, convinced that the cause of the lack of Asante-British understanding in extradition issues lay in the 1831 Treaty, Governor Hill dispatched George Blankson to Kumase in 1853 to secure the Asantehene's mark to a new treaty. Kwaku Dua Panin, however, decidedly rejected the idea on the grounds that he had "not violated any of the rules in the old treaty since it was drawn up," and that what was required was not so much a new treaty as a new spirit on the part of the British to make the old agreement work.[30]

It was against this background of first, the inadequacies of the 1831 Treaty, and second, the reemerging and unresolved question of the extradition of runaways, that an Asante embassy was dispatched in 1858 to demand the return of yet another group of fugitives from Cape Coast. The headship of this embassy was entrusted to a Kankam whose identity cannot as yet be established with confidence. While

Kankam is evidently an *asomfo* stool name and the mission's task was apparently within the domain of the *asomfo fekuo*, none of the Asomfohene of the period was named Kankam. It might be inferred from the Agyeman-Duah stool history that the *asomfo* incumbent in 1858 was Akoako Tando, who had succeeded his brother Kwabena Safo. In view of the fact that both Safo and Tando enjoyed long "reigns" as Asomfohene,[31] it might be speculated that Tando might have been too old to travel in 1858, in which case he could have deputized his Mmammahene, presumably named Kankam, to head the mission. It could alternatively be presumed that British officials might have simply preferred to refer to the *asomfo* functionary who headed the mission by the stool name of Kankam, irrespective of whether or not he was Akoako Tando himself.

The uncertainty about his exact identity notwithstanding, Kankam's mandate and status were without question. British officials recognized him as a linguist and "Chief Messenger"; he led a high powered embassy numbering fifty persons;[32] and it became clear that his mandate had apparently authorized him to set up courts of law in Fante, if need be, to try the fugitives whose extradition he was seeking. Arriving in Cape Coast in March 1858, Kankam conveyed the Asantehene's request to the British administration that a group of recent fugitives be delivered to him for repatriation. Most of the runaways were described as "slaves" who were presumably of non-Asante origins, on account of the use of the word "*donko*" to refer to them. They were all accused of either fleeing Kumase or escaping while they were on trading errands to the Coast. Governor Benjamin Pine deemed the Asante demand legitimate by reason of his belief that proper protection should be given to Asante subjects who visited the coast for legitimate commercial purposes. Consequently, he directed that two militiamen be provided as an escort for the embassy while it was on the coast and ordered that any fugitives such as might have been enticed or harbored to remain in the Protectorate by the Fante be surrendered. However, he failed to back up his directives with the action necessary to secure their repatriation, and the issue remained without settlement for weeks.

Soon after his appointment as Acting Governor, Major H. Bird resolved that unless firm measures were taken to end the continuing problem of the Fante enticing Asante slaves who visited the coast for trading purposes into remaining there, Asante-British understanding would be further endangered to the detriment of trade. He accordingly issued, with effect from 18 May 1858, a proclamation imposing heavy fines ranging from £3 to £15 and imprisonment in default of payment on any individuals convicted of "harbouring, enticing, or otherwise advising, persuading, or intimidating any Ashantee subject to remain with him or her."[33]

Although some of the runaways were successfully delivered to Kankam, it was reported that several of the refugees had sworn "the King's oath" not to return to Kumase for fear of being victimized. Meanwhile, to emphasize his stand, the Asantehene had dispatched to Governor Bird a letter dated 16 June, in which he expressed the hope that friendly relations between the two nations and between the two leaders would prevail as in the time of George Maclean. As no resolution of the matter was in sight, Kankam, with the British administrator's consent, established courts to investigate the cases of all those who refused to return home. The sessions were held on 25, 26, and 28 June 1858. Six Asante runaways initially appeared as defendants. In carefully conducted trials, the accused were called upon in turns to state their cases, after which Kankam presented the evidence against each of them. The trials were organized in such a way that both the prosecution and the defense availed themselves of opportunities to call upon witnesses. Thus, Boafo, an Asen deputy, and Akua Tawia, a Fante, presented evidence to support the claims of the refugees that they had not been enticed to remain in the British Protectorate, while several prosecution witnesses, including two former slave owners and several junior members of ambassador Kankam's staff, both identified some of the runaways and supported the government's position.[34]

British officials reported with a measure of satisfaction that Kankam himself did not personally know most of the accused and that it became evident at the trials that most of the fugitives were of good character. However, the Asante government's case was directed less at the accused and more at the Fante, the Asen, and the British. For far from encouraging the return of runaways, the Fante had actively supported Asante fugitives to remain on the coast (apparently with British backing), in contravention of the stipulations of the 1831 Asante-British treaty. And on this score, British Governor Bird himself conceded that, by their conduct, the runaways had "rendered themselves subject to punishment." [35]

Kwadwo Donko, the first accused, stated in his evidence that he had been ordered to procure an anker of rum. He had left Kumase in the company of other comrades, ostensibly to acquire the rum for his female owner, who was described as a sister of the Asantehene. However, once he crossed the Pra River and entered the British Protectorate, he declared to his companions that he had no intention of returning to Kumase.

Following the trials, the British Governor on 12 July called a meeting of the King, principal chiefs, and merchants of Cape Coast to obtain their views. He evidently succeeded in making them concur with his view: that the runaways should be afforded the protection they were seeking. Governor Bird subsequently decided to write to explain the circumstances of the matter to the Asantehene and to inform him, in accordance with existing agreements between the two nations, that he was assuming the responsibility of punishing the refugees. Ironically, however, he did not consider that the fugitives should be permitted to return to Kamase.[36]

On the following day, the British Administrator conveyed these decisions to the Asante embassy and the refugees in a meeting at Castle Hall. Ambassador Kankam took the opportunity to request that yet another refugee, Tando, be delivered to him, failing which he suggested that his case also be investigated. Tando's trial was held on 14 July. He was found guilty of violating the 1831 Treaty. The Governor therefore decided that he should be punished but characteristically concluded that there were no circumstances which justified the refugees being returned to Kumase against their will. In all, a total of eight refugees, all of whom were first or second generation *nnokofo* (slaves) presented evidence in their defense.

The significance of Kankam's embassy lay in the extraordinary steps that the Asante administration was prepared to take in seeking the return of its subjects. The decision to investigate and try the runaways in Cape Coast was itself indicative of the Government's concern to demonstrate unmistakably to the British administration that there were legitimate grounds, in accordance with existing agreements, for Asante's demand for the repatriation of fugitives. These apart, the embassy's high mandate and long stay at Cape Coast underscored Asante's determination to adhere to the 1831 Treaty, for all its imperfections. Finally, the embassy laid bare the tenuousness of Asante-British understanding, providing one more evidence of the conflicts that beset the relationships between the two nations, despite the limited incidence of open military confrontation during the Kwaku Duan period.

The Asabi Antwi Missions of 1874. Asabi Antwi had a long diplomatic career which was highlighted by two major embassies to the British: the one in 1874, which made his diplomatic mark, and the other in 1881, which somewhat dimmed his reputation. Throughout the period that he held diplomatic appointments (1872–84), Asabi Antwi built up a name for himself for his commitment to peace as the cornerstone of Asante's foreign policy. A son of Asantehene Kwaku Dua Panin,

Kwame Antwi, as he was known before his elevation to the rank of Asabihene, saw early *gyaase* training, first as an *atumtuni* (gunbearer) within the *ankobea fekuo* (royal bodyguard) and subsequently as an *afenasoani*. It was a testimony to his successful rise through the *afenasoafo* ranks that Asabi Antwi came to be entrusted with responsibility for negotiating peace with the British, after Major-General Wolseley's troops had sacked Kumase in 1874, when he was apparently in his thirties.[37]

Asante armies had pacified the southern provinces in 1873 in a move to suppress provincial rebellions. It was a two-pronged campaign in which Boakye Yam Kuma *okyeame*, Akyampon Yaw, commanded the western wing that reoccupied Denkyira and the southwest, while Gyaasewahene Adu Bofo carried responsibility for the reoccupation of Akyem and the southeast. Though the Asante action emanated from a recognition of the need for a restoration of law and order into provincial administration, it evoked an unexpected reaction from the British: the decision to invade Asante itself. Military preparations were speedily mounted under Major-General Wolseley, and by late December an armed force under his command was on its way from Cape Coast to Kumase. On 2 January 1874 Sir Garnet Wolseley wrote from Praso to inform Asantehene Kofi Kakari that he had taken over from Colonel Harley as the Queen's representative on the Gold Coast. In the letter, Wolseley accused the Asantehene of violating the terms of the Asante-British treaty of 1831 by continuing to regard the people of Asen and Denkyira as his subjects and warned that he had been sent "to demand reparation" for Asante's invasion of the southern provinces and the continued detention of Ramseyer, Kühne, and Bonnat. He demanded three conditions as the price of peace: that Asante release all captives, both European and African, held in Kumase; pay an indemnity of 50,000 ounces of gold; and sign a new peace treaty, a draft of which he personally carried to Kumase.[38]

Wolseley's demands for peace and more so the imminence of his approach to Kumase precipitated a period of intense diplomatic activity by which the Asantehene sought in vain to dissuade the British general from entering Kumase and submit to a peaceful resolution of Asante-British differences. As a gesture of Asante's good faith, Basel missionary J. Kühne was released and conducted to the British camp at Praso by ambassador Owusu Koko Kuma on 12 January. Wolseley received the Asantehene's letter per Owusu Koko Kuma and "proposed peace, whilst at the same time he was advancing with cannon," notwithstanding the fact that he learned from Mr. Kühne that except in isolated quarters, the prevailing mood in Kumase was a "desire for peace."[39]

After weighing the options in careful deliberations, the Asantemanhyiamu decided to accept Wolseley's conditions rather than risk war. The Asantehene therefore made "an expression of ready compliance" in writing, and Wolseley telegrammed the Colonial Office to that effect. But nonetheless General Wolseley decided on taking his forces to Kumase and therefore continued with his military operations. As the British advance progressed, Asantehene Kofi Kakari intensified his entreaties to the British general to halt his forces and have "everything properly arranged," that is, negotiated. However, Wolseley was adamant in his resolve to enter Kumase with force. Until all his peace conditions were met, he asserted in his reply to the Asantehene, he would not stop his advance. On 21 January the Asantehene wrote again, reiterating that he had "no quarrel of any kind" with Wolseley and expressing his anxiety to have all matters amicably settled. The letter was hand-carried by envoy Esen Buadi, who was accompanied to Wolseley by the remaining European hostages now released.[40]

Wolseley's response did not portray a desire for a peaceful settlement; on the contrary, it gave indications of a hardening of his position. He now demanded that Asante surrender the following as hostages:

1   The heir-apparent Mensa Bonsu
2.   Asantehene Kofi Kakari's mother
3.   The heir to the Dwabenhene
4.   The heir to the Kokofuhene
5.   The heir to the Mamponhene
6.   The heir to the Bekwaehene

It has been commented elsewhere that the conditions would have stood a better chance of being met if any hostages other than those listed above had been demanded. In addition, Wolseley issued an ultimatum demanding an immediate payment of one-third of the indemnity of 50,000 ounces of gold. Further correspondence and other diplomatic moves from Asante proved futile as Wolseley's forces entered and sacked Kumase on 5 February. [41]

The British action generated renewed diplomatic initiatives on the part of Asante. The governing Council decided, as a matter of urgency, to appoint a high-powered embassy to negotiate with Wolseley, and advance notification to the effect was given by envoys who caught up with the retiring general on 9 February at Dekyiaso. The envoys repeated Asante's concern for peace. Wolseley promised to wait until the 13th or 14th of the month to allow time for negotiations. He, however, cautioned the envoys that while he was prepared to drop his demand for the release of the hostages held in Kumase, he would be willing to discuss peace terms only if an indemnity was paid.

The leadership of the main embassy charged with conducting the peace negotiations with Wolseley was entrusted to Asabi Antwi, who had seen prior diplomatic appointments to the British. In October 1872 Asabi Antwi had held discussions with British Governor Salmon at Cape Coast concerning a request for Elmina resident ambassador, Boakye Yam Kuma *okyeame* Akyampon Yaw, then banished to Assini, to be reunited with his followers who had been left behind in Elmina. According to Asantehene Kofi Kakari's proposals, which were outlined before the British authorities by Asabi Antwi, the British governor was requested to arrange for the Asante's resident in Elmina to be conducted to Assini under the care of the Asante diplomat. It was seemingly in recognition of Kwame Antwi's conduct of this mission that the Asantehene elevated him to the headship of the Asabi stool in the Manwere *fekuo*, following the banishment of the incumbent, Asabi Boakye.

Now leading the mission of February 1874 with a mandate to discuss an Asante-British peace treaty, Asabi Antwi and his party arrived on the outskirts of Fomena, next to Wolseley's camp, on the 12th. In line with Asante practice, Asabi Antwi delivered only the customary greetings the first day, the formal message and negotiations being deferred until the following day. When the Asante delegation met with General Wolseley on 13 February, Asabi Antwi expressed Asante's desire to accept the terms of the draft treaty which Wolseley had earlier proposed, but with two reservations: first, he did not think that the indemnity was as large at 50,000 ounces of gold, and in fact could recall that Asante was required to pay only 600 ounces by the earlier treaty with George Maclean in 1831; and second, he objected to British encouragement for Adanse in its attempts to secede from Asante. However, as evidence of Asante's good faith, he paid 1,000 ounces as the first installment of the indemnity, after which the two representatives concluded a draft treaty of Fomena on behalf of their respective nations. Asabi Antwi returned to Kumase with a copy of the draft treaty for the government's approval, on the promise that he would present a duly ratified copy to the British administration in Cape Coast within two weeks.[43]

With the Asantemanhyiamu's formal acceptance of the treaty, Asabi Antwi was again commissioned as head of the embassy to proceed to Cape Coast for its ratification with the British administration. He arrived in Cape Coast on March 13, accompanied by a staff and a retinue numbering 300. It has been pointed out above that the inclusion on this occasion of delegates from the *aman* (states) was a mark of the embassy's broad representation, a feature that was characteristic of embassies charged with matters affecting the whole Asante nation. Also present was Kofi Nti, a sixteen year-old son of the Asantehene. In the preliminary discussions misunderstandings again arose about the indemnity. Asabi Antwi objected to its size, pointing out that the Asantehene believed that it had been fixed at 10,000 rather than 50,000 ounces. He however produced a copy of the treaty to which the Asantehene had affixed his mark.[44]

At the second interview held on 14 March, the discussion of the treaty was concluded. With Sir Garnet Wolseley refusing to negotiate the indemnity, the Asante ambassadors accepted the terms of the treaty and subscribed to it on behalf of the Asantehene. The peace treaty was signed on behalf of Queen Victoria of Britain and Ireland by Major-General Garnet J. Wolseley and by "Saibee Enquie acting on behalf of His Majesty Koffee Kalkalli, King of Ashantee." The indemnity was maintained at 50,000 ounces. By its terms Asante renounced claims to Denkyira, Asen, Akyem, Adanse, and other "allies" of Britain as well as to Elmina; guaranteed freedom of trade between Asante and the British forts; and undertook to implement steps towards the eventual elimination of "human sacrifice." Asabi Antwi, Kofi Nti, and eighteen other leading members of the embassy including three *afenasoafo*, one *nsenieni*, one *nsumankwaani,* and the representatives of Dwaben, Bekwae, Kokofu, Nsuta, and Mampon ratified the treaty by affixing their marks to it. Asabi Antwi further notified Acting British Administrator J. Maxwell that he had been empowered to resolve all problems with the British, for which reason he would remain in Cape Coast until all outstanding issues had been cleared. In consonance with his high mandate, he directed the discussion to cover a number of broad subjects, including requests that Kofi Nti be sent to England to be educated; that the payments formerly made by the Dutch to the Asantehene in respect of the "notes" be continued by the British; that some criminal executions be carried out to mark the funerals of high ranking Asante officials; and that the Adanse be permitted to return to Asante control.[45]

Though a large portion of the ambassador's train presumably returned home after the conclusion of the peace negotiations, Asabi Antwi and the core of his staff remained in Cape Coast and continued to hold regular discussions with British officials, notably Administrators C. C. Lees and G. C. Strahan. It may be presumed from Asabi Antwi's mandate which gave him jurisdiction over all Asante-British affairs that the discussions covered continuing issues like the payment of the indemnity, the repatriation of Asante fugitives, the release of Fante war captives detained in Kumase, and English education for *oheneba* Kofi Nti.[46] He returned home in late 1874, having secured British ratification for a major document in Asante-British relations and having achieved a broader understanding between the two powers beyond the confines of the stipulations of the 1874 treaty.

Asabi Antwi held responsibility for the handling of British relations shortly after Asante had suffered the setback of Wolseley's sack of the capital. His selection to lead the peace missions of January and February 1874 was largely influenced by his specialization in British affairs as much as by his faith in peace policies and the benefits of the use of diplomatic instruments. His pacific zeal, however, did not imply that he toed the line of peace at all costs. He was a hard bargainer, as was evidenced by his persistence in reducing the indemnity. The 1874 peace treaty itself was perhaps no more successful in bringing Asante-British relations to a sounder footing than its 1831 precursor, but the 1874 missions of Asabi Antwi underlined the tenets of Asante's fundamental faith in diplomacy and brought to the fore the style, form, and character of major embassies.

The Owusu Taseamandi Extradition Missions of 1881. On 18 January 1881 a refugee called Owusu Taseamandi arrived in Cape Coast from Kumase to seek British protection. He had escaped earlier in the year, possibly during the Odwira festival. The next day a high-powered mission, closely following upon his heels, arrived in Cape Coast to demand his extradition. The party was led by a senior *afenasoani* who carried the Golden Axe, and it included Yaw Anane, a junior envoy who had earlier served on the staff of ambassador Gyakye Nantwi in Cape Coast and was therefore acquainted with Fante and British affairs. The envoys first reported to senior diplomats responsible for Britishaffairs, Asabihene Kwame Antwi and Akomfodehene Kwaku Bosommuru Dwira, who conducted them to Lt.-Governor W. B.Griffith on the same day.[47]

Owusu Taseamandi was a Gyaman royal maternally and an Asante *oheneba* (prince) paternally. Tamia, his grandmother, was a sister of Gyamanhene Adinkra and one of the captives who were brought to Kumase after the 1819 campaign. She subsequently married the Adumhene Kwadwo Sampene. Their daughter, Ampomawene, was married to the heir apparent Osei Kwadwo, who died in 1859. It as out of this union that Owusu Taseamandi was born.[48] The significance of Owusu Taseamandi's royal links become apparent within the context of two considerations: first, that he was a surviving royal of Gyaman, and second, that Gyaman's relations with Asante had been those of hostility and uneasy peace at best. For these reasons Owusu Taseamandi had been held as a captive in Kumase (although all of his relatives who had been taken to the Asante capital as war prisoners had been permitted to return to Gyaman) because of the fear of the possibility of a union of the two crowns of Asante and Gyaman. Indeed, it is reported that the Gyamanhene attempted to bribe the Asantehene into releasing Owusu Taseamandi in return for 1,000 peredwans of gold.[49] It is under these circumstances that Owusu Taseamandi fled Kumase.

Owusu Taseamandi's statement to Administrator Griffith, as recorded by A. J. Quansah, a clerk at the Governor's office, was ambiguous and contradictory. He claimed that he had been banished from Kumase because of Asante-Gyaman hostility. In the same breath, he stated that the reason for his escape was that he was a wanted man in Asante for an unspecified crime.[50]

Assuming the headship of the mission, Asabi Antwi demanded the surrender of not only Owusu Tasemandi but also of Amankra, an Asen who had been living in Kumase and who was alleged to have been an accomplice in the escape. Amankra was accused of having "gone lately to Gyaman and obtained money from the King of that place upon a promise that he would try his best to persuade Owoosoo to go to Gyaman."[51] Asabi Antwi, Lt.-Governor Griffith alleged, further threatened that Asante would invade Asen if Owusu Taseamandi was not extradited. The Governor's response was that Owusu Taseamandi had not committed any crime, and, having sought British protection, he would not be surrendered. Asked if he would prevent the refugee from returning to Gyaman, Governor Griffith again declined. Thus were set the circumstances for an Asante-British misunderstanding that was to tax the energies of the two sides for the next half-year. More importantly, the consequences of this golden axe-bearing mission of January 1881 were inadvertently to create a war scare that gripped the Gold Coast for more than six months.

Among Asante diplomatic symbols the most solemn and precious was the Golden Axe. Emblematic of sovereignty and mystical powers, it was very sparingly used—indeed in times of crisis only. Its use by the Owusu Taseamandi extradition mission signified a determination to accomplish the objective of the mission at all costs. It "only indicated that the matter was one of great importance."[52] It was however misconstrued as a sign of declaration of war by Lt.-Governor Griffith, who further alleged that Asabi Antwi actually did threaten that Asante would invade Asen if Owusu Taseamandi were not returned to Kumase. Thus, the grounds were laid for the most serious war scare in Asante history out of the inauspicious circumstances of a golden axe-bearing mission.

A close analysis of statements made before, during, and after the presentation of the axe on 19 January as well as the history of the axe should have left no one in doubt that its use on that occasion did not signify a declaration of war. Owusu Taseamandi's statement, delivered and recorded on January 18, that "a son of the late Chief Amanqua Kooma [Amankwa Akuma] and three court criers arrived with an axe from the King of Ashanti for the express purpose of compelling me to return to Coomassie," made no mention of a threat of war. This explanation was reiterated in a subsequent cross-examination of Owusu Taseamandi two days later, when he declared that "the meaning of the King of Ashanti sending the gold axe is that the King will cut his way to the accomplishment of his end."[53]

W.B.Griffith based his interpretation of the significance of the axe as indicative of war on association. The axe had been used on two previous occasions:"The first was in 1863, and then the Ashantis fought the English. The second was in 1873 and again they fought." [54] What he failed to see was that on the occasions cited, diplomat Amankwa Akuma had been sent to demand the extradition of the Asante runaway Kwasi Gyani, who had taken refuge in Asen. Kwasi Gyani was a *sikani* (wealthy man) who, contrary to the law requiring the surrender of all gold nuggets to the royal treasury, was alleged to have concealed a rock gold.[55] An Asante-British war had erupted on both occasions because Asen failed to comply with the repatriation of the "criminal" Kwasi Gyani. The British became involved in the hostilities simply because they chose to enter the dispute on behalf of Asen. It is arguable that fighting would not have ensued if Asen had not given protection to a refugee in contradiction of the Treaty of 1831. It was not so much the axe being symbolic of war as the violation of agreement that caused war.

Whether Asabi Antwi did in fact issue threats of war or not will perhaps never be known. What is known is that Asabi Antwi later publicly explained that what he had said was that "a row or disturbance" might ensue if Owusu Taseamandi were not given up. [57] It is also known that two follow-up missions from the Asantehene arrived in Cape Coast soon afterwards to repudiate the alleged declaration of war. The first, led by *esen* Kwabena Awua and *afenasoani* Kwabena Nyantakyi, met with W. B. Griffith on 8 February, and the envoys were accompanied by Asabi Antwi and Kwaku Bosommuru Dwira, who again played the role of senior resident diplomats. The party expressed the Asantehene's

displeasure at the seemingly unexplained conduct of the British in beginning preparations for war. The second mission was evidently commissioned with a higher mandate. Its leading members included *afenasoani*
Akyampon Daban and three envoys from the *nsenie* ranks—Kwaku
Agyida, Kwabena Agyena, and "Akoa Ye Na," but the headship was
strategically entrusted to an envoy long committed to the peace interest, namely, Ankobea *okyeame* Kofi Bene, "who was celebrated for his
peaceful disposition.[58] Clearly as an indication of the pro-peace party,
the government dispatched this mission to give assurances of the
Asantehene's peaceful intent to the British administration.[59] In the presence, again, of Asabi Antwi and Kwaku Bosommuru Dwira, Okyeame
Kofi Bene emphasized that if Asabi Antwi had indeed used aggressive
language, such statements lacked authorization.[60]

Other evidence bore on the peaceful disposition of the Asabi Antwi
mission. For example, Acting Administrator Griffith knew by 14 February that the Golden Axe was not always associated with war. He had
learned from Edmund Bannerman, an Accra advocate who was well
acquainted with Asante practices, that the Golden Axe "does not necessarily imply a declaration of war. It is quite as often, as not, emblematic of peace, or to convince the individual to whom it is sent that the
message accompanying it really and truly comes from the King." Mr.
Bannerman intimated that in this instance the indications suggested a
peaceful disposition. "I have conversed with Ashantis who have been
in Accra for years," Bannerman declared:

> with some that have been here for a few weeks only, and
> again with others who left Coomassie after the bearers of
> the Golden Axe left, and they are all unanimous in saying
> that the idea of war never could have entered the heart of a
> single Ashanti, from the King to the public executioner; and
> that if such had been the case the whole of the Ashantis on
> the coast would have disappeared suddenly one night with-
> out a soul knowing of their intention to leave.[61]

In addition, he continued, "it ought to have been known that any invasion would have been heralded by the flight of the inhabitants of the
towns along the Prah road to seek the protection of the forts."[62]

Further, senior ambassador Owusu Ansa had given assurances
to the Lt.-Governor on 18 February that the Golden Axe was not *ipso
facto* symbolic of war. It was suggested, besides, that the Governor
could send a messenger to Kumase to satisfy himself that no preparations for war were being made in Asante.[63] Rather than heeding this
advice, the British Administrator sent repeated dispatches to England
about a "threatened invasion" of the Gold Coast by Asante and re-

quested additional military and naval officers as reinforcements to the Gold Coast forces.

Meanwhile, Asantehene Mensa Bonsu continued his efforts in the hope of disabusing the minds of the British administrators at Cape Coast. A post-haste mission under the headship of Osei Broni, a son of Akyempemhene Owusu Koko, left Kumase on 1 March, arriving at Cape Coast on the 12th. The party included Yaw Awua, presumably an *afenasoani* who acted as "speaker," and Kwame Nsia and Dantanno, both *nhenkwaa*, and was instructed to approach Reverend J. Fletcher of the Wesleyan Mission and the merchants of Cape Coast through the intermediary of Owusu Ansa with a request that they use their good offices to restore Asante-British relations to a friendly footing. In a courtesy call, the envoys, in the company of Owusu Ansa and Asabi Antwi, disclosed the purpose of the mission to Governor Rowe, who suggested that his political secretary Knapp Barrow write a letter of introduction for them. Though the merchants—Messrs. Grant, Selby, Sarbah, Wylie, Elliot, and Davidson of Cape Coast—turned down the Asante envoys on two occasions, Reverend Fletcher wrote to the Governor to assure him of the Asantehene's peaceful intentions.[64]

Boakye Tenten's Follow-up Mission. One of the earliest references that can be linked to the Boakye Tenten mission is contained in Reverend Fletcher's memorandum to Governor Rowe concerning the interview he had with the Asante envoys. Mr. Fletcher recommended the sending of a "big man" with "full hands," possibly about 5,000 ounces of gold, to apologize for the inconvenience brought about by the misunderstandings over the Golden Axe, a message that was conveyed by envoys Kwaku Bosommuru Dwira and Yaw Anane, who were sent from Cape Coast by Owusu Ansa. By 2 April information had reached Governor Samuel Rowe that the husband of the Asantehemaa and a large number of attendants were on their way to see him. This was confirmed in a letter addressed by Knapp Barrow from Akroful, dated 1 April 1881.[65] In Kumase a customary special tax was levied to cover the expenses of the embassy and an "indemnity" of 2,000 ounces of gold.

The mission was perhaps the most impressive of all Asante embassies. Governor Rowe's opinion that it was "by far the most important embassy which Ashanti has ever sent to the coast, whether we look at the rank of the chiefs composing it, or the numbers of themselves and followers,"[66] was certainly justified. Boakye Tenten, the leader, was no other personage than the Boakye Yam Panin *okyeame* and husband of Asantehemaa Afua Kobi and therefore stepfather of

Asantehenes Kofi Kakari and Mensa Bonsu. His mother, Birago, was the sister of Abena Kwaadu, wife of Asantehene Kwaku Dua Panin, and of Kofi Nti who married the Asantehemaa. Therefore, Boakye Tenten was both an *ommamma* by patrifiliation and an *ohenenana* (grandson of Asantehene Osei Kwadwo) by matrifiliation. His memory continues to this day as the King's "greatest *okyeame*," whose opinions were much respected by the Asantemanhyiamu.[67] Boakye Tenten himself apart, no such assemblage of chiefs had ever been put together on a single mission. Present were Yaw Badu, the Asantehene's personal attendant (*ahenkwaa*) and representatives of the Kumase *abirempon*: Amoako Ata and Kwame Asante, for example, as representatives of Bantamahene Kwabena Awua and Asafohene Asafo Boakye, respectively. As evidence of the embassy's broad representation, it included delegates of the Amanhene of the *amanto*—the core of Asante, composed of Bekwae, Kokofu, Mampon and Nsuta. The remaining persons of rank included Boakye and Kwaku Dua, brother and son, respectively, of Boakye Tenten.[68] The usual additions of *nseniefo*, of whom there were four, and *afenasoafo* were present. The mission was joined at Praso by envoys from Kumase who had been sent there earlier by Owusu Ansa, namely, Akomfodehene Kwaku Bosommuru Dwira and junior diplomat Yaw Anane. Of the total retinue, the figure 400 appears to be conservative and has to be adjusted to something like 900 to include the entire following. [69]

Boakye Tenten brought to the April 1881 mission a wealth of knowledge and experience in both domestic and foreign affairs. His early training was acquired in court circles, in the company of and following his father, Okyeame Oti Panin, second incumbent of the Boakye Yam Panin stool. As a boy he is known to have possessed extraordinary powers of memory.[70] After the death of his father in 1826, he may have been apprenticed to *akyeame* Kofi Boakye and Kofi Nti of the Boakye Yam Panin Stool, in which position he gathered knowledge in affairs relating to the stool. Later, as a *batani*, that is, an official trader in the service of Asantehene Kwaku Dua Panin, he became distinguished in this capacity in Salaga, particularly for his commercial abilities. Boakye Tenten succeeded to the Boakye Yam Panin stool sometime in the early 1850s, following the death of Okyeame Kofi Nti, the incumbent.

Okyeame Boakye Tenten began his diplomatic career as a resident ambassador for Salaga, an area with which he was already well acquainted through his earlier commercial activities. At home his controversial marriage to Afua Kobi, widow of his uncle Kofi Nti, aggrandized his personal influence, as he continued in office throughout the administration of Kwaku Dua Panin. He was during this period involved in a mission to Krakye to consult the Dente shrine, an event which was occasioned by the occurrence of a severe earthquake in Kumase, possibly around mid-1862. His influence continued to grow under Asantehene Kofi Kakari (1867–74), who stood in the relationship of stepson to Boakye Tenten. He took part in foreign policy decisions and appeared as signatory to a number of important chancery documents including the controversial "Certificate of Apology" and correspondence on the negotiations for the release of the European captives, Ramseyer, Kühne, and Bonnat. In late 1872 Boakye Tenten was appointed to investigate reports of unrest in Asante-Akyem. His investigations were successful and directly resulted in the trial and execution of a number of Akyem *ahene*.

Following the Asante pacification of the southern provinces in 1873, a British counteroffensive was quickly mounted under the leadership of General Garnet Wolseley. The British stratagem this time was to carry the onslaught into Kumase itself. As direct military confrontation between Britain and Asante seemed imminent, Okyeame Boakye Tenten, as a firm believer in the Kwaku Duan doctrine of "peace, open roads and trade," emerged as the leader of the pro-peace interest group in Asantemanhyiamu debates. It was he who, in one of such council sessions convened on 21 January 1874, prevailed upon the Asantehene to write to Wolseley to entreat him to halt his advance on Kumase in return for a promise to release the European captives, this time without any ransom demand.[71] That Wolseley's forces entered Kumase in early February was an attestation to British determination to demonstrate to Asante a show of force in the hope of deterring future Asante aggression rather than a negative commentary on the diplomatic skills of Boakye Tenten, who was by then already a proven negotiator.

In the wake of the setback and humiliation of 1874, Asantehene Kofi Kakari was deposed. The next Asantehene, Mensa Bonsu, was immediately faced with a secession move on the part of Dwabenhene Asafo Agyei. The new Asantehene explored and utilized a number of peaceful approaches, including employing Boakye Tenten's diplomatic abilities to successfully isolate Dwaben from Bekwae. Preferring to end the Dwaben secession move rather than contain the rebellion, Boakye Tenten dispatched four emissaries to negotiate peace with Asafo Agyei. When the envoys were all murdered in Dwaben, Boakye Tenten finally gave in to the clamoring for war. Asante forces duly subdued Dwaben in November 1875, and notification of the action was given to the British administration in a letter whose signatories included Boakye Tenten.[72]

At a time in 1881 when Asante-British relations were extremely tense and clouds of mistrust of Asante motives were hanging over the British administration owing to the controversy over the use of the Golden Axe, Asante's choice of an ambassador to settle outstanding misunderstandings could not have fallen on a better qualified person. Boakye Tenten's credentials were impeccable: firstly, as a very senior and most experienced counselor whose tenure of office spanned three successive administrations; secondly, as a man unmistakably known for his adherence to the Kwaku Duan doctrine of peace, open roads, and trade; thirdly, as a person who stood high in royal connections—stepfather to the reigning monarch and his predecessor; and fourthly, as an experienced negotiator and diplomat who combined a rare knowledge of northern and southern affairs.

Appropriately commissioned in the capital, the Boakye Tenten mission was instructed to:

i.   give the Governor unmistakable assurances of the Asantehene's friendship;
ii. repudiate Asabi Antwi's alleged threat of war;
iii. explain for the final time that the Golden Axe was not by itself an indication of war and that indeed no war had been contemplated; and
iv. request the Governor's intercession in the restoration of friendly relations between Queen Victoria of England and King Mensa Bonsu of Asante.[73]

Considering the slow pace at which such large embassies traveled, Boakye Tenten and his party did not reach Praso until 16 April. As a measure of the British administration's estimation of the embassy's importance, Governor Rowe personally went to Praso to welcome the group. The first formal meeting was held on 17 April.[74] Boakye Tenten assured Governor Rowe of his government's desire for peace. While diplomatically intimating that Asabi Antwi may have been guilty of improper conduct if he had indeed issued threats of war, Boakye Tenten cautiously pointed out that British opinion of the Golden Axe as being indicative of war was a misrepresentation. To forestall future misunderstandings, he restated his government's preference that Owusu Ansa serve as the official intermediary between the British and Asante. A second meeting between Boakye Tenten and Samuel Rowe was held at Praso on 24 April. Following Rowe's suggestion that Asante surrender the Golden Axe and also offer a sum of money in excess of the 500 ounces of gold which Boakye Tenten had carried with him from Kumase, the Asante ambassador sent Amoako Ata back to the capital to convey the British demands to the Council.

Boakye Tenten then proceeded to Elmina and Cape Coast, where he held further discussions with the British officials in April and May. In his formal address which was delivered in Cape Coast on 29 April, Boakye Tenten reaffirmed his government's anxiety for peace, in token of which he announced that Asante would pay the British 2,000 ounces of gold. Thereafter, the first installment of 500 ounces was delivered. On Amoako Ata's return from Kumase a further payment of 650 ounces was made and, along with this, the Golden Axe was surrendered to Governor Rowe at the third major meeting, which was held on 30 May at Elmina. It is a point of interest to Asante chancery studies that an English record of this meeting was given to Boakye Tenten to be carried back to Kumase and that an Arabic translation, subsequently prepared at the instance of the British, was also made available to Asante.[75]

Boakye Tenten continued to hold regular discussions with the British authorities at Cape Coast. The talks covered a wide range of subjects affecting Asante-British relations, including notably, the Asante penal code. An agreement was reached, which the ambassador conveyed back to the Asantemanhyiamu for adoption later, that "human sacrifice" at funerals was to be abolished, although the Asantehene was still at liberty to enforce capital punishment for murder and other criminal offenses.[76] Boakye Tenten is also known to have discussed with Arthur Brun, a Frenchman who served as consular agent for the French and Netherlands governments, the prospects for building a road from Assini to Kumase.[77]

It would appear from a record of the Rowe-Tenten meeting of 30 May that the basis for an understanding had been reached. However, Boakye Tenten remained in Elmina until the final installment of an indemnity which was being demanded from Asante had been paid to the British administration. Thereafter, he decided, apparently without his government's prior knowledge, but certainly in consonance with his mandate, to undertake a goodwill mission of the coast from Cape Coast to Accra before returning home. Wherever the Asante ambassador and his 400-strong party stopped—at Anomabo, Apam, Winneba, and Accra—they were the recipients of the local people's bountiful generosity.[78] They were also accorded highly enthusiastic receptions, which underscored the embassy's great success as an advertising instrument.

Coercion, Blackmail or Imminent War? In retrospect, the Golden Axe episode appears more like a case of coercion rather than imminent war. The repeated assurances of the Asante envoys as well as those of Reverend Fletcher and Mr. Bannerman should have left no one in doubt about the Asantehene's peaceful intent. All but W. B. Griffith and Samuel Rowe were convinced that Asantehene Mensa Bonsu had no plans for attacking the protectorate. For the British administration, only the payment of a price of 2,000 ounces of gold by Asante would eradicate the so-called war scare. "Without your King is [being] prepared to do this," Samuel Rowe insisted at a meeting with Boakye Tenten, "I cannot hold out to him the hope of the friendship and help of my Queen." [79] Not the payment of two installments of 500 and 650 ounces of gold nor the surrender of the Golden Axe, the subject of much controversy, could be accepted by Governor Samuel Rowe as convincing proof of the sincerity of the Asantehene' s wish for peace.

When, for a while, it appeared that no further money was immediately forthcoming from Kumase, rather than taking the payment of 1,150 ounces of gold as a gesture of goodwill and calling off the rest of the payment (as demanded by Asante custom), Samuel Rowe insisted that the ambassadors sign a bond and pawn their personal ornaments as security. The final payment was made by an embassy that arrived on 7 June, composed of envoys Yaw Mensa, Osei Broni, and Oti.[80] Thus, Asante found itself in yet another infamous example of indemnity without a military defeat. Asante was a victim of blackmail, Ellis observed as early as 1883, as "the Government kept a dispute open and then asked for money as the price of a settlement." [81] British handling of the Golden Axe episode was the very opposite of the pursuit of an honest peace.

Following the highly successful mission of 1881, which may be said to have represented the high watermark of his career, Boakye Tenten remained in office as Boakye Yam Panin *okyeame*, elder statesman and senior diplomat until his death in 1884. He served in other diplomatic roles of less consequence. In August 1883, for example, during a period of internecine troubles that followed in the wake of Mensa Bonsu's deposition, Boakye Tenten led a delegation to the Tafohene in an effort to secure his support for the candidature of Agyeman Kofi in opposition to Kofi Kakari. The mission's outcome was disastrous to Boakye Tenten, who was taken captive and might have been executed, but for the intercession of his stepson Kofi Kakari. The internal conflicts of feuding factions eventually proved to be his undoing, as he was captured in a local skirmish in late 1884 and quickly executed.[82]

The diplomatic significance of the career of Boakye Tenten lies first and foremost in his singular success in averting imminent Asante-

British war in 1881. The selection for the headship of this mission of Boakye Tenten who was well known for his commitment to a policy of peace, the ambassador's cautious diplomatic style, and the grand scale on which the embassy was undertaken were all intended as explicit affirmations of Asante's belief in the peaceful resolution of differences and the use of diplomatic mechanisms. These apart, the career exemplifies, perhaps more glaringly than others, the growth of specialization in the Asante administration. In genealogical as well as territorial terms Boakye Tenten was the fifth (following Boakye Yam, Oti Panin, Kofi Boakye, and Kofi Nti) in a stool line which held responsibility for, and acquired specialization in, foreign policy and specifically in Fante and British affairs. More notably, Boakye Tenten inherited a family tradition of specialization in foreign affairs going back through his uncle Kofi Nti and father Oti Panin to his maternal grandmother Akyaawa Yikwan.

The London Mission of 1894–1895. In 1894 Asante dispatched a high-level embassy to the British Government in London. The embassy was occasioned by a demand that Asante accept a British Resident, a symbol of authority whose presence in Kumase would have amounted to the acceptance of British overlordship. After a long and careful debate of the British proposition which was conveyed to Kumase in early 1894 by their emissary, Henry Vroom, the Asantemanhyiamu decided on a line of action that sought to emphasize the utility of personal diplomacy as opposed to written diplomacy. It considered that the question of British protection was:

> so grave and sweeping, touching as it did the constitution and construction of the King of Ashanti's independent Kingdom, that considering the unfriendly attitude already assumed by Her Majesty's Government on this Coast to the Kingdom of the King of Ashanti... it is impossible that mutual sympathy and understanding could be looked for or arrived at in the Colony for prevention of war and bloodshed, and that therefore special embassy should be sent to England to lay before her Majesty and Privy Council this and other matters of importance connected with peace and progress of Ashanti Kingdom and its cooperation with settlement of Her Majesty the Queen on the coast for full discussion and final decision. [83]

Official notification of the embassy was conveyed to the British Governor by envoys Kofi Abua and Esen Ofori. [84]

The main outlines of the 1894–95 embassy have been chronicled by Wilks.[85] What the recreation here of one of the most important events in nineteenth-century Asante diplomatic history does additionally is to underscore the principal precepts upon which Asante diplomacy was built, highlight the fundamental diplomatic mechanisms in operation, and assess their effectiveness within the context of Asante's relations with the British. The decision itself to appoint an embassy to England — notwithstanding the heavy costs involved—attested not only to Asante's commitment to a policy of the peaceful resolution of differences but also to the very belief in the efficacy of personal diplomacy.

Careful preparations were undertaken towards the trip, the cost of which was borne, according to the prevailing practice, by a special tax that was levied before the embassy's departure. The strategy employed was to carefully conceal the details of both the preparations and the embassy's objectives from the British administration beyond what was officially communicated to it. The mission's broad goals were rather grand and had a touch of an advertising and goodwill quality:

> The Embassy hopes to winter in England, and after completing their diplomatic mission to the British Government they will probably visit other European capitals, notably Paris and the Hague.[86]

The embassy was composed of John and Albert Owusu Ansa, Kwame Boaten, Kwaku Fokuo, Kwaku Nkruma, Kwabena Bonna, Akyampon Daban, and Kwadwo Tufuo. By all indications it was a high-powered mission. Each of the Owusu Ansa was an *ohenenana*, a grandson of Asantehene Osei Tutu Kwame. Kwame Boaten and Kwaku Fokuo were both "influential Chiefs," the former Kyidombene and the latter Boakye Yam Panin *okyeame*. Kwaku Nkruma was a leading member of the *abenase fekuo* and Kwabena Bonna, the Sepe Nkyetiahene of the *nseniefo*. Akyampon Daban and Kwadwo Tufuo were senior members of the *afenasoafo* and *ankobeafo*, respectively. All the members had seen earlier diplomatic service to the British administration, a fact that the Asantemanhyiamu must have considered significant in its appointment criteria, but which nevertheless was to prove inconsequential in the eyes of British officials. Kwame Boaten, for instance, was a member of the all-important 1881 mission that was led by Okyeame Boakye Tenten. The inclusion of *afenasoani* Akyampon Daban and *nsenieni* Kwabena Bonna in the embassy underlay the recognition given to the members of these *nfekuo* as essential components of all missions.

It was no mere accident that in England, Akyampon Daban along with Kwadwo Tufuo were employed to carry errands. It was the two who conveyed a letter prepared by the embassy's solicitor, J. H. Brew, which sought audience with the Colonial Office. [87] The embassy had a following of 300 to 500 from Kumase to Cape Coast.

The commissioning letter, which was addressed to the British

Queen, clearly spelled out the embassy's mandate:

> ...to lay before your Majesty diverse matters affecting the good estate of our Kingdom and the well-being of our subjects... to negotiate and conclude all such treaties relating to the furtherance of trade and all matters therewith connected....[88]

At the same time specific definition was appropriately given to each member's mandate. John Owusu Ansa was designated "head of the Embassy to Her Britannic Majesty from the King of Ashanti."[89] He directed the affairs of the embassy in that capacity and described himself as such in the correspondence he undertook on the embassy's behalf. Kwame Boaten was in a sense the real leader of the embassy, the inclusion of the Owusu Ansas being necessitated by Boaten's inability to read and write English. Indeed, oral accounts widely assert that John Owusu Ansa threatened to withdraw from the embassy unless he was appointed to its leadership.[90] The presence of the two "leaders," the one representing the modern trend initiated by the adoption of Western influences and mechanisms of communication and the other representing the persistence of traditional systems, underlay the dualism that characterized Asante diplomatic practice in the nineteenth century. Kwaku Fokuo, as an *okyeame* distinguished in the art of oratory, was the appointed spokesman.

As "co-leader" of the embassy, Kwame Boaten brought to bear on the 1894–95 mission a quarter-of-a-century of diplomatic experience with the British administration and familiarity with its officials. A son of Boakye Yam Kuma *okyeame* Akyampon Tia, Kwame Boaten had specialized in British affairs, largely because he was brought up, in the absence from the capital of his father who was on posting to Dagomba, under the aegies of Boakye Tenten, the Boakye Yam Panin *okyeame*. He had led missions to the Wesleyan society authorities at Cape Coast in 1871, served as a leading staff member of Boakye Tenten's embassy to British officials at Cape Coast in 1881, conducted protracted negotiations with the British in Accra for the return of Asante refugees from 1884–1888, and had returned to Cape Coast on another diplomatic assignment to the British administration in 1891.[91] During the 1891 mission Kwame Boaten had been accompanied by Kwaku Fokuo, who served in the capacity of *okyeame* to the embassy. The two therefore were not only well acquainted with British affairs by 1894, but had begun a diplomatic partnership which was to outlast the 1894–95 mission.

As an act of diplomatic courtesy the 1894–95 embassy to the British Government decided to call upon the British administrator at

Cape Coast before proceeding to England. The first meeting took place on 12 December, at which Okyeame Kwaku Fokuo introduced Kwame Boaten as head of the mission and J. Owusu Ansa as the leader to whom "all matters connected with the King of Ashanti have been entrusted." At this meeting Kwame Boaten reiterated to W. B. Griffith his government's belief that "mere letters to the Governor would not settle matters," hence the dispatch of the mission to England.[92] The following day the delegates held a second interview with Brandford Griffith, at which they were instructed to notify the Asantehene that his envoys would not be received in England, and that he could only communicate with the Queen through her appointed representative, the Governor. Thus were set the circumstances for an impasse that thwarted the achievement of the embassy's set goals.

At a subsequent meeting held on 15 December the Governor informed the envoys that, following correspondence he had received from the Secretary of State for the Colonies, his government did not recognize Agyeman Prempe "as the King of Ashanti, but that of Kumasi, and that the head of the embassy and his brother were dismissed from the public service."[93] This marked the beginning of a battle of status which the embassy was to fight without success for the next ten months. The Governor's strategy was a calculated one that sought to scandalize John Owusu Ansa and the other persons in or attached to the embassy. He denied Owusu Ansa the status of prince and charged that he was "dismissed" as a telegraph clerk for being "inattentive to his work" and for possessing a "reprehensible character."[94] He also suggested that John Owusu Ansa was of British rather than Asante nationality, and accused him of insisting on the embassy proceeding to England to further his own personal ambitions. In a letter to the Colonial Office, Governor Griffith summed up his design: "my object was to discredit him [Owusu Ansa] with them and thereby to induce them to return to Kumasi."[95] In response, the Asante ambassadors insisted that they had been commissioned as such: "As ambassadors we have simply been commissioned to visit England, and the above instructions we intend carrying out." They also expressed displeasure at the British design to deny them recognition and refuted allegations that "human sacrifice" was being practiced in Kumase as misrepresentations.[96] In contrast to Brandford Griffith's disparaging remarks, Asantehene Prempe I reassured John Owusu Ansa of his confidence and described him as a "very good assistant and a very good adviser."[97]

The British administration extended its campaign of discrediting the Asante mission to other individuals who were attached to the embassy. It alleged that Joseph Gattin Halm, whom the embassy had engaged as a secretary, "was convicted of a serious and most disgraceful crime at Cape Coast in 1886 and sentenced to imprisonment with hard labour for eighteen months," and that Frank S. Essien (Kofi Asaam), counsel to the embassy, was "a person of doubtful antecedents." [98]

In the hope that the Asante administration might recall the embassy, Governor Griffith dispatched a "special envoy" to Kumase to notify the Asantehene of the British Government's decision not to receive Owusu Ansa and his party. While the Council debated the issue in discussions which might have been purposely prolonged as a strategy for buying time, the embassy's own envoys who had been sent separately from Cape Coast arrived in Kumase to seek instructions. The Council's response was a reaffirmation of its position: the embassy had been appointed to proceed to England and it believed that the surest course of action, in view of recent experiences, lay in personal discussions between the embassy and the British government.[99] Realizing that the envoys' determination to travel to England was growing rather than diminishing, despite mounting obstacles, W. B. Griffith next wrote to forbid the embassy to proceed to England. [100]

Undaunted, the embassy continued with its efforts to achieve its objectives. From its office at Freemason's Hall in Cape Coast, head of embassy Owusu Ansa wrote to challenge the validity and basis of the right of the British in debarring them from entering England. He also engaged the services of solicitor James Hutton Brew (Brew of Dunquah), a Fante barrister then resident in England, and requested him to ascertain whether the members of the embassy could be restrained by force from proceeding to or entering England. The embassy also protested against the action of Commissioner Peregrin in issuing a warrant for the arrest of John Owusu Ansa on grounds of diplomatic immunity, a status which the British claimed Owusu Ansa lacked. Before their departure from Cape Coast the embassy wrote to Governor Hodgson to restate their determination to proceed to England as properly commissioned envoys and to express their displeasure at how contemptuously they had been treated by the British administrators on the Gold Coast. [101]

Ironically, unknown and unsuspecting to the Asante government or its representatives who had been deputed to proceed to England, the British government was seriously contemplating an invasion of Asante itself at the very time that Asante was making a high investment in diplomacy. When the Asante government finally had to face and deal with the British expeditionary force, the timing of this event and the discreet way in which it had been planned, seen in retrospect, must have once again undermined Asante's faith in Britain as a friendly power. In any case it is significant to note that while the embassy was still in Cape Coast, Governor Griffith telegraphed the Marquess of Ripon in February 1895, "strongly recommending for favourable consideration" of his government "the adoption of an advanced line of policy with regard to Ashanti by promptly dealing a crushing blow to that country, and thereby bringing it under complete control of Great Britain." He urged that this "important business should be dealt with without avoidable delay," suggesting that it be executed during the current dry season. In his own assessment of the situation, he considered it "doubtful whether Ashanti would offer determined opposition to expeditionary force."[102] The idea must have received the approval of the Colonial Office, for on W. E. Maxwell's appointment as Governor to replace W. B. Griffith, the Marquess of Ripon suggested that the new administrator of the Gold Coast could consider a military invasion of Asante if it did not appear that a peaceful approach would work out.[103]

The embassy of Kwame Boaten and John Owusu Ansa, Jr., finally embarked on a steamer for Liverpool on 3 April 1895, subsequently proceeding to London. Their departure was preceded by that of lawyer Frank S. Essien as "guide." Their arrival in London was formally communicated to the Colonial Office in a letter of 6 May, prepared by J. H. Brew. At the same time counsel Brew cogently argued the case of the Asante embassy, amply citing precedence and historical facts: that the British government had itself accorded Agyeman Prempe and his government due recognition in correspondence with Asante; that the British officer who had been present at Prempe I's coronation never saw or heard of a massacre of 400 persons and indeed wrote to say that "human sacrifice" had "ceased"; and that the credentials of the members of the embassy were without question.[104]

The Colonial Office refused to budge from its position of denial of recognition to the embassy, no matter how flimsy and contestable its grounds were and how naive its outlook appeared; it continued to deny Owusu Ansa and the others the status of envoys. Neither the independently conducted investigation of Mr. H. C. Richards (a Member of Parliament deputized by the House of Commons to act as an intermediary between the embassy and the British Government, who reported that the Asante delegates were sufficiently empowered) nor Owusu Ansa's assurances that "human sacrifices" at funerals were not being practiced carried weight with the British Government. J. Bramston of the Colonial Office turned down a suggestion to see the Asante ambassadors privately, saying: "No, I decline altogether to see them — they are human sacrificers — and so [like the Queen] I cannot receive them."[105] Far from receiving the delegates, the Colonial Office advised the Asantes to return home and informed the War Office of its support for a military expedition unless Asante were to submit to a British Resident.[106]

While the embassy was attempting to resolve its problems of status and recognition, it executed on 21 October an important document—the Reckless Concession—with a George Reckless and his associates. Seen from the perspective of rights, this agreement gave to the concessionaire far more legal entitlements than the British Government sought to acquire from its proposition to Asante, and for this reason Wilks has suggested that it seemed redundant for the Colonial Office to have pursued its demands on the Asantehene.[107] Indeed, barrister J. E. Harris, also representing the embassy, wrote to request the British Government to change its plan with regards to the projected invasion of Asante in view of the execution of the Reckless Concession.[108] However, it should not be forgotten that this was an age of imperialist expansion in Africa and that the British Government was prepared not to be outdone by any power, be it a rival government like France or a private company like that headed by Mr. Reckless. When the Harris representations failed to effect a departure in the Colonial Office's position, the envoys engaged the services of yet another solicitor—Thomas Sutherst. In two letters addressed to the Colonial Secretary on 15 and 16 November, Mr. Sutherst confirmed having seen the credentials of the ambassadors and being satisfied that they were empowered to negotiate and conclude on behalf of the Asantehene. He reasoned with the Colonial Office that the British Government could achieve its objective—the submission of Asante—through the ambassadors "without either firing a shot, sacrificing a life, or spending a pound."[109]

The Colonial Office was unmoved by the Sutherst representations. Determined on the imposition of British authority over Asante, the government insisted that Asante accept its ultimatum. In the end the envoys reluctantly tendered in their submission in writing, agreeing to accept a British Resident in Kumase, reaffirming their government's support for the abolition of "human sacrifice," and declaring their intention to promote trade. Yet, their bewilderment continued when they received a declaration from the Colonial Office that "the military expedition will, in the meanwhile, proceed, according to arrangements already made." The embassy understandably protested against "the preparations and lavish expenditure which is [sic] being incurred by the British Government, for no other purpose...than a demonstration of strength, which is quite unnecessary, seeing that the King, Chiefs, and people have already accepted to the fullest extent the demands of the British Government."[110]

Complying with a British order to return home immediately, Kwame Boaten, Kwaku Fokuo, Kwaku Nkruma, and Kwabena Bonna departed on 27 November for Cape Coast. Akyampon Daban and Kwadwo Tufuo, who had left earlier, arrived in Cape Coast in September and reached Kumase on 14 October. The Owusu Ansas left England later in December. News of the details of the British preparations for the invasion of Asante befuddled the Asante envoys on their return to the Gold Coast.[111]

The 1894–95 embassy in one sense marked the high watermark of Asante's policy of commitment to diplomacy, but in another light it was anticlimatic in achievement. For not only were its immediate goals unattained; British colonial designs against Asante had been intensified while the embassy was en route to England. However, its limited achievements notwithstanding, the mission's organization and conduct significantly exemplified the careful attention to detail and the complex operation of such large-scale embassies. More importantly, British persistent refusal to cooperate with the mission laid bare the obstacles, frustrations, and futilities that confronted Asante's efforts to reach an understanding with Britain. Yet the embassy did not fail to impress upon English public opinion the philosophical bases and mechanisms of Asante diplomacy.

CHAPTER 5

The Chancery: A Structural Analysis

> I swear a great oath, by the great God and Fetische, and
> that great oath of my ancestors...that that...book is what I
> approve of.[1]

This statement of unqualified approval for the Dupuis Treaty was made
by Asantehene Osei Tutu Kwame as he swore an oath of inviolable
friendship between Asante and Britain in 1820. The approbation with
which he received this treaty (in contrast to the Bowdich Treaty three
years earlier), important as it was, had a less profound effect on the
course of nineteenth century Asante-British diplomatic relations than
the belief and faith in treaties which the statement exemplified. It was a
faith so strongly characteristic of all nineteenth century Asantehenes,
a faith so pervasive and persevering, and at times so naively persist-
ing, that written agreements would work where oral accords alone had
failed. It marked a turning point in Asante's principal mechanism of
diplomatic intercourse: first, a recognition of the inadequacies of oral
agreements as a basis for a firm understanding at least with the European powers, and second, a realization of the need to reinforce "oral
diplomacy" with "written diplomacy." In adopting the written medium,
Asante in the course of the nineteenth century poured forth an enormous volume of documents. The standardization of practices and observances connected with the preparation and preservation of documents in turn brought about developments associated with the mak-
ings of an Asante chancery.

In 1975 Wilks commented upon the Asante government's use of
letters in the maintenance of its official communication in the nineteenth
century: "the Asantehenes came increasingly to conduct their correspondence in writing," he observed, "in Dutch to Elmina, in English to
Cape Coast, and in Arabic to the provincial rulers and imams of the
northern hinterland."[2] He followed this with a discussion of some of the
individuals who were responsible for undertaking this correspondence.
Elsewhere in the same work, he commented upon the preparation of
letters of appointment, citing those of Bonnat in 1875, Huydecoper in
1878, and John Owusu Ansa, Jr., in 1894. These were obviously references to the development of the Asante chancery, a subject of investigation which this chapter seeks to pursue more fully.

The principal goal of this chapter is to examine the structure of
the chancery as a bureau responsible for the maintenance of diplo-

matic communication with Asante's foreign neighbors, principally the British, Dutch, Danish, and Arabic powers. Importance will be placed on examining the backgrounds of the individuals who were engaged to undertake foreign correspondence, their role, and their eligibility skills.

Origins of the Chancery

Chancery developments in nineteenth century Asante were the outcome of the general growth in the governmental machinery which occurred during that period. The chancery, therefore, cannot be seen as existing outside the bureaucracy. It was part and parcel of an expanding bureaucratic system which developed in response to the governmental needs of the time. As the volume of governmental business in both the domestic and foreign fields expanded, so did the need for the effective management of specialized functions progressively bring into being specialized branches of administration, including the chancery. A discussion of chancery developments therefore necessarily preempts a recapitulation of the major stages in the development of the overall domestic administration so as to shed light on the salient aspects that were related to the growth of the chancery.

The major administrative reforms which changed the form and character of appointments in the nineteenth century are usually associated with Asantehene Osei Tutu Kwame (1800–1823).[3] Bowdich observed during his visit to Kumase in 1817 that this Asantehene was "considered to take better care of the treasury than any of his predecessors; he cautiously extends his prerogative, and takes every opportunity of increasing the number of secondary captains by dignifying the young men brought about his person, and still retaining them in his immediate service." [4] The implications of these developments in the early decades of the century in terms of administrative reform are threefold: first, a reorganization of financial administration that emanated from the *Gyaasewa*, which, incidentally, had overall jurisdiction over the chancery; second, an emphasis on merit and skill rather than ascription as criteria for appointment; and third, the emergence of specialized departments requiring skilled personnel to handle the increasingly specialized nature of governmental work. It was this trend towards specialization that led to the development of distinct bureaus responsible for the preparation of public records and the maintenance of foreign correspondence.

By the 1870s Asante had developed a complex administrative system with specialized departments responsible for military, financial, political, and foreign affairs. Yet, the failure to establish a firm basis of understanding and cooperation with European government officials on the coast — a situation which directly resulted in several major wars — must have cast doubts on the efficiency of the foreign bureaus or their mechanisms for conducting and maintaining external relations. It is against this background that the administrative overhaul of Asantehene Mensa Bonsu (1874–1883), which had a tremendous impact on the chancery, must be seen. Diplomat John Owusu Ansa, Sr. was very instrumental in the creation of what Wilks views as Mensa Bonsu's new "civil service."[5] In his capacity as head of the foreign bureaus, he engaged the services of free agents like M. Bonnat, whose contribution to chancery styles was seen in areas like the form for letters of appointment and commission. The rationale for the employment of foreigners like Bonnat, Nielson, Campbell, and Huydecoper in the foreign bureaus in the second half of the l870s and the early l880s, therefore, lay, first, in the inadequacies of the traditional medium of diplomacy (which had been painfully demonstrated during the Asante-British 1873–74 crisis) and, second, in the expertise of such individuals in Western modes of diplomatic conduct, including competence in European languages.

The Chancery

There is no doubt that the concept of the chancery as an office of public records existed in Asante. The chancery undertook responsibility for the preparation, preservation, and retrieval of public records on behalf of the Asante government. Its officials composed letters and other documents for the Asantehene and the Asantemanhyiamu and generally provided secretarial and linguistic services, including dictations, translations, and interpretations. As individuals who were knowledgeable about the politics of the day, it was the practice for a large number of chancery officials to counsel the Asantehene on foreign policy issues as requested. There is evidence that written agreements were made and copies retained in Kumase. The chancery, therefore, represented a general repository of international and, in some cases, national agreements involving Asante and foreign powers, or Kumase and the provinces.

Preservation and security needs required the envoy on a mission to carry his letter or document in a little box. This case or handbox, such as was carried by ambassador (*oheneba*) Owusu Dome when he arrived in Cape Coast in January 1820, was popularly referred to as a "morocco trunk." On an envoy's return to Kumase it was the usual practice that "the box containing the letters was opened in the King's presence," again for security reasons. [6] One instance involving envoy Adu Borade clearly demonstrates the professional importance attached to the regulation that the Asantehene always had to be first to see the contents of the envoy's box. Adu Borade, a nephew of Asantehene Osei Tutu Kwame, had been sent on a mission to the coast in 1819 to receive a fine imposed on the people of Komenda for wrongful behavior in accordance with the Bowdich Treaty of 1817.[7] On his return from Cape Coast the envoy refused to surrender his letters to Thomas Bowdich, despite the latter's insistence, until the Asantehene had returned to the capital from a short trip to Bremen.

The Structure of the Chancery

Structurally, the Asante chancery comprised four distinct bureaus, namely: the English, with responsibility for the British and Fante; the Dutch, responsible for Dutch, Elmina, and southwestern Gold Coast affairs; the Danish, responsible for Danish and southeastern Gold Coast affairs; and the Arabic, with responsibility for the Muslim areas to the north.[8] Each staffed by trained officials, the bureaus were distinguished by the language in which diplomatic intercourse was undertaken. While all the bureaus were operative at one time or other during the course of the nineteenth century, the demands of the varying political situation determined the degree to which a bureau was most active at any particular moment. Thus, the "Dutch Chancery" experienced its time of most vigorous activity during the period which began with the Asante invasion of the coast in 1806 and ended with the withdrawal of the Dutch from the Gold Coast in 1872. But it was the English bureau that was the most active throughout the century, largely as a result of the dominance of Asante's relations with the British *vis-à-vis* those with other foreign powers.

The "Arabic Chancery"

From the point of view of historical development, it was the Arabic chancery that was the first to evolve into an organized bureau concerned with the preparation and preservation of records. While it is impossible to date the origins of the Arabic chancery with any degree of certainty, the available evidence indicates that it pre-dated the reign of Asantehene Osei Tutu Kwame. It grew out of a literary tradition, long associated with the history of Islam in Africa, of which the recording of events by chroniclers was an essential part. Among the earliest known Asante written records in Arabic is a description of the Asante invasion of

Kpembe in 1751, which is attributable to a Gonja chronicler. Of the outcome of this invasion, Reindorf, who evidently had access to an extant copy of a treaty prepared in Arabic between the Asantehene and Kpembewura Nakpo, wrote:

> Nakawa's life was spared, but he was made to write a contract in Arabic to the effect that he and his successors should remain vassals to the kings of Asante and pay a tribute of 1,000 slaves yearly to the king, this document was signed by Nakawa and all his generals .[9]

Clearly, then, a tradition existed, dating back at least to the mid-eighteenth century, in the use of Arabic as a medium in Asante diplomatic intercourse.

While instances were known before the nineteenth century of written agreements in Arabic between Asante and the Muslim imamates to the north, it was not until the reign of Asantehene Osei Tutu Kwame that the Arabic chancery began to take definite form. Exercising a system of patronage liberally, this Asantehene engaged and personally encouraged the services of literate Muslims in the task of maintaining records. As Bowdich observed, "the anxiety of the Ashantee government for daily records" began "immediately on the establishment of the Moors, who were only visitors until the present reign."[10] This, no doubt, was a reference to Muhammad al-Ghamba's party which migrated to Kumase during the 1807 invasion of Fante.[11] The renowned Muhammad al-Ghamba, who was soon to become "the chief" of the Muslim community, came to Kumase to solicit political protection, having been driven from Gambaga by its reigning monarch. The Asantehene offered instant assistance on a *quid pro quo* arrangement: that the Imam and his party ensure Asante success in the impending war through their "prayers and charms." Thus it was that the basis of a mutually beneficial arrangement was established between the Muslim immigrant community and a non-Muslim Asante administration which was not slow to recognize the practical value of Islam.

Asantehene Osei Tutu Kwame wasted no time in recognizing the skills of the distinguished Imam and in giving him secretarial responsibilities. And in the performance of this task, the Imam was assisted by other leading Muslims who provided the staff of the Arabic chancery. Bowdich certainly recognized one of them as a "moorish secretary" and described his general responsibility as the recording of what he viewed as "the greater political events."[12] An entry in the Journal of the Dutch administrator at Elmina similarly recalls that on 15 May 1817, a Muslim, the son of a writer in the service of the Asantehene, arrived in Elmina. Born in Timbuktu, this man's father and two other Muslims were employed "to keep the necessary records" in Kumase.[13]

The "Arabic chancery" performed other functions beyond the recording of historical and political events. Among the diverse roles performed by its personnel was an apparently medical function, as was evident from the responsibilities of "an Arab medical staff" which accompanied Osei Tutu Kwame during the southern invasion of 1806–07. In the opinion of Robertson, this group was charged with the recording of a casualty list.[14] Other functions performed by the "Arabic chancery" included the synthesizing of the Asante, Christian, and Muslim calendars; the recording of court proceedings; and the preparation of a chronology and dynastic annals of the Asante monarchs.[15]

Viewed against the background of, firstly, Asante's absence of a written tradition in the pre-nineteenth century period and, secondly, the general anti-literacy sentiment prevalent in the society at the time, the chancery-related achievements of the Kumase *ulama* (Muslim scholars) were very significant as well as novel.[16] The attainments of the "Arabic Chancery" even appear more unusual and revolutionary when seen in the context of a long-established Asante tradition which forbade references to the deaths of former kings or disasters which might have befallen them.[17] It was certainly in recognition of the utility of the preservation of diplomatic documents in the Arabic medium that the British administration commissioned the translation of the record of the discussions between Governor Samuel Rowe and the Okyeame Boakye Tenten mission of 1881 in Arabic.

The "Dutch Chancery"

Next to the "English Chancery," the most important bureau responsible for European affairs was the "Dutch Chancery." While the latter may not have enjoyed the same level of institutional continuity and intensity as did the "English Chancery," the bureau for Dutch and southwestern Gold Coast affairs witnessed, nevertheless, periods of vigorous activity throughout the first three quarters of the nineteenth century.

As early as the 1810s Asantehene Osei Tutu Kwame had recognized the need for maintaining effective channels of communication in the Dutch language with the Dutch administration based at Elmina, when he appointed visiting Dutch envoy W. Huydecoper to head and organize the Dutch chancery. Huydecoper had been dispatched to Kumase in 1816 as an emissary of Dutch Governor H. W. Daendels of Elmina. He had been instructed to discuss questions relating to Wassa's relationship with Elmina, the Dutch "note" by which the Asantehene received annual groundrent (*kostgeld*) from the Dutch in respect of the land on which their fort at Elmina stood, and issues relating generally to Asante-Dutch trade.

During the period of his residence in Kumase from 1816 to 1817 Huydecoper undertook correspondence in Dutch on behalf of Asantehene Osei Tutu Kwame. In early 1817, for example, Daendels reported receiving three letters from the Asantehene written in Dutch in Huydecoper's writing and signed by the writer. A projected meeting between Osei Tutu Kwame and Daendels; the construction of the great western road from Kumase through Wassa to Elmina; the activities of Asante ambassador Tando, who had earlier been sent on a mission to Wassa; and the conduct of the Wassa people provided the subject matter of these letters. In one dated 29 November 1816, the Asantehene proposed that Daendels visit him in Kumase (rather than the two meeting halfway in Wassa), reported that construction work on the Wassa road was to begin immediately, and protested against alleged molestations of Elmina inhabitants by the Wassa. The letter also rebuked ambassador Tando for overstepping his bounds in his conduct of Wassa affairs and further authorized the Dutch Governor to settle the Wassa issue.[18]

The exact details of the nature of the administrative machinery created by Huydecoper as the nucleus of the bureau responsible for Dutch affairs are not yet known. What can be recalled, however, is that for most of the century, following Huydecoper's visit, a local Asante who was known to be competent in Dutch matters came to be attached to the "Dutch Chancery" as a general consultant on Dutch affairs to the administration.[19] Forty years after Huydecoper, Asantehene Kwaku Dua Panin in 1859 showed recognition of the importance of maintaining the links with Elmina by engaging a Dutchman, Pieter de Heer, to oversee his correspondence with the Dutch administration.[20]

The "Danish Chancery"

Before the eventual withdrawal of the Danish administration from the Gold Coast in 1850, Asante maintained considerable diplomatic contacts with the Danish authorities at Christiansborg, particularly for commercial purposes. As with other European government representatives on the Gold Coast, the demands of effective relations led Asante to adopt written communicative processes — hence the growth of a "Danish Chancery" that engaged the services of persons who were skilled in that language.

The Danish bureau, however, operated on an *ad hoc* basis, as indeed did the "English Chancery" in the early phase of its development, when local Asantes trained in that language were yet to appear. As a result, it relied on visiting Danish officials for its personnel. Such was the case of Henrik de la Palm, who served in the "Danish Chancery" from February to late June or early July 1819.[21] Arriving in Kumase on 4 February on a mission from Danish Governor Christian Svanekiaer, which was intended to reciprocate an earlier one from the Asante government to the Danes at Christiansborg, de la Palm was conveniently drafted into the Danish bureau. The Asantehene must have been impressed by the negotiating and linguistic skills of the Dane who, in addition to his native language, was reputed to have been competent in Twi, Fante, Ga, Ewe, and Adangme.[22] In this capacity, he undertook official correspondence in Danish on behalf of the Asantehene. It was he who drafted Osei Tutu Kwame's letter of 17 May addressed to Governor Svanekiaer.[23] The letter affirmed Asante's friendship with the Danes and thanked the governor for gifts lately received from him. The major subject of this communication, however, dealt with a matter which was then of great concern to the Asante government: preferential trade rates for the *batafo,* the official traders. The Asantehene requested that goods received from the Danish administration in respect to the "*gage*" (ground-rent) should be valued at prices lower than the regular commercial rates. Henrik de la Palm hand-delivered this letter to the Governor on his return to Christiansborg on 14 June 1819.

As with the "Dutch Chancery," the bureau responsible for Danish affairs lacked an institutional growth with clearly identifiable structural outlines, operating as it did in an *ad hoc* manner. Beyond the recruitment of individuals with competence in Danish to prepare official communications in that medium and beyond the surviving evidence of extant documents to that effect, it is indeed doubtful whether the Danish bureau ever developed as a distinct department. Yet, the Asante government's decision itself to adopt the dual mechanisms of the preparation and preservation of documents in Danish represented one more step in its efforts to maintain more effective links of diplomatic communication with a European power.

The "English Chancery"

The largest and by all indications the most active foreign bureau was the "English Chancery." It also enjoyed the greatest measure of continuity. An examination of chancery documents gives a strong indication of the wide range of officials who were responsible for the English correspondence of the Asantehenes as well as their role in the Asante administration. They carried responsibility for the drafting of letters and other documents pertaining to Asante's relations with the British and generally served in a secretarial capacity. The intensity of Asante-British relations in the nineteenth century made the "English Chancery" by far the most important foreign bureau, and for this reason the head of the English bureau came to be generally referred to as *ohene krakye*, that is, "the king's secretary."

Three major categories of *ohene krakye* can be recognized, the first of which comprised trained Asante civil servants, examples *par excellence* being the Owusu Ansas and Owusu Nkwantabisa. In 1831 John Owusu Ansa, Sr., then aged about nine, and Owusu Nkwantabisa, a few years older, were given into British custody as a condition of the Asante-British peace treaty of that year, to be educated.[24] The two youths were sons of Asantehene Osei Tutu Kwame and Asantehene Osei Yaw Akoto, respectively. Osei Akoto refused to let the two *ahenemma* leave the Gold Coast. Under Kwaku Dua Panin, however, Owusu Ansa and Owusu Nkwantabisa finally left Cape Coast in 1836 for England where, according to Freeman, they became the beneficiaries of a "liberal and religious education."[25] At Kwaku Dua's request, the two were returned to the Gold Coast in 1841 to put their education to the benefit of their country.

Back in Kumase in 1842, Owusu Nkwantabisa had a brief and unspectacular life before his premature death in 1859. His reputation suffered as a result of an adultery incident, shortly after his arrival in Kumase, that involved him and a wife of counselor Kwame Poku Agyeman. Although Owusu Nkwantabisa's life was spared, partly because he was an *oheneba* and partly because of his education, the incident must have shaken the Asantehene's confidence in him. For it was not until the 1850s that he was seen again in any prominent administrative role — as *ohene krakye*; and even then there are no indications of a sizeable number of letters signed in his name for a decade or so that he spent in Asante's "English Chancery" before his death.[26]

In contrast, John Owusu Ansa, Sr. had a longer and more distinguished, if also a more eventful, career in the Gold Coast. Trained under Wesleyan ministers, Owusu Ansa became a catechist, school master in charge of Cape Coast Boys' School, and a customs officer before coming to dominate the Asante "English Chancery."[27] By 1853 he had acquired the role of the principal person who drafted and signed the Asantehene's letters as well as counseled the king on foreign policy issues.

Owusu Ansa's return to Kumase in 1853, apparently on a three-week leave of absence from his Wesleyan Missionary Society station at Abakrampa, coincided with a period of hostilities in Asante's relations with the southern provinces. Writing to Governor Hill on behalf of the Asante government in March, he requested safe conduct for Akyampon Tia of the Boakye Yam Kuma stool, who was to be sent on an official visit to Jukwa.[28] Owusu Ansa returned to Cape Coast soon afterwards on a mission from the Asantehene. This was followed by a period of residence in Cape Coast during which his apparently waning interest in missionary work led him to take up an appointment as master at the Cape Coast Boys' School.

Owusu Ansa returned to Kumase in March 1862, accompanied by his little son John, Rev. William West, and Rev. Robert Johnson Ghartey, a Fante minister who was later to become King Ghartey IV of Winneba. The visit itself lasted only eight weeks and is not known to have involved the prince in any service in the chancery. However, the enthusiastic reception he received in Kumase reassured him of the friendship of his homeland, and he might not have been unmindful altogether of the fact that the premature death of Owusu Nkwantabisa bereft Asante of literate citizens who were capable of undertaking the Asantehene's official correspondence for him.[29]

Following the death of Asantehene Kwaku Dua Panin in 1867, Owusu Ansa returned to Kumase, having been recalled by the new Asantehene, Kofi Kakari, to head the "English bureau," in which position he received the assistance of the Wesleyan minister J. S. Watts. In this position, Owusu Ansa's major responsibility as *ohene krakye* was the preparation of that large body of letters that emanated from the Kumase court at that time. The Rev. Tregaskis aptly perceived that Owusu Ansa was retained in Kumase at this time because he was the only Asante "able to communicate in writing with the coast Government in matters then pending."[30] Examples of Owusu Ansa's official correspondence prepared during this period include a letter of 23 March 1868 from Kofi Kakari to Governor Ussher, in which the Asantehene explained the delay in the anticipated return to the coast of Fante war prisoners then held in Kumase as being caused by the blockade of the road to Cape Coast through the activities of "some mischievous persons."[31]

Meanwhile, by early 1869 hostilities were developing in eastern Gold Coast, initially originating as a Krepi revolt against Akwamu overlordship. The combatants in the fray widened, as Akyem joined the side of Krepi, and Asante on behalf of Akwamu. Frederick Ramseyer, a Basel missionary, his wife Rosa, their infant son, and Johannes Kühne, a German merchant, were captured at Anum by Osahene (General) Gyaasewahene Adu Bofo on 12 June 1869.[32] Late the same month, Joseph-Marie Bonnat, a French trader, was also taken captive.

The four-year period immediately following was one in which Owusu Ansa, as the Asantehene's secretary and foreign policy advisor, increasingly played a vital role in the official correspondence and negotiations relating to the release of the European captives.

In November 1870 Owusu Ansa addressed three successive letters to the British Governor on behalf of the Asantehene. The first, dated 2 November, explained the delay in releasing the captives: the matter could not be properly discussed until the return of Gyaasewahene Adu Bofo. The second, written two days later, requested safe conduct for a messenger who was to be sent to usher the resident ambassador for Elmina, Akyampon Yaw, back to Kumase. The third, dated the 24th, registered the Asantehene's protest against the impending Anglo-Dutch transfer of forts, which could bring Elmina under British jurisdiction. Owusu Ansa, in this letter, firmly established Asante's historic claim to Elmina:[33]

> The fort of that place have from time immemorial paid annual tribute to my ancestors to the present time by right of arms, when we conquered Jutim Gackidi, king of Denkera.

Owusu Ansa did not doubt that the continued need for his secretarial services led the Asantehene to restrain him from leaving Kumase and, on occasion, had reason to reveal his displeasure at his detention. Expressing sympathy for the European captives during one of the numerous visits he paid them, Owusu Ansa commented that "he was himself detained in Coomassie, but daily hoping to be allowed to return to the coast." [34] He eventually left Kumase for Cape Coast on 2 February 1871. On March 31, as an *ex-officio* member of an embassy to Cape Coast and Elmina headed by Kofi Afrifa, he participated in the exchange of prisoners that took place in Cape Coast.[35]

Owusu Ansa was back in Kumase in December 1871, charged with responsibility from the British to negotiate the release of Ramseyer, Kühne, and Bonnat. He carried with him a written message from British Administrator Salmon, expressing the hope for an immediate settlement of the issue. The Asantehene's response, which was drafted by Owusu Ansa, was also hand-carried by the prince to Cape Coast on the expiration of his mission in April 1872. The letter was a firm statement of the Asantemanhyiamu's position on the issue:

> Respecting the release of the Europeans, I requested Addo Boffoo (through my linguist) to hand them over to me to send them to the Governor, my friend. Addo Boffoo refused to give them to me (saying he demands 6,480 pounds ransom). Your Excellency's messenger asked to know from me con-

cerning other matters of peace and when peace shall be
finally settled; My answer to him is, "Tell the Governor that I
and my great chiefs have decided this: after the ransom is
paid to Addo Boffoo, then peace between us shall be finally
settled, and not before."[36]

This letter's authenticity was witnessed by the European captives.

Following an attack on his house in Cape Coast by a band of
enraged Fantes during a period of Asante-Fante hostilities in 1873,
Owusu Ansa briefly left Cape Coast, first for Sierra Leone and subsequently for England, for safety. He was back in Kumase from May 1875
to March 1876, ostensibly to undertake business ventures in partnership with M. Bonnat who was revisiting the Gold Coast. Of greater
concern, however, was the subject of Asante-Dwaben relations which
were clearly drifting towards open hostilities at the time, and it was this
political situation that occasioned the prince's return to his homeland.

As before, the chancery benefited from the invaluable services of
Owusu Ansa, and now of Bonnat also. Commenting on the role of the
two in the drafting of official correspondence, M. Johnson has observed
that there is evidence of the Asantehene's dispatches to the Governor
"being the composition of M. Bonnat or Mr. Ansah or not improbably
both."[37] Indeed, with the return of Owusu Ansa to the Asante chancery
service in 1875, Asantehene Mensa Bonsu himself raised the hope
that the correspondence between the two governments would improve:
"As my grand-uncle J. 0. Ansah is at Coomassie now, I shall from thence
communicate with you in writing, and beg earnestly your Excellency to
answer me in writing."[38]

Acting on the Asantehene's orders, Owusu Ansa drafted a letter
of 11 June 1875 to Governor-in-Chief Strahan at Cape Coast, remon-
strating against the Dwaben rebellion. With the growing clamorings of
the pro-war party, the Asantehene warned of the difficulty that he might
have in the future in restraining the cry for revenge. The letter announced
that the Asantehene had dispatched Dane McEacheren, an American
gold prospector, to ascertain the extent of the depredations caused by
Dwabenhene Asafo Agyei's men. This letter was cosigned by Bonnat,
McEacheren, and Kofi Nkan, an official of the Asante administration
whose position is unclear.[39]

A month later the Asantehene had occasion to write again to
Strahan on the escalating tension created by the Dwaben insurrection.
The letter which was dated 16 July 1875, once again bore Owusu Ansa's
print, together with those of Bonnat and Campbell as witnesses. In the
letter the Asantehene made reference to Owusu Ansa's continued role
in the chancery: "I beg your Excellency to give me an early answer, in

writing, as my uncle, Prince Ossoo Ansah is here, who can read and interpret it to me."[40]

Owusu Ansa also apparently collaborated in the drafting of Mensa Bonsu's letter of 19 July 1875 to G. J. H. Lyall and other merchants at Cape Coast. The letter charged Asafo Agyei of Dwaben of molesting traders and inciting hostility against Asante in contravention of the existing treaty between Dwaben and Asante. The Asantehene sought the intercession of the Cape Coast merchants with the British government in bringing Asafo Agyei to order. Owusu Ansa signed this letter, along with A. H. Campbell and M. Bonnat, both of whom were anticipating a visit to the inland territories.[41] This was followed in August by yet another letter of protest from the Asantehene about hostilities committed against Bonnat's party, en route to Atebubu, by Asafo Agyei's men. The letter in addition announced the imposition of certain trade controls on the sale of gold to eliminate illicit trading in base metals which were circulating as pure gold. Owusu Ansa once again authored this letter.[42]

Owusu Ansa's final phase of service in the chancery was from April 1878 to August 1879, which coincided with a time when Asante was embroiled in an effort to suppress an Adanse secessionist movement. As *ohene krakye,* he dispatched three letters in March 1879, in which the Asantehene protested against alleged molestations of Asante traders on the Kumase–Cape Coast route by Adanse and requested the Governor to use his good offices in persuading the Adanse to desist from such activities.[43]

Meanwhile, the 1870s were witnessing an expansion in the commercial activities of European trading companies and individuals in the Gold Coast and Asante. Reference has been made above to the reentry of Bonnat, in the company of Owusu Ansa, into Kumase in June 1875. With them was another entrepreneur, Alister H. Campbell. The details of their commercial ventures lie outside the scope of this discussion. However, there was one direct connection between the growth of commerce in Asante at this time and chancery work. The danger of Asante losing lands through the granting of reckless concessions to foreign nationals had never been more imminent. Worse still, there was a general speculation that some of the prospectors might have been operating as agents of European governments The suspicion that Bonnat could have been a disguised agent of British imperial expansion, for example, was rumored.[44] In the circumstances, the Asante government responded to the situation by ensuring that the chancery provided proper documentation in respect of all concessions and appointments.

If Bonnat's letter,[45] reproduced below *in extenso*, is in any way representative of the form and content of such commissions, then the attention to detail was impressive:

> We, Assai Mensah, King of Achanty, in our name and in the name of our chiefs, having received the oath of M. M-J. Bonnat, attaching him to us and wishing to extend our relations, establish the said N. Bonnat as our governor in our name, conjointly with another chief, to be named by us.
>
> The jurisdiction conferred upon him extends from 40 miles above Accrono to develop and to extend as far as possible our commerce with the interior of Africa, and to establish the bases of a financial system regarding importation and exportation.
>
> To do this and facilitate his duty, we, King and Chiefs of Achanty, give to the said N. Bonnat, agent of N. de Cardi, for six years the entire monopoly of commerce and the right of navigation on the river Volta through the regions under his jurisdiction, that is to say from 10 miles south of Accrono to Jegui, near Salaza.
>
> N. Bonnat has to pay 3% on all kinds of goods imported, and will levy for us in our name 5% on all merchandise of exchange and native produce.
>
> At the expiration of the six years, the monopoly will cease and the coutry will be open to all Europeans desiring to trade in this part of our territory, provided they submit to the laws and customs then established.
>
> We further guarantee to N. Bonnat, as to our Governor, the right of possession for 20 years of all sites necessary for the construction of their establishments, whether on the banks of the river or on the islands of the said river. After the expiration of twenty years, these establishments will become our property and that of our successors.
>
> Given under our name, mark and public seal, Coomassie, 31 July 1875.

This document is strikingly specific as to name of officer being commissioned, extent and limitations of his jurisdiction, duration of the concessionary rights, and other details.

The same vein of specificity characterized Huydecoper's letter of appointment of 1876, by which he assumed headship of the Gyaman mission:

> KNOW ALL MEN by these present I, Ossai Mensah, King of
> Ashantee and its dependencies in my name and in the name
> of our Chiefs do hereby nominate, constitute, and appoint J.
> J. C. Huydecoper as our Commissioner and headman of our
> Mission of Peace to the King of Gaman, in the room or place
> of the late C. Nielson our late Commissioner and headman
> of our Mission of Peace to the King of Gaman, who died on
> Thursday 13th June 1878, to act for us and settle all matters
> between Ashantee and Gaman according to the *objects* of
> our Mission under his charge.[46]

This document bore Owusu Ansa's name and was executed on 9 July 1878.

With the death of Governor Ussher in Accra in December 1880, all notions of Owusu Ansa's intermediary role disappeared in the eyes of the British administration. Suspicion for the prince's motives, already generated in previous decades, now mounted in the minds of the British. Unable to obtain further permissions from the British administration to visit Kumase to serve in the English bureau, Owusu Ansa remained in Cape Coast until his death on 13 November 1884. Although he continued to the last to comment on Asante political affairs in writing, his career as *ohene krakye* was effectively over by 1880.

John Owusu Ansa, Jr. John Owusu Ansa, Jr. continued in his father's footsteps by serving in the "English Chancery." Born in 1851, the younger Owusu Ansa was educated in Cape Coast, where he served as a teacher at the local Government School. He was subsequently known to have worked with the Audit Department in Cape Coast before leaving the country to undertake trading ventures on the Lower Niger.[47] This phase of Owusu Ansa's career, when he took up residence outside the Gold Coast, lasted from 1880 to about 1887 and was interrupted twice by periods of repatriation: first, on a recall by Governor Rowe to join his administrative staff in 1881 — during which time he participated in the diplomatic discussions between the Boakye Tenten mission and Governor Rowe's party at the Pra River —and second, in 1883, for a brief appointment with the telegraph service.

It was, however, not until 1889 that Owusu Ansa, Jr. was to return to Kumase, apparently on the invitation of Asantehene Agyeman Prempe. Asante's independence was being threatened at the time by expanding British imperialism, and it was to Owusu Ansa that the Asantehene turned for counseling in foreign matters as well as secretarial service through the "English Chancery."

Late in 1888 the British-controlled Gold Coast Government had made to Asante a proposal for protection, which was propped up by an offer of a "gift" of 80 ounces of gold. The validity of a British claim that the offer of gold was based on an earlier request by Asante for a loan is suspect, as this claim was decidedly repudiated by the Asantehene.[48] Agyeman Prempe both sought and received the advice of Owusu Ansa, who initially counseled Asante's acceptance of the British proposition. In a series of developments which quickly followed, Owusu Ansa rose to dominate not only the foreign policy decision-making process, but also the mechanisms involved, as head of the "English Chancery" and ambassador. He recommended to Agyeman Prempe the preparation of a document accepting the offer of British protection, although it was never drawn up. Next, he obtained appointment from the Asantemanhyiamu as envoy to the British government on the subject.[49] Having received the appropriate commission, he proceeded to Accra in June 1889 on an official mission to the British administration. Though Owusu Ansa met with Governor Griffith, no "protection" agreements could be concluded as his credentials were rejected by the Governor. In the circumstances, Owusu Ansa returned without any Asante-British document, perhaps a happy fortuitous event for Asante, whose independence was thereby preserved for at least a few more years.

From this time on, Owusu Ansa was clearly the person who ran the English Chancery. He became the Asantehene's principal letter writer and official channel of communication with the British administration in the Gold Coast, and later in England. As his stature with the Council steadily grew, Owusu Ansa assumed full control of the direction of diplomatic matters with the British within the "English Chancery." It was he who prepared the document by which Asante made a firm rejection of the protection idea as presented through British Travelling Commissioner Hull:

> The suggestion that Ashanti in its present state should come and enjoy the protection of Her Majesty the Queen and Empress of India, I may say this is a matter of a very serious consideration and which I am happy to say we have arrived at this conclusion, that my kingdom of Ashanti will never commit itself to any such policy; Ashanti must remain independent as of old, at the same time to be friendly with all white men.[50]

It was therefore no accident that the head of the English bureau should have resided during this period at the house of Asomfohene Kwaku Wo, who was himself head of the *afenasoafo*.[51] Owusu Ansa's functions extended beyond "secretary to the King of Ashanti," that is, *ohene krakye*, to those of "principal advisor to the King in everything."[52]

In 1894 the British administration renewed its efforts to bring Asante under its "protection." The new plan centered around the posting to Kumase of a British resident whose approval was to be sought in all political matters, particularly those pertaining to war and peace. Included in the British plan were also proposals under which the Asantehene and the Asantehemaa were to become recipients of annual stipends from the British government.[53] These stipulations would not only have seriously circumscribed the authority of the Asantehene and his council, but would also have pawned Asante's sovereignty in the conduct of foreign policy. At a session of the Asantemanhyiamu convened on 5 April 1896, Owusu Ansa cautiously debated the implications of the new British proposals and counseled the dispatch of a mission to discuss the issue in full with the British administration. At a subsequent extraordinary session held two days later when British emissary Henry Vroom announced the specific monetary value of the stipends proposed for the Asantehene, the Asantehemaa and the senior *amanhene*, Owusu Ansa was able to effect a postponement of the Council's decision on the proposals to a later date in June, by which time Agyeman Prempe would have been formally enstooled as Asantehene.

Owusu Ansa was clearly instrumental in shaping the particular course of action which the Asante response to the British proposals assumed. Writing in January 1895 on behalf of the Asantehene, he expressed the Council's awareness of the dangers the British proposition posed for Asante's independence. The issue of British protection, he argued, "was so grave and sweeping, touching as it does the constitution and construction of His Majesty's Independent Kingdom" that, in view of the absence of "mutual sympathy and understanding" in recent Asante-British relations, a special embassy had been appointed to discuss "important matters connected with the peace and progress" of Asante with the English Government in London. As one of the two leaders of this embassy, Owusu Ansa was accorded the full power of "ambassador extraordinary and minister plenipotentiary." In this capacity he undertook the responsibility for inquiring into the credentials and legal status, in England, of the members of the embassy, in view of Governor Griffith's deliberate attempts to discredit the envoys and his threats that they would be denied diplomatic recognition by the English Government. Towards this end, the embassy engaged the legal services of the Liverpool firm of Radcliffe and Durant, to whom Owusu Ansa wrote from Cape Coast to inquire whether the ambassadors could be legally prevented from leaving Cape Coast or landing in England and whether they could be arrested in England.[54] Owusu Ansa continued to direct the affairs of the embassy to England personally and in writing. His English training and familiarity with British modes of diplomacy, and his knowledge of Gold Coast and Asante affairs made him especially suited for the headship of the foreign bureau responsible for British affairs.

A second category of *ohene krakye* embraced non-Asantes, usually Fantes, who were drafted into the "English Chancery" on an *ad hoc* basis. It has been pointed out above that the Owusu Ansas did not enjoy uninterrupted periods of residence in Asante. The failure of Asante to produce a sufficient cadre of literate citizens who could read and write English meant that the government had to look elsewhere for secretarial assistance whenever the services of the Owusu Ansas were not available. Such men as Henry Ata Plange, George Kuntu Blankson, Joseph Dawson, and J. S. Watts, all of whom undertook letter-writing duties for various Asantehenes, were Fantes who had received English training at Cape Coast. Their appointments to the "English Chancery" occurred at times when they had been sent to Kumase as agents of European governments. That they were often required to assist in drafting Asante's replies to various pieces of correspondence which they had themselves conveyed to Kumase from foreign governments created a situation which was inherently fraught with dangers. The Asante government therefore had to institute measures to ensure that while these agents of rival governments were writing on behalf of the Asantehene, they recorded only statements which were dictated to them.

Described as "an Elmina man and a Dutch agent," Henry Ata Plange was dispatched by Dutch Governor Nagtglas in 1871 to Kumase to seek Asante's renunciation of its claim to Elmina.[55] Plange's visit lasted from June to October and, from Asante's point of view, he apparently failed to obtain the renunciation. However, as far as the Dutch administration was concerned, Plange's visit was successful, for a document entitled "Certificate of Apology" and purporting to disavow Asante's claim to Elmina by right of conquest, found its way to Nagtglas. Henry Plange was engaged by Asantehene Kofi Kakari in the "English Chancery" while he was in Kumase, and during the preparation of the document he may well have taken liberties with his position to include statements that were not dictated to him and therefore distort and misrepresent Asante's response.

Plange returned to Kumase in July 1872 on a second mission, this time as an agent of both the Dutch and English administrations. His mission's primary object was to give official notification of the Anglo-Dutch transfer of forts to the Asante government. However, he was also charged with responsibility for securing the release of Ramseyer, Kühne, and Bonnat. Having incurred the extreme suspicion of the Council on his earlier visit, Plange was this time slighted by the Asante government and treated in a way unbefitting the diplomatic profession. There was considerable delay in having his credentials accepted, and official response to his message was delayed indefinitely. He was also confined to his residence and forbidden to undertake any correspondence for several months.[56] It was not until September that the Asantemanhyiamu lifted the restrictions on him and asked him to write again for the government. Plange accordingly drafted the Asantehene's response to the British and Dutch request for the release of the European captives. In this letter which was carried to the coast by the confidential envoy Owusu Koko Kuma, the Asantehene expressed the wish that the English Governor would accept a reduction of the ransom demand from £2,000 to £1,000, and suggested that payment could be made partly in goods and partly in gold-dust or cash.[57]

An Anomabu merchant prince of considerable reputation and well acquainted with Gold Coast and Asante affairs, George Kuntu Blankson was sent on several missions to Kumase as an emissary of the Gold Coast administration.[58] During periods of his residence in Kumase, various Asantehenes took advantage of his presence to engage him in the "English Chancery." In 1834 Blankson arrived in the Asante capital with presents from Governor Maclean to Asantehene Osei Yaw Akoto. He was detained in Kumase for eighteen months by the Asantehene, who "utilized Mr. Blankson's services in carrying on important political correspondence between himself and the Government."[59]

In November 1853 the Asantehene sent envoys to the British administration with a letter in which Asante rejected British proposals for a treaty of friendship. The British proposition had been conveyed to Kumase by Blankson, who now accompanied the Asante envoys to Cape Coast with the Asante response. Though the author's name is not mentioned in the Asantehene's letter, the style of writing seemed to have been that of Blankson, who was on this occasion again detained in Kumase for a period of time longer than necessary. Asantehene Kwaku Dua's official explanation was that Blankson was delayed in Kumase because his visit coincided with the yam festival.[60] The truth of the matter, however, was that Blankson's services were required in the chancery.

Joseph Dawson represents another example of a Fante who, while serving as a British emissary to the Asante court, was drafted into the "English Chancery." Among the letters prepared in Dawson's name was one dated 20 March 1873, in which Asantehene Kofi Kakari expressed his displeasure at an allegation that the British administration was planning to transfer control over Elmina to the Denkyirahene. The letter established the Asantehene's claim to Elmina on hereditary grounds as a descendant of Osei Tutu. It further requested the restoration of Akyem and Asen to their previous relationship of dependency on Asante. To dispel rumors about the safety of the European captives, Kühne, Bonnat, and Ramseyer, for himself as well as his family, signed the letter as evidence of their being alive.[61]

From about the 1830s the Asante government increasingly drew upon the ranks of Wesleyan ministers stationed in Kumase for secretarial services. Writing to the Wesleyan Committee on 17 October 1836, Mr. Wrigley commented that a young man was resident in Kumase at the time "as the king's writer or secretary." This person is not named and his exact identity is not known beyond the fact that he is said to have continued to be under the direction of the Wesleyan Society's President.[62] However, slightly better known to us is J. S. Watts who served in the "English Chancery" between 1862 and 1879. Although his nationality is not absolutely clear, he was in all probability a Fante. Watts composed several letters for the Asante government during his long period of residence in the capital. The question has been raised as to whether Watts stayed in Kumase on his own volition or was restrained from leaving the city. While references to his activities are sparse, the available evidence points to a Rev. Watts who, while ministering in Kumase, voluntarily served Asantehenes Kwaku Dua and Kofi Kakari in the capacity of *ohene krakye*. Writing in Kumase in 1870, Ramseyer and Kühne commented that Watts had already been "detained" for eight years as a "hostage."[63] The word "detain" appears here to have been used in a free sense, in much the same way as Plange and Dawson were said to have been "detained" because their visits were delayed until their assistance had been obtained in the drafting of replies to messages they had conveyed. Had Watts been indeed involuntarily detained as a "hostage," he would have protested. On the contrary, the fact that he assumed the title of "linguist" in some of the letters he authored[64] would seem to indicate that he had taken up an official appointment as "counselor" of sorts in the administration. Ramseyer and Kühne provide further evidence of Watts serving in an official capacity, apparently not unwillingly: the two had the privilege of observing an official reception in December 1871 at which Watts, in conjunction with John Owusu Ansa, Sr. took up positions as government functionaries next to the Asantehene.[65]

Be this as it may, Watts' years with the chancery were not altogether prolific, as few letters appear in his name from this period. Indeed, Ramseyer and Kühne observed that for four years prior to 1871, Watts "had been prevented from communicating with the coast." This would seem to suggest that because he was in an official and sensitive position, Watts was prevented from engaging in private, unsanctioned correspondence, especially at a time when security decisions and preparations respecting war were being made. Watts finally left Kumase, accompanied by some liberated Fante war prisoners on 4 February 1879, after seventeen years of unspectacular service in the "English Chancery."

A third category of chancery officials consisted of Europeans whose literary expertise qualified them for appointment. A combination of emphasis on talent and pure necessity accounted for the government's recruitment of persons like Bonnat in the mid-1870s and Ramseyer in the early 1870s: the one because he was free and skilled, the other because he was unfree but possessed the requisite skills at a time when other qualified personnel were unavailable. Owusu Ansa had recognized Bonnat's potential during his association with him in the years of Bonnat's captivity earlier in Kumase. It is an indication of the close collaboration the two were to enjoy in the chancery subsequently that Owusu Ansa housed Bonnat at his residence during the time that the latter was in Cape Coast en route to the Asante capital.

In Kumase adventure-seeking Bonnat took up various *ad hoc* appointments, including those of an envoy and the Asantehene's letter writer within the English bureau now headed by Owusu Ansa. In July 1875 Bonnat, in conjunction with A. B. Campbell and Owusu Ansa, signed Asantehene Mensa Bonsu's letter which was written preparatory to a projected visit to Dwaben by Bonnat and Campbell. The letter was addressed to G. J. H. Lyall and all the European merchants at Cape Coast to seek their support in approaching the British Government with a request to bring Asafo Agyei of Dwaben to order. In the event that the British Government was disinclined towards interceding in the interest of Asante, Mensa Bonsu requested its neutrality.[67]

A second letter which came out of the chancery on the Dwaben issue was the product of M. Bonnat. The letter informed the Governor of the failure of the mediation efforts of Bonnat and Campbell. The Asantehene reported:

> Asafu Agal by refusing my proposal of peace has shown to me that he means war, and to continue kidnapping, plundering and destroying my villages.[68]

The Governor commented about this letter being "a joint composition of M. Bonnat and Mr. Ansa." [69]

In captivity in Kumase, Basel missionary Ramseyer was expediently engaged to draft letters as an *ad hoc* chancery official for Asantehene Kofi Kakari whenever such services were required. In November 1871, following the outbreak of civil war in Appolonia (Nzema) between two local chiefs, the Asantehene wrote to Acting British Administrator C. S. Salmon to assure him of his peaceful disposition. To convince Salmon of his determination to bring order to Appolonia, Kofi Kakari vowed to invoke the capital punishment on Ahuru Kwame, who was alleged to have been the cause of the hostilities. This letter, which was dated 23 November 1871, was composed by Ramseyer and "written by order of the king before the linguists."[70] Ramseyer was particularly useful to the chancery at times when Owusu Ansa was away from the capital. There were, however, occasions when he signed chancery letters as a witness even though the documents were prepared by Owusu Ansa. Such was the case with the Asantehene's letter of 20 February 1872, which was written to explain to Governor Salmon the continued detention of the European captives.[71]

It is clear from the above evidence that the Asante chancery of the nineteenth century should be thought of as four distinct bureaus that operated for the most part on an *ad hoc* basis rather than as a single, integrated office. It had not developed well-defined structural features beyond the existence for each bureau of a staff that operated along accepted procedures. The lack of a single organized system would seem to suggest, at first thought, the absence of an overall office of head of the chancery. However, the size and importance which the "English Chancery" acquired in relationship to the other foreign bureaus seemingly gave to its head a status that closely approximated to that of chancellor. Indeed, the position and functions of heads of the "English Chancery" like the senior and younger John Owusu Ansas were, to all intents and purposes, those of a chancellor. They were responsible, like heads of the Roman Curia, for the preparation and preservation of official documents. Although, unlike their counterparts in the Roman Curia, they performed limited non-secretarial functions such as financial and judicial administration, they were certainly caretakers of public deeds and documents. They were also advisors to the Asantehene, thereby exercising patronage. Nonetheless, these officials performed such chancellor-like functions in *de facto* rather than *de jure* roles. As such, there was no direct Asante equivalent of Dahomey's office of the Yovogan, who, as the appointed "white man's chief," exercised overall responsibility for the direction of foreign affairs. Asante's closest equivalent to this position was the *akyeamehene,* who, as head of the whole administration, had general jurisdiction for the all important foreign bureaus. For an *akyeamehene* like Kwaku Poku Agyeman, who showed a keen interest in foreign policy matters, he also performed the role of "chief of protocol" with conspicuous effectiveness.

The chancery was based in Kumase as part of the general administrative machinery. However, the sedentarization of the chancery does not mean that it ceased to function whenever the political situation made it necessary for its officials to be away from the capital. In much the same way that the government functioned outside Kumase during occasions when the Asantehene and his *akyeame* happened to be away, the chancery continued to operate beyond its Kumase base when circumstances so demanded. Considerable evidence is available indicating chancery activities and letters being undertaken in Cape Coast, Elmina, and other places outside Kumase. Indeed, it might be said that when the 1894–95 embassy to the English Government left Kumase, the chancery practically moved with it. It would appear from the use of the seal on some chancery letters written by the embassy in London in 1895 that "Chancellor" John Owusu Ansa, Jr., as custodian of the seal, kept it in his care while he was on this mission. For a young and developing institution, the Asante chancery was flexible enough to allow for occasional mobility. It was perhaps this character and the absence of a truly professional personnel in the modern sense that accounted for the possession of private archives by some chancery officials. John Owusu Ansa, Sr. had his own archives in Cape Coast, and the same can be said of Muhammad al-Ghamba, who maintained a personal collection of a "great number of Arabic manuscripts" in Kumase.[75]

The chancery's significance must be seen in terms of the creation of a distinct governmental agency employing new diplomatic instruments — the written medium. Asante's willingness to adopt and fully utilize this medium betokened a government that was dedicated to the quest for more effective means of maintaining diplomatic communication with its European neighbors, notably the British. Yet, the absence of hesitation with which Asante employed Europeans in chancery-like roles must not be interpreted as a manifestation of a government that was readily pursuing a conscious policy of "modernizing" its administrative institutions. Faced with the need to communicate in writing with European administrators with whom Asante shared no common language, the choice of English, Dutch, or Danish appeared a more plausible alternative to Asante than Twi. Once this decision was made, it became imperative that the government look for individuals skilled in the use of such European languages. Had Asante possessed an adequate cadre of its own nationals with competence in English, Dutch, and Danish, it would not have turned to men of the likes of Bonnat, Ramseyer, de Heer, and de la Palm — and, by the same token, persons like Plange, Blankson, Dawson, and Watts — for secretarial assistance.

Regulations governing the appointment of chancery officials and the performance of their functions point to a development in the direction of the standardization of procedures. This trend in itself is an indication of the gradual creation of established traditions. Between father and son, the two John Owusu Ansas by themselves gave the "English Chancery" five decades of tradition, and permanence — necessary ingredients in institutional development. However, even as one sees evidence of institutional growth, in view of the limitations in the structural development of the nineteenth century Asante foreign bureaus, it would be more accurate to speak of "institutionalization" rather than of an "institution," and of "chancerization" rather than the "chancery." Our evidence so far is limited to an incipient chancery.

CHAPTER 6

The Chancery: A Functional Analysis

This chapter complements the preceding one by providing a functional analysis of the "English Chancery." It examines the measures employed to ensure accuracy in the transmission of messages from Twi into European languages; discusses the literary styles that became standard in the preparation of chancery documents; and attempts to evaluate the extent of use of the written medium in Asante diplomatic communication. An important consideration is an assessment of the degree to which the chancery became a vehicle by which the administration's foreign policy concerns found expression. In this respect, this study of chancery documents presents a tool for identifying the issues that became pronounced in Asante's foreign policy. The emphasis, therefore, is on the role of the chancery in the maintenance and adjustment of Asante's relations with the European powers.

Chancery Documents and Literacy

It is impossible to obtain accurate statistical data on the volume of official correspondence that emanated from Kumase in the nineteenth century from a study of the contemporary records. The frequency with which copies of the Asantehene's letters are found through a reading of the British Parliamentary Papers alone leads the investigator to believe that the volume of correspondence was enormous. As early as the mid-nineteenth century Governor Hill observed that "many letters and messages pass between this Government and Coomassie."[1] As the political and military confrontation between Asante and the British intensified in the second half of the century, so did Asante resort more frequently to written correspondence as a means of reaching understanding with the British Government.

The available evidence relating to the structure of the chancery does not suggest that it developed into an efficient, integrated office that maintained an inventory of incoming and outgoing letters. However, even in the absence of such record-keeping mechanisms, the number of extant letters provides the investigator with a valid indicator of the volume of official correspondence. Copies of nineteenth-century Asante chancery letters found today in the principal archival sources in Ghana (National Archives of Ghana and The Furley Collection, Balme

Library), the United Kingdom (Public Record Office and Methodist Mission Archives), The Hague (General State Archives), Denmark (National Archives), and Switzerland (Basel Mission Archives) might collectively total several hundred. That more documents have reached us from non-Asante than Asante sources can be explained by the fact that a preponderant number of the Asantehene's letters found their way to the European cities of London, The Hague, Copenhagen, and Basel as enclosures in communications from European Governors and missionary agents on the Gold Coast to their home governments or headquarters. If it is to be assumed that only the Asante documents that the colonial governors and other European representatives considered worthy of the attention of their headquarters were forwarded to Europe, there is reason to believe that these documents that have reached us from European centers represent only a fraction of the total volume of correspondence prepared by the Asante chancery.

Further, although it is known that copies of major international agreements and important communications were retained in Kumase, the destruction of the Asantehene's palace by English forces in 1874 may have seriously affected documents that might have been kept there. Reporting on his sacking of Kumase in 1874, British general Garnet Wolseley confirmed: "I gave orders for the destruction of the palace and the burning of the city.... The demolition of that place was complete."[2] It is reasonable to speculate that the double attack on the Asantehene's residence by English forces in 1874 and 1896 dealt an irreparable blow to the Asante chancery. Official documents may have perished in the general destruction and looting which the residence of the Asantehene suffered. Besides, a great volume of Asante official correspondence may also have been destroyed when a Fante mob attacked the Cape Coast residence of John Owusu Ansa, Sr., Asante's foremost chancery official, during a period of hostilities in 1873. It is suggested that the documents that were prepared by the Asante chancery in the nineteenth century could have totaled several thousand. This enormous volume of correspondence that came out of Kumase and in particular the strong faith that Asante reposed in written agreements were almost paradoxical, in view of the low level of literacy in the society at large. Not only was Asante a preliterate society; the Council's complexion towards Christian education throughout the nineteenth century was persistently one of opposition. Western education was viewed as potentially corrosive to the Asantehene's authority, in that it was capable of inducing disloyalty among the people.[3]

The decision of the Asante administration to promote the written mode of diplomatic communication was in itself a significant one insofar as it ran counter to the long-established traditions of the people and the deeply entrenched prejudices of the governing Council. In adopting and even seeking to encourage the written tradition, the government was showing itself cognizant of the need to infuse efficiency into its diplomatic mechanisms, for which purpose it was prepared to compromise its traditional mechanisms in the interest of the quest for an understanding with European powers.[3]

Veracity and Authenticity in the Preparation of Chancery Documents

A preliterate Asante court committed to the written medium of external communication found it necessary to devise measures for ensuring veracity in the recording of message dictated from Twi into English and other European languages. Letter-writers were sworn on oath each time they were required to write in an official capacity. They took the traditional oath, the "fetische" of Bowdich and Dupuis, and, as if this were not enough, they were also required in some instances to swear in Muslim fashion, as Bowdich came to realize in Kumase in 1817. He and other members of his mission were asked to swear on the Qur'an that they would not record any deceitful matter. Failing to do so because of religious considerations, they were asked to touch the book three times, which they did.[4]

One of the most effective checks against falsification of documents was the Asantehene's own supervision. All letters were written not only by the king's orders but also in his presence. When the letter was concluded, it was "sealed in the king's presence." It was the practice in the early nineteenth century to conclude the exercise with a long Muslim prayer.[5] The Asantehene directed the whole process of dictation, often interjecting it with exhortations like: "Put down in the book what is true."[6] The dictation process itself followed a specific format, again designed to ensure accuracy in the transmission of oral messages into writing. Brodie Cruickshank learned from George Blankson who was sent as a British emissary to Kumase in 1853 that the Asantehene "dictated his letter... sentence by sentence," which afforded "ample proof of his talent, and the extreme caution of his diplomacy."[7]

Other mechanisms which were implemented to check the veracity of recorded messages included the practice whereby the king's *okyeame* periodically interrupted the dictation of a message and asked the recorder to repeat what had been said. Bowdich himself seemed to have been impressed by the effect of the *okyeame's* sudden interruption of the Asantehene's dictation of a letter to him in May 1817, and thus reported: "Here the King's linguist ceased, and by his desire requested us to repeat all the King had said; he was much pleased with our accuracy...."[8] When a letter was not completed, it was locked up and the following day the *okyeame* had it read by the recorder to verify that it had not been altered before the writing was resumed.

Regulations were also enforced to ensure that incoming letters were not tampered with in transit or until the Asantehene had seen them. Thus, on envoy Adu Borade's return from his mission to Cape Coast in 1819, his men retained the dispatches from the governor, knowing very well that they were not to be read until the Asantehene who was away had returned. Bowdich, however, prevailed upon Adu Borade's men to be given the letters in spite of the objections of Gyaasewahene Opoku Frefre. The incident excited the court's suspicion — a suspicion which Bowdich knew he merited —so much so that Bowdich was required, on the Asantehene's return, to swear that he had not tampered with or altered any part of the letters. [9]

Because nineteenth-century Asante kings could not read or write, their marks which were affixed to the letters they caused to be written for them served as signatures. It was the usual practice for the letter writer to be identified as such and his signature appended. As a large number of chancery officials were neither Asantes nor members of the Asantemanhyiamu whose honesty could be readily taken for granted, it was also the practice to have letters written in the presence of witnesses, many of whom were signatories to the documents. An examination of the names of the individuals who signed chancery documents sheds considerable light on chancery procedures and officials, on the personality and political authority of the monarchs, and on the sway of influence within the Council.

Two types of witnesses can generally be identified: first, non-Asantes who were either resident in Kumase at the time or were members of visiting missions; and second, *akyeame*, many of whom were members of the Asantemanhyiamu. In the early decades of the century most witnesses to letters were non-Asante visiting diplomats, the Asantehene's *akyeame* being conspicuously absent from the list. Bowdich, in particular, and Dupuis undertook a number of correspondence for Asantehene Osei Tutu Kwame. In his *Mission From Cape Coast to Ashantee*, Bowdich reproduces four letters he wrote for the Asantehene between May and September, 1817.[10] In none of these do we find the mark of a single counselor as a witness; all were signed by William Hutchinson and Henry Tedlie, members of the James-Bowdich mission, as witnesses. It cannot be said that the contents of the letters did not deal with subjects that were important enough to warrant the attention of the councilors. On the contrary, the letters were concerned with political and economic issues that were of vital significance to Asante—the effective incorporation of the southern provinces, particularly, Fante, Elmina, Komenda, Denkyira, Wassa and Akyem into Greater Asante; the future of the relationship between Asante and the British on the coast; and groundrent paid through the "notes," a steady source of revenue for the government.

There is ample contemporary evidence that the letters as well as the treaties of the time were preceded by lengthy council discussions of their contents, and that both the "Preliminaries" and the final version of the Bowdich Treaty, for example, were witnessed by Gyaasewahene Opoku Frefre and Gyakye *okyeame* Kwadwo Adusei Kyakya. The absence of the marks of councilors from chancery letters of the 1810s cannot therefore be linked to a lack of interest on their part. The explanation lies in the incipient nature of the chancery. In the slow, institutional development of the chancery, standardized procedures by which the marks of councilors were to be appended as witnesses to documents had not yet become a regular feature at the time of Bowdich and Dupuis.

By their very nature treaties were accorded greater ceremonial importance than letters, and right from the beginning of the century it became a chancery procedure for treaties of friendship between Asante and other powers to be witnessed by important members of the royal house and council representatives. Thus, the signing of the Bowdich Treaty of 1817 was witnessed by four *akyeame,* including Opoku Frefre and Adumhene Adum Ata, who were "deputed by the General Assembly of caboceers and captains to swear with the King."[11] In another instance we find an even larger number of witnesses to a treaty. The Asante delegation which witnessed and ratified the Asante-British 1874 Treaty on behalf of the Council was headed by Kwame Antwi and included two akyeame, two *afenasoafo,* one *nsenieni,* and one *nsumankwaani.*[12] To make treaties legally binding on all of Greater Asante rather than the district of Kumase, it became a chancery procedure to have such documents witnessed by representatives of the provinces. Thus, the 1817 Asante-British Treaty was cosigned by the Dwabenhene, Kwame Boaten.[13] Similarly, the 1874 Treaty was witnessed by representatives from Dwaben, Bekwae, Kokofu, Nsuta, Mampon, and other districts.

It is also significant to note that, whereas Asantehene Kwaku Dua Panin was usually the only signatory to his letters, it was the pattern to see Kofi Kakari's letters signed by others besides the Asantehene. Hence, a letter written by Owusu Ansa, Sr., to explain to the British Governor that the Asantehene thought it improper to release Ramseyer,

Kühne, and Bonnat before the return of Gyassewahene Adu Bofo, was signed by Akyeamehene ("Nsuase") Kwaku Poku Agyeman for Kofi Kakari and witnessed by J. S. Watts; a letter written on the Asantehene's behalf to request safe passage for an escort to recall Boakye Yam Kuma *okyeame* Akyampon Yaw in 1870 was witnessed by J. S. Watts and John Lindsay; a letter of 24 November 1870 in which Asante established claim to Elmina through Osei Tutu's conquest of Ntim Gyakari, was signed by both Kofi Kakari and Owusu Ansa, Sr. and witnessed by "Nsuase" Poku and J. S. Watts; the "Certificate of Apology" (which was in all probability prepared by Henry Plange, who was himself a signatory to it) was supposed to have been signed by Kofi Kakari and five of his *akyeame* including "Nsuase Poku, Boakye Tenten, and Yaw Nantwi; a letter of 20 February 1872 in which the Asantehene maintained the Council's determination to accede to Adu Bofo's demand of a ransom, was written by Owusu Ansa, Sr. and attested to by the European captives; and the Asantehene's letter of 24 September which also dealt with the issue of the release of the captives was signed by Plange, the writer, and witnessed by envoys Owusu Koko Kuma and Kwaku Bosommuru Dwira.[14]

An even larger number of officials had witnessed an earlier letter in which the Asantehene announced that his Council had decided to maintain its position of demanding a ransom of £2,000 as a condition of peace. Five councilors headed by Akyeamehene "Nsuase" Poku either signed or affixed their marks to this letter.[15] And when, in another letter two months later announcing an arrangement for the release of the European captives, the names of the councilors did not appear, Akyeamehene "Nsuase" Poku affixed his mark on behalf of all the *akyeame*.[16] Kofi Kakari' s correspondence throughout the rest of his reign continued to bear the marks of his *akyeame*, notably "Nsuase" Poku and Boakye Tenten.

By late January 1874, with Wolseley's forces closing in on Kumase and with the Asantemanhyiamu apparently dispersed, the Asantehene's mark disappeared altogether from the chancery letters. Thus, a letter of 21 January, which announced the Esen Buadi mission with the release of the second batch of European prisoners, was signed for and on behalf of Asantehene Kofi Kakari by Akyeame Yaw Nantwi, Kwaku Poku Agyeman, and Kofi Boakye.[17] A second letter in the name of Kofi Kakari but without his mark was prepared by the chancery on 4 February 1874. The letter announced the Asantehene's preparedness to comply with General Wolseley's demands for hostages if proper arrangements could be worked out as in the time of Governor Maclean. It was signed on behalf of Kofi Kakari by *abenasefo* Yaw Bosommuru Tia and

Kwaku Bosommuru Dwira, as "private counselors" to the Asantehene.[18]

Reade characterized Kofi Kakari as a young man who "could not resist the united will of so many powerful chiefs."[19] A more objective critique was that of Governor Ussher who described the Asantehene as a young man under the influence of his generals.[20] Kofi Kakari, without doubt, lacked decisive action, and his indecision was borne out in the large number of signatories to his letters. The unusually large number of signatories was in reality suggestive of the fact that the contents of the letters represented the majority rather than the unanimous decision of the Asantemanhyiamu. The plurality of signatories may even have evidenced a split in the council in addition to the Asantehene's own weakened position. Plange perceptively stated the Asantehene's ineptitude in a report on one of the Council sessions which discussed the release of the European captives. "I am willing to let these white men go to their country free," he reported the Asantehene as saying, "but the chiefs stick upon the said money."[21]

An examination of the signatories to chancery letters also provides a valuable index to the control of influence in the government. Among the recurrent signatories to Asantehene Kofi Kakari's letters, particularly during the politically tense period of 1870–1874, were "Nsuase" Poku, Boakye Tenten, Yaw Nantwi, Kwasi Apea, Bosommuru Dwira, and Bosommuru Tia. The first four were counselors, the last two councilors. Okyeame "Nsuase" Kwaku Poku Agyeman of the Domakwai stool, Okyeame Boakye Tenten of the Boakye Yam Panin, Akankade *okyeame* Yaw Nantwi, and Butuakwa *okyeame* Kwasi Apea were the most powerful non-military counselors in the state. The four constituted what Ramseyer and Kühne termed "the king's general council" — that is, the inner council, or what Bowdich preferred to call the aristocracy in his day. Bosommuru Dwira and Bosommuru Tia were senior *abenase* officials, that is, "chamberlains" to Asantehene Kofi Kakari.[22] All six were members of the Asantemanhyiamu, the main legislative and judicial body that administered Asante. It was therefore understandable that these influential members of the Council should have signed Asantehene Kofi Kakari's letters and attempted to give direction to the nation's foreign policy at a time when the Asantehene himself patently lacked a sense of direction.

Restrictions which were periodically imposed on letter-writing represent another measure by which the central government attempted to give authenticity to chancery documents and security to foreign policy decisions. Though Ramseyer and Kühne were assigned chancery responsibilities during their period of detention in Kumase, general limitations were imposed on them regarding when and what they could write. Thus, in a letter addressed to Governor Ussher at Cape Coast in October 1870, the two indicated their satisfaction that they were then at liberty to resume writing: "the king has given us now at our request, allowance to write you again."[23] Notwithstanding his high position and influence in the administration, Owusu Ansa, Sr. in turn did not enjoy unbridled license to write as he pleased. On the contrary, during his residence in Kumase from 1867 to 1871, he had reason to lament that despite the fact that he still held an appointment from the Asante administration, he "had not been allowed to write any letters in his official capacity for three years." [24]

Besides the need to regulate official letter-writing as a means of safeguarding the authenticity of the correspondence purporting to originate from the Asantehene's chancery, certain political conditions also periodically necessitated embargoes on communication. Thus, it was Asante's traditional practice to forbid all external communication shortly before major wars.[25] Total bans included complete prohibitions both on the movement of people and on the flow of correspondence into and out of Asante. Such restrictions were imposed to prevent leakages of information relating to military preparations. It might not therefore seem altogether improper that letter-writing restrictions were imposed on the head of the English bureau at a time (1869–1871) when Asante was involved in the invasion of the southern provinces and possible preparations towards another impending war. This situation was certainly confirmed by visiting envoy J. E. Crawford in 1871. Writing from Kumase as an emissary of the British and Dutch administrations sent there to discuss the transfer of forts between the two governments with Asante, Crawford observed:

> There is difficulty in obtaining pass for letters from us to the coast, especially, unless the King is acquainted with its contents.[26]

A further allusion to the subject is provided in another letter from Kumase two years later. Communicating to the British Governor in March 1873 a letter in which the Asantehene reaffirmed his claim to Elmina as a hereditary right, Joseph Dawson, British agent to Kumase, noted in a postscript that "Mr. Plange being not allowed to write," acknowledged receipt of a stipend of £30 through Dawson.[27] Henry Plange, it might be recalled, had fallen from favor because of his wording of the "Certificate of Apology" by which Asante seemingly surrendered its traditional claim to Elmina, and was regarded with extreme suspicion at the time.

Smuggling of Letters and Forged Documents

Notwithstanding these controls against unsanctioned letter-writing, instances were known involving the smuggling of letters and the forgery of documents. A few illustrations would suffice. One instance which involved the Wesleyan minister T. Laing seriously impaired the implementation of the government's course of action recommended for dealing with the Asen situation in 1853. Asante was concerned with settling once and for all the long-standing problem of reasserting its authority over Asen, which had fallen under the British Protectorate's sphere of influence. After decades of unsuccessful resolution of the matter with the British administration and after lengthy debates in the Asante-manhyiamu between the pro-war and pro-peace factions, Asantehene Kwaku Dua Panin decided to give in to aggression. The plan of action, initially, was a concealed one. Boakye Yam Kuma counselor Akyampon Tia, brother of the Asantehene and *okyeame* with jurisdiction over the foreign bureau for Dutch affairs, was to be dispatched, with the support of a military contingent, under the pretext of performing funeral rites for the late Denkyirahene Kwadwo Tsibu, but in reality to capture the two Asen chiefs, Kwadwo Tsibu Kuma and Gyebi. Meanwhile, Reverend Laing had secretly smuggled information concerning the Asante plan, conveyed in letters which were concealed in sandals. Laing's own detailed admission of improper conduct with regard to this incident is cited:

> The road was stopped, so that no person might go from this to the coast to carry the report. (I think the king intends to take the people of the coast by surprise); no sooner I heard this than I got a messenger ready with a letter to acquaint you with the affairs here, but my messenger was stopped, searched, whether he had any letter, and sent back. It was lucky that I had the precaution to divide the sole leather of a sandal and hid the letter there, and sewed it up again, and the messenger wore the sandal as he was going, and by this means the letter was not found out, the king would have been angry with me.[28]

Having been apprised of the situation, British Governor Hill ordered troops to counteract Akyampon Tia, who in consequence was unable to execute the Asante strategy as originally planned.

The so-called "Certificate of Apology" of 1871, which sought to repudiate Asante's claim of sovereignty to Elmina, has often been cited as the example *par excellence* of forged documents. Attention was drawn as early as 1883 by Ellis to the fact that the document might have been a forgery.[29] In 1963, however, Coombs strongly presented a contrary view, contending that there is evidence to suggest that the Asantehene might have authorized a retraction of his earlier position of sovereignty over Elmina through conquest of Denkyira. Coombs argued that the Asantehene might have apologized for the sake of a continuation of the "notes," and that the authenticity of the "Certificate" is "supported by strong circumstantial evidence." [30] However, the forgery view persisted and was upheld in 1975 by Wilks, who described the document as "spurious" and contended that "its fabrication had involved collusion between Dutch officers, their agent Plange, and at least one Asante official."[31]

A close examination of the trend of contemporary events in London, The Hague, Elmina, Cape Coast, and Kumase, and of official documents of the period, including confidential correspondence, should lead the investigator to the following conclusions: first, that the English and Dutch governments were determined to secure a disavowal of the Asante claim at all cost; second, that although Henry Plange was authorized by the Asantehene to prepare Asante's response to the Dutch request for a renunciation, the particular form in which the document appeared was the letter-writer's own creation; and third, that Asante at no time actually renounced its sovereignty to Elmina. It is therefore contended that the "Certificate of Apology" was not a forged document as such, although it nevertheless misrepresented the Asante position on Elmina. It is argued, then, that the true picture lay neither in the view of a fake document on the one hand, nor in that of an outright renunciation of sovereignty on the other; it lay somewhere in the middle. The "Certificate" nonetheless represented a case of distortion in the recording of messages at a time when increased precautionary measures were being taken by the government to ensure veracity in the transmission of official communications. In view of the controversy surrounding the subject, a full discussion of the issue is warranted in order to establish this new position.

Without the knowledge of either the Asantehene or the British and Dutch Governors on the Gold Coast, secret negotiations had begun in Europe between the governments of the two European powers as early as November 1869 for the cession of Dutch forts to the British.[32] By November 1870 the convention had been concluded and might have been ratified soon after, but for a domestic crisis in the Netherlands involving the resignation of the Minister for the Colonies and for Foreign Affairs. Only two impediments stood in the way of the final transfer of forts: first, clarification of Dutch assets and liabilities other than the settlements themselves; and second, fear of Asante opposition owing to its sovereignty over Elmina.

On 9 October 1870, Governor-in-Chief Arthur E. Kennedy wrote to Dutch Governor Colonel Nagtglas to ascertain his views on a number of issues, including, *inter alia*, the possible reaction of the people of Elmina and the trading community and the financial obligations the Dutch were making to the Asantehene. Governor Nagtglas' report was framed to encourage his British counterpart. Although indicating that he paid the Elmina chiefs £100 annually, he suggested that they could be silenced by being bribed into accepting £25 more. As regards the "paynote," he indicated that the Dutch paid the Asantehene £80 per annum, but it was a stipend rather than groundrent. In any case, if it became necessary, he would prepare the people of Elmina for the change of allegiance.[33]

Writing under "Confidential" cover to the Governor-in-Chief in Sierra Leone, Administrator H.T. Ussher expressed extreme uneasiness over the Asante claim. At the same time he intimated that to be able to "authoritatively meet the King's claim," he would ask Governor Nagtglas to reexamine the Asante claim and hinted: "Upon his [Nagtglas'] reply will be framed my answer to the King." For Colonel Nagtglas, however, "the King's party [Akyampon Yaw] is the only one likely to be troublesome," he speculated.[34] It is in this set of correspondence, dated 15th and 16th December 1870, that we find the seeds of the Anglo-Dutch conspiracy that ended in Asante's alleged renunciation. By the end of February the Earl of Kimberley was suggesting positively that "if this claim is renounced, they would not object to grant to the King of Ashantee an annual stipend as an inducement to him to maintain peace and encourage trade."[35]

The main threat in British estimation was not an intangible claim, but Akyampon Yaw's presence. "There is a war party in Elmina," reported Administrator H. T. Ussher to Arthur Kennedy, (in an obvious reference to resident ambassador Akyampon Yaw), "who are much opposed to such a step [the cession] and who would possibly attempt hostile proceedings." The Governor-in-Chief's response was plain but firm; he would not be a party to any transfer of territory, he declared to the Earl of Kimberley, so long as Akyampon Yaw's party remained in Elmina. In almost every correspondence between the British administrator and the Dutch Governor, and between the former and his superior in Freetown from October 1870 to June 1871, Akyampon Yaw's removal was consistently discussed.[36] To make the Anglo-Dutch cause appear a little palatable, Akyampon Yaw was maligned as the disturber of peace, a nuisance, and a villain.

Asante's connection with and claim to Elmina was sentimental, strategic, and historical, dating from the time of Asantehene Osei Tutu in the seventeenth century. By the victory over Denkyira, Asante had acquired the right to groundrent by the same right of conquest as that by which its Denkyira precursor had acquired the notes. Apprehensive about the prospect of the cession, Kofi Kakari protested in no uncertain terms.

> The fort of that place have from time immemorial paid annual tribute to my ancestors to the present time by right of arms, when we conquered Jutim Gackidi, King of Denkera.[37]

In March 1871 ambassadors Kofi Afrifa and Kotirko arrived in Cape Coast at the head of a mission to discuss peace and the exchange of Asante-Fante prisoners. Negotiations protracted into May, with ambassador-at-large Owusu Ansa Sr. participating. Colonel Nagtglas' record of meetings he held with the Asante envoys on 18th and 19th May 1871 alleged that the envoys declared:

> The Ashantees have never quarreled with Elmina, consequently they could not have conquered Elmina, as they never fought with Elmina. [38]

The Dutch Governor then took this statement as being indicative of a retraction of the Asante claim based on conquest. It can be recalled, however, that the Asantehene based his right to sovereignty on the conquest of Denkyira and not directly of Elmina. Apparently under coercion, and possibly to save Akyampon Yaw from further harassment, Kofi Afrifa and Kotirko were reported to have made the ludicrous statement that the Asantehene could not have written the letter under question because he was not by custom permitted to "see a piece of writing paper." However, not even the "unauthorized disavowals" of Kofi Afrifa and Kotirko could save Akyampon Yaw from Colonel Nagtglas' hostility, as he was re-arrested and imprisoned in June.[39]

Early in August, Administrator Ussher dispatched J. E. Crawford to discuss the settlement of outstanding disputes with Asantehene Kofi Kakari. Crawford's record of a meeting he held with Kofi Kakari on 5th August was obscure in places, but the Asantehene's reiteration of his claim through right of conquest was not obscure. Crawford quoted Kofi Kakari as having reasserted:

> It was Intim Gachedi, my great-grandfather Osai Tutu conquered, and his Intim Gachedi's customary paid note was transferred to him, my great-grandfather.[40]

It was against this background that, contrary to the trend of events, the highly suspicious document known as "Certificate of Apology" appeared. The Dutch Governor had in the meantime hastened to dispatch Henry Plange to Kumase to obtain Asante's renunciation of the claim to Elmina. The renunciation of sovereignty was ostensibly obtained and appeared in the extraordinary document reproduced here *in extenso*:[41]

Certificate of Apology

1. *These are to certify that the letter addressed to his Excellency H. T. Ussher, the Administrator of Her Britannic Majesty's Settlements on the Gold Coast, dated Coomassie, 24 November l870, by me Coffie Calcalli, King of Ashantee, reside at Coomassie kingdom, was totally misrepresented in the part of parties entrusted with the writing and the dictating.*
2. *I therefore do solemnly declare, in the presence of your Excellency's Ambassador Mr.H. Plange, profession writer of the Government's Office at St. George d'Elmina and my Chiefs, that I only meant board wages or salary, and not tribute by right of arms from the Dutch Government.*
3. *On account of circumstances relative to my ancestor, Osai Tutoe the 1st, having conquered Intim Gackadi the then King of Denkerra, a friend or kind of commission agent of some transactions for His Netherland Majesty's Government on the Gold Coast, the said Intim Gackadi's liabilities with the Dutch Government on the Gold Coast, to the amount of £9000, my said ancestor was caused to make it good by the said Dutch Government, and in virtue of which the Custom pay-note of the said Intim Gackadi was transferred to my said ancestor, who enjoyed it in times immemorial, and became heritable to his heirs the Kings of Ashantee, who now hold the said Custom pay-note in possession to this present moment.*
4. *The said £9000 was paid to ensure friendship and goodwill, or feeling, toward the Dutch Government on the Gold Coast Settlement in Elmina Fort, castle or fort.*
5. *Tradition tells us that Ashantee and Elmina are relatives; offspring of one mother; they are brethren; also they are not to have hostilities against each other by oath of allegiance.*
6. *In conclusion, I must acknowledge that the aforementioned letter, dated Coomassie, 24th November, 1870, about my communication to his Excellency H. T. Ussher, concerning Elmina Fort is vague, formal, or nominal expression, the sentiments of which I therefore must now write that the whole is a mistake*

Signed in the presence of the Ambassador and the Chiefs. Coomassie, 19th August, 1871.

Chiefs:

(Signed)	*Insuas*	his + mark	*Pokoo*
(Signed)	*Booachie*	his + mark	*Turtsin,*
	Yoar	his + mark	*Nychwie.*
(Signed)	*H. Plange, Ambassador*		
(Signed)	*Coffie*	his + mark	*Calcalli,*

King of Ashantee,
Reside at Coomassie Kingdom

The "Certificate of Apology" sought to retract the Asantehene's letter which had established Asante's hereditary claim to the notes in respect of Elmina through the right of conquest over Denkyira as a mistake, a misrepresentation on the part of the letter-writer. It now attempted to establish that the payment made annually by the Dutch administration to Asante was a salary or a stipend rather than rent or tribute. Since this trend of thought was diametrically opposed to the known position of the Asantehene and his Council at the time, it is maintained that the "Certificate" did not represent the true sentiments of the Asante government. The prevailing evidence supports the view that although Plange was authorized to prepare Asante's response, he distorted the government's position by making the reply an outright renunciation of claims so as to satisfy his Dutch and British mentors. On the same day that the Asantehene was alleged to have caused this document to be written, that is, on 19 August 1871, Kofi Kakari addressed to Acting Administrator C. S. Salmon a letter in which he supported the claims of Elmina against Fante. Within two weeks Kofi Kakari again upheld the same position in a second letter to Mr. Salmon. "As this claim was utterly irreconcilable with the alleged renunciation," Ellis contended as early as 1883, "it ought to have aroused some suspicion of the true facts."[43]

Further evidence bearing on the subject leaves no doubt that the document did not represent the Government's position. It has been argued elsewhere that Ramseyer and Kühne, whom the Asantehene always asked to read and translate documents to him before affixing his signature, would have known about the renunciation if indeed Kofi Kakari had caused the "Certificate of Apology" to be written. When Mr. Plange announced the cession, a bewildered Kofi Kakari asked if the chiefs of Elmina and its surrounding areas knew about it!

The Dutch at no time denied that they made annual payments to the Asantehene. In 1870 they suddenly found it necessary to obtain a statement to establish a shift from the official Asante view of the payments and argued that it was a "stipend." Though the Dutch administration sought to place new emphasis on the significance of the "notes," it never doubted that Elmina owed allegiance to Asante, hence its concern to prepare the people of Elmina for the takeover. To the end Asantehene Kofi Kakari opposed the transfer of control of the forts; to the end he also consistently reaffirmed his nation's claim to Elmina by right of conquest. Like Maria Theresa's emotions over the loss of Silesia, Kofi Kakari could never forget, nor forgive Plange for, the "renunciation" of Elmina. Ramseyer and Kühne observed:

> His Majesty had never pardoned this young man for the in-
> jury which he alleged had been done to him by the wording
> of this letter. [44]

The "Certificate of Apology" represents an example of distortion in the recording of messages from Twi to English by *ad hoc* chancery official Plange, rather than a case of outright fabrication, although the instigation of British and Dutch administrators is hardly disputable.

Types of Chancery Documents

An examination of nineteenth-century Asante chancery documents provides us with fascinating insights into the workings of the foreign bureaus of the time—the scope of functions performed, procedures for the preparation of specific documents, the thrust of Asante foreign policy concerns and priorities, and acceptable literary styles pertaining to the drafting of official documents. The variety of documents itself gives evidence of an institution that responded to the diversified needs of a government that increasingly showed a preference for the written medium in the conduct of relations with its European neighbors. In addition to regular letters, specialized documents were prepared by the chancery, including, notably, letters of introduction, felicitation, appointment, knighthood, safe conduct, and protest; others were treaties and policy-statement letters.

The regular correspondence, expectedly, dealt with a wide range of issues. For a society whose members by and large could neither read nor write, its foreign bureau had not yet assumed the character of a modern-day civil service that is dependent on daily written communication. Consequently, a large body of the regular chancery letters became mainly a function of misunderstandings which they sought to resolve with foreign powers, particularly Britain. Indeed, the chancery communicated with successive British administrations on the coast in an attempt to reach a settlement of the issue, for example, of the relationships of the former provinces of Asen, Denkyira, Adanse, Akyem, Dwaben, Atebubu, etc., with Asante.[45] The subject of the secession of the provinces from Greater Asante was directly related to other jurisdictional issues: the extradition of Asante nationals, a recurrent theme of nineteenth century chancery correspondence, and the maintenance of Asante sovereignty in the face of expanding British imperial designs in the second half of the century.[46] Other questions of misunderstanding that became pronounced in the chancery correspondence of the "English bureau" included the detention of Ramseyer, Kühne, and Bonnat in Kumase in the early 1870s, and capital punishment.[47]

Since the major function of written correspondence was the resolution of differences, chancery documents abound with letters of protest. The subject matter of such letters embraced a wide spectrum of issues ranging from molestation of peaceful traders and extradition of criminals to the secession of the southern provinces and the preservation of Asante independence. Complaints from various Asantehenes to British administrators presented a recurring theme in nineteenth-century Asante official correspondence. In February 1863, for example, Asantehene Kwaku Dua Panin addressed to Governor Pine a firm letter in which he demanded to know "the reason why your Honour's subjects seized all my people whom trade business call them to visit your coasts, on the road."[48] On another occasion Asantehene Kofi Kakari wrote to Administrator C. S. Salmon to protest against unprovoked attacks by the Fante and Asen on Asante:

> At the time of the death of the late King of Ashanti, I sent messengers to the coast to announce it, of which the Elminas, having received the message, sent to make custom.

> When I sent in order to inform the Governor and others in Fanti of the same sad event that had happened in Ashanti by one Ananee, my messenger, who was accompanied by some Elminas that came to make custom; but when they reached halfway close to the frontier as far as Assin Aseerman, they were plundered and detained by the Assins and Fantis.[49]

A great volume of chancery letters was taken up with the government's efforts to reassert its control over the southern provinces. The cession of the former districts of Greater Asante was symptomatic of the slow disintegration of the nation. Worse still for Asante, what it lost territorially went to strengthen its imperial rival Britain, through the incorporation of the districts into the gradually expanding Gold Coast Protectorate. The strategic location of some of the provinces like Asen, Akyem, Adanse and Wassa on the great commercial routes linking Kumase to the coast made Asante economically and militarily vulnerable to the effects of interruptions and blockades of the roads. Asante to the very end, therefore, continuously worked for a restoration of these provinces through its diplomatic channels, including written communication.

The surviving documents are replete with letters in which the government protested against the movement of the southern provinces away from Asante, not uncommonly with British encouragement. In one example, Kofi Kakari's letter-writer urged Colonel R. W. Harley to return Denkyira, Akyem, and Asen back to Asante control:

> His Majesty further states that, your Honour's restoring him these tribes, viz., Denkerahs, Akims, and Assins, back to their former position as his subjects... will be the only thing or way to appease him.[50]

The adjustment of peaceful relations with Dwaben engaged a considerable portion of the attention of Asantehene Mensa Bonsu and the "English bureau." Unprovoked assaults from Dwabenehene Asafo Agyei in the 1870s drew sharp criticism from Mensa Bonsu. Writing to the Governor-in-Chief on the subject, the Asantehene moaned the failure of his peace initiatives to the Dwabenehene:

> By my last messenger, Captain Bawooach, I informed your Excellency that Assafoahjie, the Chief of Djuabin, had openly broken the oath which was asked from him by Captain Lees, your Excellency's Commissioner, to the effect that from thence we should live peaceably together, by commanding his people to kidnap and kill my people, and to destroy some of my villages who had remained loyal to my authority. By the same messenger I asked your Excellency respecting the gold stool which had been given to the Chief of Djuabin.
>
> Since that the Djuabins, seeing that I do not retaliate, are bolder and bolder every day. [51]

In a further development, Mensa Bonsu warned of the possible dangers, if the situation were to continue unchecked:

Asafu Agai, by refusing my proposal of peace, has shown to me that he means war, and to continue kidnapping, plundering, and destroying my villages. Asafu Agai's ambitious projects are well known to me; ... I, lawful King of Ashantee and its dependencies, do energetically protest against that presumption and usurpation of Asafu Agai, Chief of Djuabin; and in the name of the Treaty signed by my brother and predecessor with the English Government, and that Treaty which is my duty to see observed. [52]

Asantehene Agyeman Prempe's policy towards the provinces followed lines established by previous administrations. His government continued to work for the retention of the provinces still under Asante's suzerainty and the recovery of those already lost. A letter addressed to Governor F. M. Hodgson in December 1889 expressed the Asantehene's sentiments on the loss of Mampon. "I am very sorry to say that it is not my single wish that the British Government should allow the King of Mampon to come to the Protectorate," he wrote, adding that "even those that have come already I am earnestly praying for their safe return." Continuing with Kwahu in the same letter, the Asantehene inquired:

You stated in the 6th paragraph of your letter that the King of Kwahu have signed treaty with the British Government; may I ask, for what cause, have I had any palaver with him, or it is only the wish of the British Government that he should do so.[53]

Unceasing diplomatic efforts through written (and personal) communication failed to prevent the secession of the southern provinces. In the end, the irony of the issue of the relationship of the provinces with Asante was that the breakaway of Akyem, Asen, Fante, Denkyira, Adanse, Mampon, Kwahu, etc., represented not so much their dislike for Asante overlordship as the success of British imperial policy in the Gold Coast.

The extradition of Asante criminals who sought refuge in British protected areas provided another source of protest from the Asante chancery. It was a subject of grave political consequence to Asante because of its inherent national security risks. Numerous pieces of correspondence were undertaken to extradite both runaway individuals like Kwasi Gyani and Owusu Taseamandi, and whole groups of people.[54] One of the futilities of nineteenth century Asante-British relations is that British administrators successively exhibited neither a willingness to enforce reciprocal agreements entered into with Asante concerning the return of criminals nor a desire even to understand the subject. It took several decades and volumes of chancery effort before

Agyeman Prempe appraised the British attitude:

> I find that it is the policy and firm determination of Her Majesty's Government not to advise any Ashanti subject that sought refuge in the Protectorate on the Gold Coast Colony to return to Asanti.[55]

From the position of a sovereign power that sought to achieve seemingly mutual objectives of trade with an independent Asante in the early nineteenth century, the British administration on the Gold Coast slowly moved in the direction of increasing commitment towards colonial domination as the century gained in years. By the 1870s the British had shown clear signs not only of entrenching themselves but also of eliminating Asante. Having realized that military confrontations had given them no edge over Asante, British administrators in the 1880s and 1890s devised a concealed strategy for the colonization of Asante. This was presented in the form of "protection" — a design that was characteristic of the era of the scramble for Africa. The issue of the preservation of Asante independence therefore became one of the concerns of the government in the last decades of the century and one to which the chancery addressed considerable energies. Although Asante was eventually to come under British authority at the turn of the century, Asantehene Agyeman Prempe for the moment did not mince words about his objections to the British design. "The suggestion that Ashanti in its present state should come and enjoy the protection of Her Majesty the Queen," he affirmed in a letter to Governor Griffith, "is a matter of very serious consideration.... My Kingdom of Ashanti will never commit itself to any such policy," he firmly protested. Concluding, he declared: "Ashanti must remain independent as of old," although remaining friendly to all white men.[56]

    Letters of introduction represent one category of the "specialized" correspondence undertaken by the chancery. Such letters comprised two types: first, letters introducing envoys whose anticipated arrival was announced or who carried the letters themselves to their recipients; and second, letters that sought interviews for specific diplomats, examples of both of which abound. In March 1853, for example, Asantehene Kwaku Dua addressed to Governor S. J. Hill the following letter of introduction concerning Akyampon Tia of the Boakye Yam Kuma stool.

> The King of Ashantee's best compliments to your Excellency, and begs to introduce to your Excellency Akampon, his brother and captain, whom he mentioned in the last letter, that he will send him down to make "custom" for Chibboe, the late chief of Denkra. The King begs your Excellency to

be so kind as to spare him a soldier to conduct Akampon and his men to Djuquah to be present at the "custom," so that the ceremony may be conducted and finished with quietness.[57]

In a similar letter of introduction prepared by the chancery in June 1894, Asantehene Agyeman Prempe announced the dispatch of a mission headed by *afenasoani* Kofi Abua and *esen* Ofori to inform the British administration that their offer of "protection" was receiving the attention of the Asante government. The same letter gave the Governor advance notification of the 1894–95 mission of Owusu Ansa and Kwame Boaten to the British government on the Gold Coast and in England. Characteristic of letters of introduction of the time, the beneficiaries were named and the nature of their missions specified:

I send by Sword Bearer "Kofi Buar" and Court Crier "Ofori" with this to inform your Excellency that my district Kings, Chiefs, and principal men of Ashanti have come to the capital, and the important subject of the British Government have being laid before them, and I am preparing to send my grandsons, prince Ansah, together with two of my influential Chiefs, Chief "Boatin," and Chief "Kwaku Fokoo," Linguist, Inkrumah, Kojo Tufoo, Akempon Daban, Sword Bearer, and Bondar, Court Crier, to you with the final decision of the important letter per Mr. Vroom....[58]

Agyeman Prempe's letter of 7 April 1894, which introduced Nseniehene Kofi Apea's mission to Governor-in-Chief W. Brandford Griffith, represents the less common and less specific type in which the beneficiary was not mentioned by name:

I have sent one of my influential Chiefs, together with many messengers from every Chief in the kingdom of Ashanti, coming down to you. As I find that the number of them with their servants will be about a thousand, their expenses will be too much on us, so I beg to ask your kind favour in order to meet them at Elmina Castle to have the palaver settled there....[59]

Letters of introduction which sought interviews evidenced the diplomatic norms and etiquette of the day in both the Gold Coast and Britain. Thus, conforming to prevailing diplomatic conventional practice, John Owusu Ansa Jr., wrote on behalf of himself and other members of the Asante embassy to request an interview with William Griffith, although the Asantehene had earlier introduced him in writing.

Myself and colleagues consisting the Ashanti Embassy are now on the way to meet your Excellency; we, therefore, beg to inquire where it will be convenient to meet your Excellency, learning that your Excellency is at Cape Coast at present.[60]

In England the Asante ambassadors formally wrote through their legal representative, "Brew of Dunquah," to introduce themselves to the Colonial Office and to inquire about a convenient time for an interview:

> At the request of Prince John Ossoo Ansah of Ashanti, I have the honour to announce to your Lordship the arrival here of the Embassy despatched by His Majesty Kwaku Dua III, King of Ashanti, to treat with the Government of Her Britannic Majesty on matters affecting the relations between the Empire of the Queen and his kingdom....
>
> I am further directed to ascertain from your Lordship what day and hour after Wednesday next will be convenient to you for them to make a formal call.[61]

Another type of chancery document is what may be described as a letter of felicitation. Although there was a somewhat tacit understanding in the nineteenth century requiring the sending of notifications about assumptions of office by heads of administration to neighboring friendly leaders, such practices were not regularly followed. Even so, a few of such letters of felicitation were exchanged, including Asantehene Kwaku Dua's, which is reproduced below:

> I have received your kind letter regarding your arrival from England; I am agreeably happy to hear of your safe arrival, I also rejoice that we may live together in unity of mind, and resume our domestic business in friendly terms, without any disturbance and interruption about your cooperating with me in trade, or to promote me anything I shall be in need of... I am quite well, hoping you are the same, with my best compliments to you.[62]

Among the traditional letters of felicitation can be listed that of Asabi Antwi and Kwaku Bosommuru Dwira to Governor Ussher on 17 November 1880. The two Asante ambassadors wrote from Elmina to H. T. Ussher in Accra "to inquire after your Excellency's health." The envoys ended the letter on a friendly tone: "Hoping this will find your Excellency in good health."[63]

Also falling under the category of "specialized" documents are letters of safe conduct or passage. Akyampon Tia's letter of introduction (see Ch. 5), which also requested Administrator Hill to provide a soldier to conduct Akyampon Yaw and his men to Jukwa, may be taken as an example of a letter of safe conduct.[64] A further illustration is seen in a letter of 4 November 1870 from Asantehene Kofi Kakari to the

Governor, written on behalf of Akyampon Yaw, then stationed in Elmina as resident ambassador for Dutch affairs:

> His majesty requested me further to ask your Excellency's kind favour, whether, if he sends a messenger through you to Elmina to recall Ackampon, he will have pass to go to Elmina safe, and return with Ackampon by Cape Coast up to Kumase....[65]

In another letter subsequently written in 1872 the Asantehene requested safe passage for Akyampon Yaw, who had been exiled from his Elmina base by the Dutch Governor.[66] Letters of safe conduct specified by name the officer on whose behalf the right of free passage was being sought. Such precaution for unmolested right of way became necessary only during periods of hostility when inviolability for the persons of the diplomatic corps had to be guaranteed in writing.

Letters of appointment or commission prepared by the chancery showed a remarkable degree of specificity. M. Bonnat's appointment letter, which specified his title, rights, and jurisdiction in distinct terms, has been cited above. In the preparation of such documents the chancery showed in an amazing degree an understanding of contractual agreements between the donor and the recipient and a remarkable grasp of issues of legality inherent in such arrangements. Equally specific was the letter by which J. J. C. Huydecoper was commissioned to the headship of the Gyaman mission in 1876 (see p. 147). The document was clearly a legal one in the form of an affidavit, opening with the declaration: "KNOW ALL MEN by these present ...."[67]

John Owusu Ansa, Jr.'s letter of appointment by which he assumed formal headship of the mission to London (1894–95) was, like other commissions of the period, demonstrative of the chancery's concern for authenticity and proper authorization:[68]

> (Seal)
>
> To the MOST GRACIOUS AND ILLUSTRIOUS SOVEREIGN, VICTORIA, QUEEN OF GREAT BRITAIN AND IRELAND.
>
> Kwaku Dua III., King of Ashanti, wisheth health and prosperity. We pray Your Most Gracious Majesty to know that we have appointed our trusty and well-beloved grandson, Prince John Ossoo Ansah, son of the late Prince Ansah, of Ashanti, on our behalf to lay before your Majesty divers matters affecting the good estate of our kingdom and the well-being of our subjects with full power for the said Prince Ansah as our ambassador extraordinary and minister plenipotentiary to ne-

gotiate and conclude all such treaties relating to the furtherance of trade and all matters therewith connected as your
Majesty shall be pleased to entertain.

We therefore pray that your Majesty will be pleased to receive the said Prince Ansah on our behalf and to accord to
him your Majesty's most royal favour.

Given at our Court at Kumasi this 8th day of September 1894.

        KWAKU DUA III.,   my
        King of Ashanti.   X
                             mark

What is not clear is whether this document was truly executed in Kumase
with the knowledge of the Asantemanhyiamu. There is reason to suspect that Owusu Ansa might have prepared his own letter of appointment after the mission had left Kumase. The document was not witnessed by any of the *akyeame* or any of the ambassadors who formed
the delegation to London. However, even granting that the document
was not authorized by the Asantemanhyiamu, Owusu Ansa's action
would not have lacked legality, since the Council had earlier formally
appointed him as head of the embassy, commissioned him *viva voce*,
and confirmed his appointment in writing to the British Administrator in
Accra before the embassy's departure from Kumase. Certainly, at no
time during the mission to England did any of the envoys fail to give
Owusu Ansa the recognition due him as head of the embassy. As ambassador extraordinary, it was within Owusu Ansa's discretionary exercise of jurisdictional powers to introduce himself in writing — a mode
that was in consonance with the accepted conventions of British diplomatic intercourse.

Before their return home from Britain, John Owusu Ansa, Jr. and
the five members of his delegation executed a concessionary agreement with a British firm headed by George Reckless. The agreement
was intended to be the basis for the establishment of a British Char-
tered Company "for the purpose of opening up and developing"
Asante.[69] In form and style, the Reckless Concession, although apparently drafted by "Brew of Dunquah," followed the pattern established by
the chancery for the preparation of such documents, and bore close
resemblance to that of Bonnat two decades earlier.[70]

Operating governments that exhibited the trappings of a modern
administrative system, nineteenth-century Asantehenes recognized
merit, which they encouraged and amply rewarded. Thus, besides their
policy-making function, the annual Odwira festivals were occasions not
only for instituting the more publicized investigations into misconduct,

but also for rewarding meritorious service. A form of reward about which evidence of chancery involvement survives is in the preparation of letters of knighthood. Asantehene Mensa Bonsu thought it fit to initiate the Sierra Leonean Surgeon and one-time acting head of the British administration in the Gold Coast, Dr. J. A. B. Horton, into the order of the princes of Asante in 1879, although he was not an Asante national. Owusu Ansa, Sr. was authorized to prepare the document which conferred the distinction of an honorary Asante prince on Dr. Horton, in recognition of his services towards the people of the Gold Coast:[71]

> Coomassie, June 18, 1879
> To Doctor J. A. B. Horton, M.D., Edin., F.R.G.S., Surgeon-Major of the Army Medical Department, etc., etc.
>
> Sir, - His Majesty the King of Ashantee has heard with much pleasure the great interest you have always taken in the material advancement of his people and country, and the prompt assistance you rendered to the great Chief of Mampom, when written to about the Chief's sufferings, who had been laid up for such a long time. His Majesty the King has also been informed of your endeavours, extending over several years, towards the general improvement of your countrymen throughout the whole coast, and express a hope that you may yet continue to be of great service to them. His Majesty is informed that you are likely to leave the Gold Coast shortly, and not to return to it. He has therefore commissioned me to offer for your acceptance the *Title and Dignity of a Prince*, and trust that, wherever you may be stationed, you will continue to manifest great interest in Ashantee affairs.
>
> J. Ossoo Ansah, Prince of Ashantee.

Policy statements provided another variant of the more formal type of chancery documents. In February 1894, for example, following the dispatch of a British expeditionary force to Atebubu in 1893, Asantehene Prempe I deemed it necessary to address a policy statement to Governor F. M. Hodgson regarding the passage of foreigners to and from the districts north of Kumase. The statement was a reminder that state security, if not diplomatic courtesy, required foreign visitors to the interior, whether in private or official capacities, to make the customary call on the Asantehene:

> I will consider this in feature as a good policy, that when any official is send out to visit me he must come through the main road, as has been done always, but any one that has

been sent out to countries either in the interior or not within my Ashanti Kingdom that I have nothing to do, or interfere, I am sorry to say, it is not polite that he should pass through my capital, for if they had passed from my capital to the interior, surely they may pass through here to the coast, therefore, as your officer did not pass through here to Attabubu, I beg your Excellency most sincerely to send to recall your officer, for it is not my wish that he should pass through my capital from Attabubu.[72]

A further example of a policy statement is provided in Agyeman Prempe's letter to Governor W. B. Griffith in which he declared formally his goals for the maintenance of friendly relations with the British administration and for the development of his nation:[73]

I pray and beseech my elders, as well as my gods, and the spirits of my ancestors, to assist me, to give me true wisdom and live.. and that my friendship with Her Majesty's Government may be more firm and more closer than hitherto had been done, that bye-gones will be bye-gones, that Ashanti nations will awake herself as out of sleep, that the hostilities will go away from her, that the evils which the constant wars has brought upon her, like destroying our jewels, may die everlastingly from her, and that I shall endeavour to promote peace and tranquillity and good order in my Kingdom, and to restore its trade, and the happiness and safety of my people generally, by making it to the advantage of the refugees to return, inhabit, and cultivate their respective countries, and thus raise my Kingdom of Ashanti to a prosperous, substantial, and steady position as a great farming and trading community such as it has never occupied hitherto, and that the trade between your Protectorate and my Kingdom of Ashanti may increase daily to the benefit of all interested in it.

This statement, coming immediately after Prempe's formal enstoolment, in a sense represented the Asantehene's inauguration address.[74]

Chancery Styles

Two easily identifiable trends in chancery styles become recognizable in an examination of the records of the time. First, a progressive improvement in literary style becomes visible. As an illustration, compare the following two extracts of letters written on behalf of Asantehenes Kwaku Dua Panin and Mensa Bonsu, respectively. The first, written in 1863, shows a pretty low literary level:

Yours was received safely by Ahmanquah Akkoomah on the

answer of Quasi Gainie's case, because the case is between himself and his wife, who was pawned to him by his family; and it happened some quarrels between them about gold, which his wife said took from the ground and had given him, but Quasi Gainie said his wife have told lie; and the woman sworn the King's great oath, that she did not tell a lie. Quasie Gainie also sworn that he likes the case should be brought forward in the presence of the King; in the meantime they were King's messengers who were coming from different places happened to be present there instant to bring him, and he set them eight days time, and after the time fulfilled he set them a time of 10 days more; again fixed them 15 days time to come with them; and if he did not come then he is guilty; according as he said, the 15 days fulfilled and refused to come, the messengers condemned him to be guilty...[75]

The second, authored by John Owusu Ansa, Sr. in 1883, gives indications of a higher literary level:[76]

ACCORDING to your request, I have the honour to lay before you the facts which have caused the present difficulties of my country, Ashanti.

2. Coomassie has been from the commencement of the Ashanti confederacy the capital of that kingdom and the seat of the general Government, and it is there that the King has always resided, and there also has the great stool always been deposited.

3. On this account the people of Coomassie have always arrogated to themselves rank and prestige superior to that of the other provinces forming the empire, and they have from time immemorial considered themselves as representatives of the whole Ashanti nation, and have invariably assumed towards their neighbours of the other provinces a bearing which the latter, although they submitted to it, never liked.

Although individual officials could be distinguished by varying degrees of literary skills and style depending on their own level of training in English, nineteenth-century chancery records as a whole were marked by a vertical trend towards increasing literary sophistication. Contemporaneous with this development was an increasing adoption of literary expressions and styles pertaining to official or documentary literature, again an evidence of growing sophistication.

It is also in the light of the wholesale acceptance of British literary procedures as well as the chancery's concern for authenticity that the use of the seal must be understood. Unfortunately, no visual representation of the Asante seal survives. The only available evidence is the word "seal" which appears on some documents. As a result, we have no basis for creating an image of what the Asante seal looked like. Nor do we have an accurate indication of when the practice of sealing Asante documents began. The use of the seal on M. Bonnat's letter of commission (1875) might be taken as one of the earliest extant references to the subject. J. J. C. Huydecoper's letter of appointment (1876) was also sealed. Thereafter, no evidence survives of the use of the seal until the 1890s. There is an interesting reference to a letter of J. Owusu Ansa, Jr., dated 5 April 1894, which was dispatched to the Governor "under a flying seal."[77] A further indication of the seal appears in Owusu Ansa's letter of appointment to the headship of the mission to London. The limited nature of our evidence on the subject notwithstanding, it can be concluded that the chancery had come to adopt a seal to give authenticity to its documents by the last quarter of the century and that the use of the seal might have been limited to contractual documents like letters of appointment, much in line with modern-day practice.

Also evident in chancery documents was a fundamental awareness of legalities. The chancery portrayed a familiarity with questions of international law, jurisdiction, representation, diplomatic inviolability, and the like. Detailed attention has been drawn to the appointment letters of M. Bonnat, J. J. C. Huydecoper, and J. Owusu Ansa, Jr., all of which carefully defined the jurisdictional powers and rights of the appointees and their legal responsibilities towards the appointing authority. That the embassy to London engaged the services of solicitors was itself indicative of the delegation's concern that it both receive and act within the jurisdictional rights and obligations pertaining to their position. One instance bearing on the subject further illustrates the awareness of legal issues. In January 1895 a warrant was issued for the arrest of ambassador J. Owusu Ansa, Jr. in Cape Coast while his embassy was on its way to England. Owusu Ansa was charged with being a few minutes late to court. Fortunately for Owusu Ansa, there was no need for the use of the warrant because he himself appeared in court soon afterwards. Registering its disapproval of the action, the embassy remarked to the Governor that "although the court took a lenient view of the matter and dismissed the action we exceedingly regret that the warrant above referred to was issued out at all from the fact that the said Prince being known to your Government as one of the special ambassadors accredited to your Excellency and Her Britannic

Majesty, and as such we believe the law should have been inoperative on his person according to the general usages of international courtesy."[78]

Another facet of Asante chancery studies which is worth commenting upon is the tone of letters. Despite the overall preference for expressions characteristic of diplomatic courtesy as discussed above, and the generally pacific tone of the Asantehenes' letters, one finds an occasional departure from this trend. During the protracted debate between the Asante and British governments over the ransom of the European captives, for example, Asantehene Kofi Kakari, apparently under the influence of his councilors, wrote the following response to the British administrator, who had evidently decided upon not making any ransom payment:

> Your Excellency's messenger asked to know from me concerning other matters of the peace, and when peace shall be finally settled; my answer to him is, "Tell the Governor that I and my great chiefs have decided this: after the ransom is paid to Addoo Boffoo, then peace between us shall be finally settled, and not before."[79]

The tone of this communication was decidedly firm in the negative.

The Elmina question presented another source of irritation to the Asantehene, which was borne out in the strong tone of his correspondence. Writing to Colonel Harley in March 1873, Kofi Kakari indicated that he had "been made angry" by the suggestion that Elmina was being removed from his jurisdiction. He insisted that Governor Harley "restoring the Elmina fort and people back in the same manner as they were before, will be the only thing or way to appease" him. He cautioned that "should your Honour come in to interfere, as he hears you are, that you have not to blame him, because he will then start himself." It is significant to note that while the tone of this letter is admittedly strong, in view particularly of the threat of war, the Asantehene was firmly convinced about the legality of his hereditary claim to Elmina. Further, notwithstanding the strong bearing to conditional aggression evidenced by the tone of the letter, the Asantehene repeated his fundamental disposition towards peace, reaffirming that "he has no quarrel with white men."[80]

When Asante began to perceive a British threat to its sovereignty in the l880s and 1890s, the determination to remain independent was manifested in the strong tone of chancery letters. Asante rejected the British offer of "protection" in no uncertain terms. The Asantehene affirmed his nation's commitment to "remain independent as of old" and supported this resolve with an old saying:

so it is our Asante proverb, that what the old men eat, and
left, it is what the children enjoyed. [81]

Oral Retrieval Mechanisms

The efficiency demands of Asante's foreign relations, especially with
the British on the coast, were to necessitate adaptations and changes
in its mode of diplomatic intercourse itself. Asante's traditional diplomatic medium had been oral. The commissioning instructions of the
envoy were oral and so was his "code" of professional ethics, which
was still unwritten and largely based on precedents. Similarly, even the
international agreements Asante made with its neighbors before the
nineteenth century were to a large extent unwritten.

However, the problems of the nineteenth century brought increased stress on Asante's relations with the British. In particular, British imperial policies and questions of sovereignty and judicial right in
the southern Gold Coast resulted in conflicts which made the seemingly mutual objectives of Asante-British trade not easily attainable. As
the weakness of verbal agreements as a basis for a firm, unambiguous
relationship came to be seen, Asante employed another diplomatic
medium — the written form — in its search for a workable understanding with the British. With the acceptance of letters and treaties, a new
dimension by way of "written diplomacy" came to be introduced into
Asante diplomatic practice. It was a testimony to the integrative and
adaptive capacities of Asante's administration that the new system was
employed to supplement rather than supplant the already existing oral
mode of diplomacy. As British Administrator C. S. Salmon noted in 1871,
"no letter containing anything important is likely to come from the King,
unless brought by one of his own special trusted messengers capable
of giving verbally the contents."[82]

The numerous occasions when Asante envoys were dispatched
with letters so that they could convey their contents orally as well should
leave no doubt whatsoever about the dual development being a preferred diplomatic practice with the Asante in the nineteenth century. On
the return of Mr. Blankson from Kumase in 1853, for instance, he was
accompanied by envoys of the Asantehene, who also carried a lengthy
letter from him. The envoys, we are informed, were sent "to confirm it
verbally."[83]

The adoption of "written diplomacy" therefore did not mean the
abandonment of "oral diplomacy." Indeed, the oral medium continued
to be an essential component of Asante diplomatic practice throughout
the nineteenth century, and numerous instances can be cited in support of the continued importance which Asante attached to its tradi-

tional mode of diplomacy. After the Gyaman campaign of 1818, for example, the Gyaman royals who had been captured during the war were set free after they had affirmed "by solemn oath and written treaty" that they would never show hostility to Asante again.[84] In 1820 the Asantemanhyiamu deputed a delegation to accompany British Consul Joseph Dupuis to England to assure the English Government of the goodwill of Asante. Although the mission was never permitted to leave the shores of Cape Coast, its appointment, coming shortly after the conclusion of the Dupuis Treaty of 1820, was intended to reinforce the written agreement made in Kumase by personal diplomacy. The Asante-British agreement of 1874 similarly gave evidence of dual diplomatic mechanisms. The draft treaty which was presented to Asante by Sir Garnet Wolseley was first debated by the Asantemanhyiamu and then negotiated between Asabi Antwi and Wolseley at Fomena, before the final version was approved in Kumase and subsequently ratified in Cape Coast by a high-powered embassy led again by Asabi Antwi. When the British administration accused Asante of threatening war in 1881, Asante once again had a recourse to oral diplomacy in the grand style of the Boakye Tenten mission, to support its written assurances of peace. Similarly, the Asantehene's faith in the conduct of diplomacy through both the written and oral modes underlay his appointment of the London mission of 1894–95. Outlining the purpose of the embassy during an interview between the Asante envoys and Governor W. B. Griffith at Cape Coast on 12 December 1894, Okyeame Kwaku Fokuo, as spokesman, stated.

> His Majesty thinks that if he keeps writing to your Excellency that will not settle matters for good. Therefore he has deputed them to Her Majesty the Queen so that every matter may be entirely settled. Mere letters will not settle matters....[85]

Though "written diplomacy" is generally expected to give guarantees against misrepresentation and inaccurate delivery of messages, "oral diplomacy" is not without obvious advantages. It is forthcoming and more frank. The approach of the envoy, his wording of the message, responses to questions, and the ceremonial setting, all add color to the advantage of the living, physical presence, whereas a letter is merely a "dead" instrument. In all respects "oral diplomacy" is more flexible than a letter. It always has some limited degree of discretion, irrespective of the rank of the envoy.

The concurrent use of both the written and oral modes of communication meant that Asante had to retain a dual retrieval system. It is this element of retrieval that gave an added dimension of importance to the diplomatic career of Asabi Antwi. His prolonged stay in Cape

Coast in the 1870s and 1880s had a significance far outweighing the intelligence function which could have been performed by any other Asante diplomat in Cape Coast at the time, such as John Owusu Ansa, Sr. or Kwaku Bosommuru Dwira. Asabi Antwi had seen the Treaty of Fomena through its important stages, draft and final. Being readily available for questions of recollection or interpretation with regards to the treaty, his role was that of an instrument of retrieval.

It has been pointed out above that Asabi Antwi led the Asante embassy that negotiated a draft treaty of peace with British General Wolseley at Fomena in February 1874 immediately after the sack of Kumase. After the treaty had been duly approved by the Asante-manhyiamu in Kumase, the choice of a diplomat to head a mission to Cape Coast for its ratification naturally fell on Asabi Antwi, who had been associated with its earlier developments. His selection, therefore, depended not so much on his position as one of the government's senior diplomats as on his utility in matters of recollection with regard to the treaty's stipulations. For Asabi Antwi wasted no time at the embassy's first meeting with Acting Administrator J. Maxwell on 13 March 1874 in raising objections of interpretation, insisting that the indemnity had originally been fixed at 10,000 ounces of gold (though he appears to have been wrong in this instance) rather than the 50,000 being claimed by Maxwell.[86]

Asabi Antwi is less remembered, however, for his role in the negotiations connected with the Treaty of Fomena than for the Golden Axe episode of 1881. The major trend of events in this controversy has been outlined above (Chapter 4).[87] It is significant to point out, however, that throughout the discussions involving the so-called "threat" of war in 1881, Asabi Antwi was used as an instrument of retrieval, interestingly, by both Asante and the British. He was in attendance at meetings of subsequent Asante missions to the British not only to clarify his position but also to testify whether his action was in contravention of the Treaty of Fomena. At a meeting, for example, between Lieutenant-Governor Griffith and members of the Okyeame Kofi Bene mission, the British Administrator is reported to have said to Asabi Antwi: "Give me the paper [i.e., treaty]....Is your name Enquie? are you Enquie, the man who signed the treaty that Assin, Gaman, and Denkera should be under the English? and you come to tell me this, and break the treaty...."[88] What the British Administrator failed to see was that the Asante mission was on those occasions not reclaiming sovereignty over its lost provinces of the southern Gold Coast. What he failed to see and what Asabi Antwi, as an oral retrieval instrument was trying to emphasize, was that Asante action in demanding the return of its refugees was not in violation of the Treaty of Fomena, with which he was so well acquainted.

Asabihene Kwame Antwi was not the only Asante official engaged in the oral retrieval of information. As early as 1820 Asantehene Osei Tutu Kwame had found the need to call upon a young man to verify a critical issue in connection with the Bowdich Treaty of 1817. The Asantehene's interpretation of the 1817 Asante-British Treaty was based on the fact that a condition existed for the imposition of fines on violators. It was this conviction that had led him to demand fines from Komenda and Cape Coast for contravening the treaty. The Dupuis Treaty of 1820 was preceded by lengthy debates which were marked by differing interpretations of the 1817 treaty, the Asante side insisting that a clause in the agreement called for the imposition of fines, and Dupuis contending that no such condition existed. It was in support of his position that Osei Tutu Kwame brought in a boy, said to have been of Fante origin, who had been present at the time the Bowdich Treaty was read and interpreted to the Asantehene.[89]

Like the Bowdich and Dupuis treaties before it, the Maclean Treaty of 1831 failed to provide a firm basis for the maintenance of friendly relations. However, until it was replaced by the 1874 treaty, the Maclean Treaty, for all its imperfections, was the frame of reference by which Asante sought to carry out its responsibilities and obligations towards the British. Two issues arising out of the 1831 treaty remained unresolved throughout: the extradition of refugees, and British responsibility for ensuring proper behavior among the Fante, Asen, Akyem and other people living in the British Protectorate. The Asante position was again one that British administrators failed to see and agree with: that the Maclean Treaty imposed reciprocal obligations for ensuring the return of runaways, and that it also placed upon the British responsibility for the elimination of improper conduct within the provinces. A letter addressed by Asantehene Kwaku Dua Panin to the English Governor in 1863 clearly summed up the Asante stand on the issue:[90]

> But in poor George Maclean's time, I made agreement with him in certificate, the one in Cape Coast Castle, and another in my hand therein stated, that any Fantee person run up to me to deliver him and to bring him to Cape Coast. And if any slave of mine also run away to Cape Coast, you are to deliver him back also to me....

In support of this contention, the Asantehene added:

> But one of my slaves, named Quarquah, who was witness to the said agreement, and who was the bearer of the certifi-

cate for me, is absent in the town, and I have sent messenger after him; but when he comes I will let him come with the
book, that you may see your guiltiness.[91]

When Kwakwa was not available soon enough, the Asantehene, anxious to prove his point, provided the name of another witness —
Adansehene Oben, who also "knew and present at that time when
agreement of peace note was made."

"Quarquah," the instrument of oral retrieval in the chancery records
of the 1850s and 1860s, was a senior diplomat of the Osei Yaw Akoto
administration, a signatory to the 1831 peace treaty, and therefore a
person well acquainted with its stipulations. In the company of
afenasoani Amankwa Akuma, Owusu Nkwantabisa, and three other
envoys, Kwakwa had arrived in Cape Coast in September 1827 to discuss peace terms. The Asante embassy was involved in long negotiations, first in Cape Coast and later in Accra, where objections about
the omission of an Asante indemnity forced the party to return to
Kumase. When a second mission returned to Cape Coast to conclude
the Treaty of 1831, diplomat Kwakwa was again a leading member.[92]

Asante in the course of the nineteenth century accepted and fully
utilized the written medium in its diplomatic communication, adopting
with it literary styles associated with the European tradition. In its adoption of "written diplomacy," the non-literate Asante administration recognized the need for, and enforced measures for, ensuring accuracy in
the transmission of oral messages into the written medium. The large-
scale use of written communication by the Asante chancery led to the
production of a wide variety of documents whose total number, despite
the unavailability of accurate figures, was by all accounts enormous.

The government's adoption of the written medium, no less than
its engagement of Europeans, was dictated by the necessity of employing communicative strategies that were familiar to European officials in the hope of reaching a workable understanding with them.
Though this course of action itself represented a momentous departure from tradition, it was a development that was determined by the
unavoidable necessities of the time rather than a decision by choice.[93]
Notwithstanding the revolutionary character of the adoption of written
communicative strategies, it was an affirmation of the continuing faith
Asante reposed in its traditional mechanisms of diplomacy that the
written medium, as well as the oral, were employed concurrently, with
the result that dual information retrieval processes had to be maintained.

CHAPTER 7

Conclusion

This is a chapter outlining the major observations and conclusions to this study. It identifies the main issues which dominated Asante's diplomatic activities with foreign powers, evaluates Asante's diplomatic institutions, instruments, and mechanisms, and assesses their efficacy in terms of the search for a working basis of understanding with Asante's neighbors.

Determinants of Asante Diplomatic Policy

In this study of nineteenth-century Asante diplomatic history a number of issues have surfaced. These issues may be regarded as determinants—not so much as critical factors which predetermined Asante's foreign policy decisions, but as the dominant variables that loomed large in diplomatic activities and provided the thrust of the diplomatic effort. They were also determinants in that they were often the points of controversy, departure, or contention in Asante's relations with foreign powers and therefore impeded the drive towards the ideal of peaceful and mutually beneficial relations. These determinants can be identified as capital punishment and extradition; the cultural, political, military, ideological, and commercial variables; and what I choose to call the trinity of peace, open roads, and trade.

Capital Punishment. The British Government was firmly convinced that Asante regularly slaughtered people for sacrificial purposes at funerals and other ceremonies. The subject was one about which the British administration at Cape Coast consistently expressed concern. During Captain Winniett's governorship, for example, he paid a visit to Kumase to urge Asantehene Kwaku Dua Panin in 1848 to end "human sacrifice."[1] The issue impinged larger and larger upon Asante-British relations as the century wore on, until it inflamed in the 1880s and 1890s with newspaper reports charging Asantehene Prempe I with the killings of hundreds of innocent people.[2] Finally, the British Government made capital out of the issue of capital punishment by making it grounds for refusing to receive the Asante mission of 1894–95:

> In no case would Her Majesty the Queen receive mission from a ruler who is accused, on apparently good grounds, of allowing human sacrifice.[3]

At issue was the question of whether or not Asante continued to practice human sacrifice.[4] Bowdich's description of horrifying scenes involving the tormenting of a man "previous to sacrifice" was contradicted by Hutton who was in Kumase at the same time as Bowdich: "no such tortures or sacrifices were committed, either on our arrival in the capital, or during our stay here."[5] Besides, Bowdich later had the occasion elsewhere to examine the subject more critically and to conclude that such victims of executions "are not as might be supposed, indiscriminately chosen; they pass, indeed under the name of delinquents and are so far deserving that anathema, as having been convicted of speaking disrespectfully of the King, or of his government; of having harboured secret intentions inimical to the prosperity of the state; of having violated the civil laws; or of having invoked the wrath of their gods upon the heads of their oppressors."[6] The "Gold Coast Methodist Times" publication alleging that three hundred virgins were slaughtered at Prempe I's coronation in 1884 did not appear in the columns of that paper until six years after the supposed occurrence of the event. While it might be difficult to argue that all sacrificial killings had been eliminated, British accusations were not substantiated by proof or firsthand evidence. Indeed, there were even indications that the British administration itself seemed to have received reports of "human sacrifice" at Prempe I's enthronement with a grain of salt.[7]

The argument, besides, ran much deeper than that. The Asante Government clearly distinguished between "sacrifice" and "executions," a distinction which the British administration apparently failed to draw. Thus, British officials and contemporary European visitors and authors alike tended to misconstrue capital punishment as human sacrifice. Akyeamehene Kwame Poku Agyeman, chief of protocol, had the opportunity of explaining his government's position to Reverend Freeman in January 1842 during a discussion of the Asante penal code. After Freeman had remarked that "those who were guilty of treason in England were generally made public examples of, and that it was a sad thing to see men so rebellious," Poku Agyeman appeared satisfied that capital punishment was carried out in Europe, too.[8] Though Reverend Freeman seemed to have accepted the Asante position, the British administration at Cape Coast was never convinced that what they viewed as human sacrifice was indeed capital punishment, and the subject continued to loom large in and mar Asante-British diplomatic relations. In January 1874 Sir Garnet Wolseley had the occasion of reminding the Colonial Office that "it is remembered in the country that during Governor Pine's time two native Kings were condemned for treason by this Court (at Cape Coast), and were actually executed under native law." He thought the question could legitimately be raised: Why could Asante, under identical legal systems, not practice capital punishment?[9] The fact remained that the Asante government saw no reason why individuals convicted of criminal offenses after the due process of law had been exercised could not face the death penalty.

To assure the British Government of its opposition to sacrificial killings, Asante formally proclaimed the abolition of human sacrifice in November 1876. A high-powered embassy headed by ambassador Gyakye Natwi and including representatives of the Mamponhene, Bekwaehene, Kokofuhene, and Nkoransabene was dispatched to give official notification of the decree to the British administration on the Gold Coast. Arriving in Cape Coast on 15 December 1876, Gyakye Nantwi announced his government's action, explaining that human sacrifice was an obstacle to the Asante-British friendship necessary for the good of the country and the promotion of trade. He added, however, that the prohibition did not relate to capital punishment which would be maintained, but only in cases of murder and other serious crimes like treason and adultery.[10] Both the Asante government's action in decreeing a prohibition (on human sacrifice) which it already observed and in informing the British administration of the event through a high level embassy were gestures intended to appease the British and emphasize the Asante distinction between criminal executions and sacrificial killings.

In 1894 Albert Owusu Ansa restated his nation's case.

> Happily the sacrifices of days gone by have long been done away with, and for the present only persons who are tried and found to be murderous and conspirators suffer the capital punishment.[11]

To the end, the British failed to see the Asante viewpoint, and although a detailed discussion of the Asante judicial administration is outside the scope of this analysis, it is significant to recognize that the "human sacrifice" controversy was one that impeded Asante-British understanding, despite the fact that it was the subject of a considerable volume of Asante diplomatic effort. In view of the immense effort made by Asante through its diplomatic channels to present its views on the subject to the British, the human sacrifice issue, seen in retrospect, appears more like a case of British duplicity and less a matter of the inability to communicate effectively.

Extradition. As we have seen, nineteenth century Asante diplomatic history abounds with missions and letters demanding the return to Kumase of fugitives who had taken refuge within the southern provinces or under the protection of European flags on the coast. There is no doubt that extradition was a persistent theme of the reigns of the nineteenth-century Asante kings and the subject of innumerable embassies like those led by Amankwa Akuma, Kwame Antwi, Gyakye Nantwi, and Kwame Boaten. Extradition took two forms: the return of specific individuals such as Kwasi Gyani and Owusu Taseamandi, and the repatriation of whole groups or provinces like the Akyem and Kokofu.

Diplomatic activity in the area of extradition centered on attempts to seek the surrender of either fugitives from Asante justice or individual citizens over whom the Asantehene had claims of sovereignty. British reasons for failing to extradite Asantes tended to be based in the main on questions of justice; their administrators persistently expressed the fear that extradited Asantes might be denied the due process of law and be summarily executed. To Asante, however, extradition was a complex issue that often went beyond questions of law and justice. The right to expect the cooperation of friendly governments in extradition cases was rooted in traditional notions of friendship and reciprocity. According to prevailing practices, when a subject offended his "lord" and ran away to seek the protection of his lord's friend, the latter was enjoined to assist in the return of the offender.[12] Agyeman Prempe's expression of surprise about Governor Hodgson's failure to respect this fundamental practice between friends glaringly indicated the frustrations that beset Asante-British extradition issues:

> Your true and firm friendship you stated in your letter with me I am sorry to say it wants wanting, for I believe that when two persons are keeping friendship each of them seeks the interest and welfare of the other, but it is not the case here. I thought that my subjects that had come to you came to solicit your intercession for their safe return, for I believe that when a friend's boy or servant offends his lord he runs to his lord's friend to ask pardon for him, so when there is any punishment whatever, through the intercession of the other friend, the offended servant is pardoned, and then he returns to resume his former duties; this is real friendship, but I am extremely sorry it is not so with us.[13]

In addition, reciprocity in the exchange of runaways and prisoners was an accepted aspect of neighborly peaceful coexistence in the Gold Coast, which Asante fully cooperated in. Extradition further touched on national security. The fear that elements of discontent could easily be harbored in next-door states and utilized against Asante was ever present. Thus, the British Governor at the time rightly perceived of the threat posed by Owusu Taseamandi's escape in 1881:

He has lived all his life in the King's palace. He knows all that has been passing in Ashanti for years, and would be a valuable acquisition to Gaman, Schue [Sehwi], and Owoin [Aowin], to the thrones of which he is next heir, and whose people are at enmity with Ashanti. And no doubt the King suspects that this Government would obtain valuable information from the Prince about Ashanti, which the King of that country would prefer should not be known. [14]

It was the element of national security risk ever present in extradition cases that underlay, for example, the unyielding determination of the Asante government for decades in pursuing the repatriation of the *sikani* refugee, Kwasi Gyani. By 1865 British Administrator Pine had learned from a Dutch agent stationed in Kumase that "the King had been impatiently awaiting...the delivery by me of 'Ganin' the refugee;" that Asantehene Kwaku Dua had vowed to seek the return of Gyani as long as he lived; and that he was contemplating sending an envoy to "come with the treaty to prove my guiltiness on the subject of non-delivery of runaways."[15] Yet, successive British administrations consistently displayed a want of the spirit of cooperation in the matter of the extradition of runaway Asantes. Finally, at the crux of most extradition cases were interrelated issues of political right and sovereignty. British refusal to aid in the return of the provinces to their former position of dependence on Asante was in effect a question of whether sovereignty over those areas and peoples rested with Asante or now with Britain.

Throughout the period under study, Asante-British relations were seriously strained by the failure to reach a permanent diplomatic arrangement for resolving the issue of extradition, and the great volume of diplomatic effort expended in this area proved ineffectual. For the most part, British administrators did not appear to have understood the full scope of the issue. Few shared the concern expressed by Governor Richard Pine in 1862:

> The refuge afforded to runaway slaves and pawns under the British flag has, during my long experience, proved the source of the greatest irritation and annoyance to the native kings and chiefs.[16]

By the last quarter of the century, however, the desire for understanding the issue on the part of the British was clearly being overshadowed by their increasing commitment to empire-building designs. Nevertheless, extradition remained one of the major constraints on Asante's full realization of the benefits of international diplomacy.

The Cultural Variable. A number of Asante traditional practices, taboos, and concepts either directly affected the maintenance of friendly relations with European nations or indirectly impaired diplomatic communication through the latter's lack of knowledge or understanding of such practices. Cultural factors were potentially both positive and negative in their impact on the efficacy of Asante's external diplomatic mechanisms, although for the most part the majority of such traditional observances operated in the negative. Space limitations would permit a discussion of only a few of these cultural variables that became pronounced in Asante diplomatic relations.

Among the prevailing customary practices was one of sending a young man or woman to be brought up by a friend in token of confidence. The observance was intended to cement the friendship existing between the two parties. It was perhaps out of such a consideration that Asante voluntarily asked in 1874 that Kofi Nti be educated in England, although Owusu Nkwantabisa and Owusu Ansa had been trained under British auspices as a condition of the treaty of 1831. There were other instances when Asante resorted to this old practice in the hope of solidifying its ties of friendship with its neighbors. Early in the century, for example, Asantehene Osei Tutu Kwame had entrusted his "favourite nephew" Adu Borade to the care of Colonel Torrane at Cape Coast. Adu Borade accordingly grew up to become an "adopted son" of Torrane. Upon the English Colonel's death, Osei Tutu Kwame wrote to his successor, Mr. Hope-Smith, that he considered his nephew to "stand in the same relation" to him.[17] It was therefore on solid grounds stemming from intimacy with the British that Adu Borade was subsequently appointed Asante envoy to treat with the British administrators in 1819. The failure of this mission has been discussed above, which indicated that the anticipated positive impact of this cultural variable was not realized.

European misrepresentation or lack of understanding of several Asante practices was clearly an obstacle in the achievement of mutually satisfactory relations with Asante. The pace of the decision-making process in Kumase was a slow one by European standards. The time needed to convene representatives of the *amanto*, some of whom lived at distances of over thirty miles from the capital, and the careful stages by which political decisions were reached during Asantemanhyiamu sessions inevitably entailed some delay. But European officials portrayed no understanding of this process. Thus, when Asantehene Kofi Kakari expressed genuine difficulty in meeting Sir Garnet Wolseley's demands for peace in early 1874 owing to the dispersal of the Council, the English general was wont to misrepresent the Asante decision-making process as "the dilatory forms of Asante

diplomacy."[18] Earlier, Governor Cruickshank had similarly characterized Asante diplomacy as "dilatory" when an immediate response was
not forthcoming from Kumase to British proposals for peace made
through Mr. Blankson in 1853.[19]

Among Asante practices to which faithful observance by all was
expected was the prohibition on engaging in any important business
on a *da bone* ("bad day"). This meant that embassies could not travel,
nor could the Asantemanhyiamu be convened on such inauspicious
days. Bowdich made a detailed observation of this practice and its origins:

> The Ashantees have their Fasti and Nefasti, or lucky and
> unlucky days, as the Romans had. The former consecrated
> by some good fortune, the latter condemned for some na-
> tional calamity, as Saturday, for instance from the defeat and
> death of Sai Tootoo. They are also otherwise marked than
> by the week; for I was told that our month of September
> contained fewer bad days than any other, and was besides
> deemed auspicious to traveling. [20]

European travelers and visitors to the Asante capital found this observance an irritating encumbrance, although they generally complied with
it. Hence, because of the *da bone* observance, Bowdich's return from
Kumase was delayed; Dupuis' party to Kumase interrupted its travel on
Friday, 11 February 1820, on the instigation of the Asante guide; the
Asantehene refused to discuss the Fante palaver with Dupuis on 16
March 1820; and British Traveling Commissioner Hull was required to
delay his entry into Kumase until 2 April 1891.[21] Compliance with this
observance naturally caused considerable loss of time in the speed at
which diplomatic business was conducted.

European government representatives encountered difficulty in
comprehending another cultural variable: royal relationships. Royal links
in Asante were seen in terms of relationships to the stool rather than to
the individual Asantehene's person. Thus, the much younger Prempe I
referred to John Jr., and Albert Owusu Ansa as his grandsons. Administrator W. B. Griffith ultimately realized that "this degree of relationship
is merely a local arrangement, the fact being that whilst the King is
about 24 years of age, (John) Ansa is 43 years old."[22] But, it was not
until after the Colonial Office had relentlessly rejected the credentials
of the Owusu Ansas and the other Asante ambassadors, charging,
inter alia, that the two princes could not possibly have been "grandsons" of the reigning Asantehene. The notion of royals tracing relationship to the stool also found expression in the way individual Asantehenes
conceptualized the acts of their predecessors. Bowdich's extended stay

in Kumase in 1817 enabled him to understand this notion, thereby observing that "the King always spoke of the acts of all his ancestors as his own."[23] Thus, Osei Tutu Kwame spoke of the Asante conquest of Denkyira and the acquisition of the "notes" to Elmina as if they were achievements of his reign. But even as late as the 1870s British administrators at Cape Coast were baffled by Asantehene Kofi Kakari's claims in letters that "we" conquered Denkyira.

Further cultural constraints become discernible through a study of nineteenth-century Asante diplomatic history. European preference for royals as ambassadors on the false assumption that non-royals were of inferior rank was at variance with Asante diplomatic ranking procedures which, as we have seen, recognized *afenasoafo* and *nseniefo* as accredited envoys, and by which domestic status as councilor or counselor was considered a high rank. In bargaining processes such as took place during the ransom discussions of 1870–73, the Asante practice "to ask much more than they expect to obtain" was quite unfamiliar to European officials. During the crisis period of December 1873 to January 1874 when Asante-British relations clearly drifted towards war, Sir Garnet Wolseley's ultimatum that Asante surrender the heir apparent Mensa Bonsu, the Asantehemaa, and the heirs to the Kings of Dwaben, Kokofu, Mampon, and Bekwae as a condition of peace clearly lacked an understanding of local cultural practices. It was for this reason that Joseph Dawson, a Fante who acted as a British agent and who was better acquainted with local customs than the British officials, wrote to Captain Buller to entreat Wolseley to accept substitute hostages and explained:

> I know the Ashantees will yield to all the terms of the Major-General for peace, except the sending of their Royal lineage out of the Kingdom, which is against their superstitious notions, so much so that they would rather die or perish foolishly than doing it.[24]

Some familiarity with Asante cultural practices on the part of European government officials on the Gold Coast might have predisposed them to a degree of tolerance and appreciation which were essential for the establishment of mutual respect and understanding. A recommendation made in 1843 urging Governor Hill to an "adherence to the customs prevalent" in Asante as "necessary for the preservation of a good understanding" went unheeded.[25] Part of the difficulty from the European viewpoint might have been the fact that Asante cultural values were often not only directly observable but also inferable.

The Political Variable. Since international diplomacy functions in the national interest, political variables were significant in Asante's diplomatic activities. Asante recognized and sought to develop the national interests upon which its foreign policies were grounded. In this regard national security was an important consideration, and it is in the context of the threat to Asante's political integrity posed by the southern provinces that their insurrections and secessions must be seen. The sovereignty of the provinces was a critical variable, as Asante diplomacy was continuously brought to bear on objections to "the idea of treating with the allied tribes upon a footing of equality."[26] The 1824 Asante-British war, for instance, was caused in part by the attempts of Denkyira, Wassa, and Fante to withdraw from Asante sovereignty. Asante diplomacy throughout was therefore a function of the maintenance of national sovereignty in the face of threats to it from seceding and rebellious provinces.

Other political variables influenced Asante diplomacy within an Asante-British context. Colonialism or the perception of a threat to Asante independence surfaced as a critical variable as the century wore on. By the time of Prempe I's administration, Asante was marshaling all its diplomatic resources to reject the British offer of "protection" and strive to remain independent. The ill-fated mission to England in 1894–95 represented the climax of Asante diplomatic efforts to save a dying political independence.

At the same time individual events or developments like the ransom negotiations of 1870–73, upon which a great deal of diplomatic activity was centered, provided subtle insights into Asante's perception of the political uses of diplomacy. Throughout the delicate and protracted negotiations involving the conditions for the release of the European captives, Asante showed itself to be cognizant of the utility of the prisoners as a pawn in the diplomatic game for the acquisition of territorial gains; Asante is known to have contemplated the possibility of receiving "the whole coast of seaboard" in return for the release of the Europeans.[27] It did actually make some diplomatic gains, such as temporarily securing the release of Akyampon Yaw and the security of his property and people.

Asante was not altogether unmindful of the fact that it stood to benefit from the rivalry of the European powers amongst themselves or with Asante collectively or individually, if it could score diplomatic triumphs. It certainly played the diplomatic game creditably, sometimes courting the friendship of the Dutch against the British and obtaining supplies of powder and guns from the Dutch settlements, with commercial regularity, to build its military strength against the British.

Diplomacy was also employed to bolster the Asantehene's image and the national image. In the embassies of Gyakye Nantwi and Boakye Tenten and in the careers of men like Kwame Boaten and Kofi Apea we find a dedication to the revival, through the medium of diplomacy, of what a correspondent of the "Gold Coast Methodist Times" called Asante's "past glory and renown"[28] — an imperial glory that had been dimmed by the military setback of 1874. It is in this light that the extraordinarily large and glamorous embassies of these men must be seen. Their advertising quality was meant to impress upon the residents of the coast that the grandness of Asante had not deserted it yet.

A final political variable warrants discussion: the issue of the "notes." Whereas their nature and origin were generally not in doubt, the significance of the notes suddenly became a subject of controversy between Asante and its European neighbors during a critical period in the 1870s. Dupuis regarded them as "title-deeds" by which the late Africa Company made certain obligatory payments in respect of the settlements to local chiefs — an analysis that was hardly contestable. Separate notes existed for the major settlements — the Dutch at Elmina, the English at Cape Coast and Anomabu, and the Dutch, Danish, and English in Accra. In the nineteenth century Asante held all these notes by right of conquest — over Denkyira, Fante, and Akyem. During the early part of the century the European administrators generally recognized Asante's claim to the notes and made regular payments in cash or goods in lieu of monetary payments to Asante envoys who were sent to collect them. As long as no attempt was made to give definition to what the notes represented, the European officials were prepared to pay for the notes without question. In the early nineteenth century at least, there was general acceptance of the notes as "rent" in respect of the ground on which the settlements stood, or so they appeared to Dupuis, who also considered that the object was "to purchase security of person and property."[29] By the 1870s, however, it had become apparent that the significance of the notes was hardly an issue upon which there was general agreement. Asante certainly saw the payments as a form of "tribute," a fact that was hotly disputed. In 1871 Henry Ata Plange, a British emissary, was dispatched to Kumase to request the withdrawal of the word "tribute" from Asante written claims to Elmina, failing which Asante was threatened with a discontinuation of payments.

Although different interpretations were at the time placed on the notes ranging from rent through tribute to presents, it might not have been altogether accidental that their significance, hardly a disputed fact in the early half of the century, should have become a subject of controversy in the 1870s, a time when ideas of colonial expansion were gaining ground in the Gold Coast (as elsewhere in Africa); tribute definitely implied notions of sovereignty. Yet, the Asantehene's rent-based interpretation was not that inconsistent with pre-capitalist concepts of tax-rent which presupposed some form of subordination.[30] Be this as it may, groundrent collection in respect to the notes, disagreements over the value of European goods Asante received in kind instead of cash payments, and the controversy over the symbolic importance of the notes were subjects which engaged the attention of the Asante diplomatic institutions and personnel and provided a point of departure between Asante and European administrators.

The Commercial Variable. A further use of Asante diplomacy was as a tool in the advancement of national commercial and economic interests. Asante was committed to a policy of promoting foreign trade, and since trade and war could not coexist in the same locales, successive governments sought to maintain friendly relations with foreign powers through the medium of diplomacy geared towards the furtherance of commercial activities. Writing to the English Governor in 1871, Asantehene Kofi Kakari summed up his nation's views on the importance of trade and the responsibility of foreign partners towards the maintenance of conditions congenial to trade development:

> As your Excellency has undertaken the responsibility to negotiate peace between the Fantees, Ashantis, and others, it is the best policy on your part, and my desire also that you can go so far as to remove all difficulties thoroughly, to cause hostilities to cease in these most neighbouring friends and relatives of the coast tribes and nations, viz., the Fantis, Ashantis, and Elminas, so that all roads for commerce may be reopened, inasmuch as war is a doubtful career, but trade, which is the best support of nations, should be well and universally established amongst these nations, tribes, and kingdoms.[31]

Indeed, this was a statement not only on trade but on the interrelatedness of three Asante foreign policy variables — peace, open roads, and trade. This was a "trinity" which was the cornerstone of the foreign policy of successive Asante administrations and the subject matter of volumes of chancery letters and personal embassies to foreign government representatives on the Gold Coast. So closely interwoven were these three issues and so important were the roles of the diplomatic personnel in the realization of the "trinity" that envoys and resident ambassadors traditionally announced the closure of roads and the cessation of trading activities during periods of hostilities.

Asante Diplomatic Practice: An Assessment

There is no doubt, from the foregoing chapters, that the Asante governments of the nineteenth century drew upon the ranks of a variety of *nfekuo* (departments) for diplomatic personnel. Yet, although diplomatic appointments were theoretically open to practically all individuals, a body of functionaries from specific *nfekuo* emerged who increasingly came to be associated with diplomatic activity and came to be recognized as envoys when they were appropriately commissioned. The increasing use in the nineteenth century of *afenasoafo* for the dispatch of messages, as opposed to traders, gave to members of this *fekuo* recognition as official envoys of the Asantehene. Other office-holders, notably from the ranks of the *nseniefo* and *akyeame*, acquired specialization as individuals engaged in diplomatic communication. *Afenasoafo* and *nseniefo* became heavily engaged in diplomacy, not only in the conveyance of oral messages and written dispatches, but also in the reception of visiting dignitaries. The diplomatic roles of the *akyeame* extended from leadership of the more powerful embassies, particularly those sent to areas over which their individual stools held jurisdiction, to protocol responsibilities, such as were performed by *akyeameahene* like Kwame Opoku Agyeman and Kwaku ("Nsuase") Poku with conspicuous effectiveness. Yet, as has been pointed out above, despite the increasing specialization of certain individuals and *nfekuo* in diplomatic activity, practically all persons who held appointments as envoys saw themselves as serving in diplomatic roles as an extension of their domestic positions.

Though none were in principle debarred from foreign service, the discussion about skills amply demonstrates the eligibility criteria that were placed upon diplomatic appointments. Actual skills and competence as well as apprenticeship in the form of understudying were emphasized as necessary requisites. At the same time, the analysis of the diplomatic careers of some functionaries undertaken above illustrates the opportunities that existed for upward mobility. Asante envoys, as elsewhere, were distinguished by status and rank, the most important determinants of which were the officials' domestic status and the mandates with which they were commissioned. In line with the general usage of diplomacy, Asante envoys expectedly performed a myriad of functions as determined by the foreign policy demands and priorities of various nineteenth century administrations.

The evidence is abundantly clear that the nineteenth century saw the development and standardization of procedures regulating diplomatic appointments and conduct. Matters relating to the commissioning of an envoy, his management of a mission, the message delivery, traveling pace, and the like, were all governed by accepted and established regulations having the force of law. That the envoy's "code" of behavior was based on oral directives rather than written stipulations made it no less binding in a society where the law of the land was itself unwritten.

In consonance with diplomatic service everywhere, Asante envoys had and used a set of emblems which served as their credentials: the "large crooked sabres" with golden hilts of the *afenasoafo*, the monkey skin caps of the *nseniefo*, the golden staffs of the *akyeame*, the round, gold plates of the *akradwarefo*, and so forth. It is important for any discussion of credentials to note that these emblems were recognized as symbols of authority not only by the appointing government but also by the host governments of Asante envoys. In West Africa where the use of symbolic credentials was a prevailing practice, host governments of Asante ambassadors did not find the use of Asante official swords, staffs, and plates at variance with local systems. But even representatives of European governments whose home countries were more familiar with a system of written credentials quickly came to accept the symbolic credentials of Asante ambassadors and in some cases actually insisted on their use so that persons on official business could be easily identifiable.

An essential component of Asante diplomatic appointments and accreditation to foreign governments was the acceptance of the principle of representation by both sender and recipient. In this respect, the governments of Asante and those of the host states fully understood that the actions of Asante ambassadors entered them into contractual relations. Although there were occasional instances of repudiation of the acts of envoys, such as those that involved Tando and Kwame Antwi, the mere fact that the individual Asantehenes at the time took prompt actions to rectify wrongs that may have been caused by the misrepresentations implied a fundamental acceptance of responsibility. However, with rare exceptions (notably John Owusu Ansa Sr. and Jr.), political necessities did not make for that immense flexibility of diplomatic roles envisioned in the concept of *plena potestas* in its fullest sense, hence the Asantehene's ratification of agreements and an envoy's reference to Kumase for instructions while on a mission. But the concept of juridical representation was fully understood and practiced in nineteenth-century Asante.

One of the indispensable props of international diplomatic practice is inviolability, which alone accords diplomats certain immunities and sets them apart from private individuals. It is a highly favorable commentary on the state of the "profession" at the time that Asante envoys expected to receive and did enjoy immunities to their persons, families, and properties. Undeniably, there were occasions when diplomats were victims of assaults of various kinds, but diplomatic practice, even in the 1990s, is not entirely devoid of breaches of inviolability. If instances of perversions of the right to inviolability which Asante envoys suffered in Asen, Fante, Elmina, Ga, Gyaman, and other places appear numerous to the reader, they can be considered as such only by present-day rather than nineteenth-century standards. The incidence of violations of the right to diplomatic immunity was a reflection on the problems of peaceful coexistence and political rivalry rather than an indication of the non-recognition of the principles underlying international representation; the rarity of violations of inviolability, by the standards of the day, was a favorable reflection on the general awareness of diplomatic norms.

Diplomacy for Asante envoys entailed the acceptance to its fullest extent of the elaborate protocol that is so much a part of the profession. Thus, notification of the dispatch of embassies, requests for audiences, the holding of the audience itself, and the message delivery all followed prevailing conventions and accepted formats. To a society that was used to formality even in private receptions and greetings, and to members of a profession that was drawn largely from a group that was well acquainted with the art of court ceremony, diplomatic protocol must have seemed a normal and familiar practice.

Asante showed full reciprocity in its reception of visiting diplomats. Elaborate receptions were at the core of the treatment of visiting dignitaries like Bowdich, Dupuis, Freeman, W. and J. J. C. Huydecoper, Plange, and Dawson, etc., who invariably showed their appreciation for a practice that Asante deemed necessary by the demands of international friendship no less than local hospitality. That the Asantehene summoned visiting dignitaries to audiences through the medium of the *afenasoafo*, received them only on appointments, requested to examine their credentials and insisted that they depart only after proper leave-taking procedures — all underlie an understanding of diplomacy as operating within a reciprocal framework.

Sovereignty, Nationality, and Loyalty. Sovereignty, citizenship, and loyalty are issues that are usually critical to diplomatic service. In nineteenth-century Asante, ideas of diplomatic representation and their recognition were expectedly based on sovereignty. However, the ambivalent role played by J. Owusu Ansa, Sr., the duality of Ata Plange who served the needs of two governments, the absence of qualms or conflict that characterized the ease with which individuals such as Nielson, Bonnat, Campbell, and the Huydecopers switched or intermingled loyalties all illustrate the contention that no definition had yet been given to the concept that citizenship was indispensable to diplomatic service. The recruitment of foreigners like Bonnat and Campbell further illustrates that service, skills, and loyalty rather than national identity were the values looked for in foreign or diplomatic appointments.

The question has been raised as to whether the Owusu Ansas, Asante's foremost ambassadors, had not lost their national identity because of their British education, their long attachment to European modes of conduct, their civil service positions in the British administration, and the fact that John senior received a British pension.[32] Some discussion of the subject is appropriate in view of the prominence which the Owusu Ansas occupied in Asante diplomatic service. Admittedly, when John Owusu Ansa, Sr. felt that the Asantehene had let him down in that he was not being adequately compensated for his services, it was to Governor Ussher that he turned, pleading for any suitable position in the British administration. However, in doing so, Owusu Ansa considered that he was not portraying "any want of patriotism and faithfulness to his country." On the contrary, he was convinced that since the two governments were professedly pursuing the seemingly identical interests of trade through peaceful coexistence, he could promote them from either end. Thus, as long as he continued to work towards "the maintenance of peace and good understanding between the [British] Government and the King of Ashanti," he was content that he was doing his duty to his country. He must be judged, he contended, by what he described as "true faithfulness and justice," that is, devotion to duty rather than the modern notion of national identity.[33]

No less loyal was Albert Owusu Ansa. When, for instance, reports of human sacrifice spread in the Gold Coast and England, following a newspaper publication in 1894, Owusu Ansa was aroused to a deep sense of rage and patriotism. He published a rejoinder, refuting the allegation as a pure fabrication without a "particle of truth," and concluded that the reports were a "bogus trumped-up business to get Christian world against our nationality."[34] Later, when the British Government began raising questions about the nationality of the Owusu Ansas as an objection to their inclusion in the 1894–95 mission to England, Albert again found the need to clear the air on the subject of his citizenship. He argued that the allowance of £100 per annum which his father received never made him a British subject and emphatically stated:

> I must here publicly state, and I say so on behalf of my brother
> John Osso Ansah, that never have we naturalized ourselves
> as British subjects, nor considered ourselves as such at any
> time.[35]

It may be pointed out, similarly, that the fact that many of the African leaders of the movement for independence from colonialism in the 1940s and 1950s received British training and held civil service positions within the colonial administration did not make them any less nationalistic or loyal.

If nationality was not a critical variable in the selection of ambassadors, loyalty was. Utmost loyalty to the person of the Asantehene and his government was demanded of all envoys, both of Asante and non-Asante origins, and rigid standards were enforced to ensure that the ambassador served the interests of his sender throughout. The instances of misconduct and the corresponding penalties discussed in Chapter 3 illustrate the emphasis placed on loyalty.

Diplomatic Institutions

It can be deduced from this discussion of diplomatic practice that a foreign office, as a distinct branch of government in the modern sense, failed to develop in nineteenth-century Asante. Despite the intensity of diplomatic activity, the increasing specialization of certain individuals and *nfekuo* in diplomatic appointments, and the standardization of procedures regulating appointments and conduct, a separate department of the foreign office did not come into being. As has been pointed out above, foreign service personnel—whether *ad hoc* or career oriented—ultimately reverted to their domestic appointments. However, to argue the absence of a foreign office is not to contend that Asante did not recognize that the needs of foreign policy called for individuals with specialized skills. Asante fully recognized and utilized the benefits of individual expertise and territorial specialization in the conduct of foreign policy. The compartmentalization of national affairs into the distinct domains of foreign and domestic was alien (and perhaps even unnecessary) to the nineteenth-century Asante administrations. After all, the *afenasoani's* functions, for example, were related to the official use and custody of swords. Within a twentieth-century framework, if his conduct of a particular task confined him to Kumase or its environs, the *afenasoani* may be said to have performed a domestic role. If his assignment took him to a foreign power, he may be regarded as having been involved in foreign policy. In terms of nineteenth-century Asante, however, such an office-holder was essentially a swordbearer, whether he operated in the capital or was sent as an envoy to a foreign land; one function was seen as an extension of the other. Given the Asante conceptualization of both domestic and foreign policies as coming under one umbrella (over which the Asantemanhyiamu exercised jurisdiction) , the lack of the development of a distinct department of foreign office might have emanated from the non-existence of a true need for such a separate institution.

The absence of a "foreign office," however, did not impede the development of four distinct bureaus (English, Dutch, Danish, and Arabic) that were responsible for Asante's written communication with foreign powers. Each independently accountable to the Asantemanhyiamu, the most important was the "English bureau." The bureaus were not part of the decision-making process, although some members were influential and their advice carried weight with the Council on foreign policy matters. Below the Asantehene and the Asantemanhyiamu, Asante's foreign (and regional) representation was essentially one of delegation of power, with ambassadors for the European powers as well as the former provinces of Fante, Akyem, Yendi, Elmina, etc.

Diplomatic Mechanisms

Asante's pre-nineteenth-century diplomatic mechanisms were almost exclusively oral, the only exceptions being forms of official communication undertaken in Arabic prior to that time. The nineteenth century saw an intensification of diplomatic activity, and with it came growing stress on the mechanisms of intercommunication. The difficulties Asante had in reaching a basis for a permanent understanding with its European neighbors, and in particular the repeated conflicts with Britain in the first three decades of the century, provided enough grounds for a reassessment of the modes of diplomatic communication. The continual espousal of a policy of commitment to peaceful coexistence with its European neighbors led Asante to adopt and apply some aspects of European processes of communication — the written medium. Thus, by the 1870s there was a widespread acceptance by the government of not only the written medium but also the form, style, and the whole tradition consistent with diplomatic correspondence in the written mode. To facilitate the implementation of such major changes in the mechanisms of communication, the government found it necessary to have a cadre of Asantes trained under the auspices of the British in Cape Coast and England. It was also within the context of the search for a body of individuals who were familiar with European modes of conduct, thought, and communication that one should find the justification for the recruitment of non-Asantes like Bonnat, Nielson, Campbell, and J. J. C. Huydecoper in foreign-service roles.

It is, however, clear from the preceding chapters that neither the engagement of Europeans nor the adoption of the written medium succeeded in bringing about the desired understanding in Asante-British diplomatic relations. Written communication did not entirely eliminate ambiguities in diplomatic relations, nor did it resolve Asante-British differences. Indeed, far from the elimination of conflicts, the century progressively saw a deterioration of relations until Asante was colonized at the end of the century. The failure of Asante to reach an understanding with the British must be interpreted more in the light of British unwillingness to faithfully operate existing agreements and less in the context of the inefficacy of Asante's diplomatic mechanisms.

As has been pointed out above, "written diplomacy" was not a substitute for "oral diplomacy," and the new form of written communication was only employed to supplement the traditional oral medium. To this day Asante has amply manifested its undying faith in oral communication with all its external trappings of ceremony, protocol, and expressions of oratorical skills. If the adoption of foreign mechanisms was indicative of Asante's determination to seek more effective ways of communicating with its European friends, the concurrent retention of the oral mode was an affirmation of the utility of traditional diplomatic mechanisms.

Professionalism

Current notions of professionalism devolve on a number of determinants which, among others, emphasize that the position must be a full-time, paid occupation; that it must be the main source of income for the officeholder; and that he should belong to a group of workers who are regulated by a code of behavior that marks them out as a body distinct from persons in other professions. To nineteenth-century Asante, however, professionalism was seen in the context of specialization; in terms of the existence of a recognized body of regulations governing diplomatic appointment and conduct; and in the light of identification with a dominant rather than exclusive activity. Notions of a full-time, salaried diplomatic official were yet to emerge. It can be seen from the preceding chapters, therefore, that nineteenth-century Asante diplomatic practice met the prevailing criteria for professionalism to an appreciably high degree.

Recruitment and appointment processes followed set procedures that insisted on specialized skills and eligibility standards. Specialization, a necessary aspect of professionalism, occurred, both in functions and in roles. Thus, individuals came to be engaged in the various foreign bureaus based on their command of a body of expertise necessary for conducting affairs within the language of the Dutch, English, Danish, or Arabic-speaking peoples. The *ohene krakye*, for instance, emerged as the official specializing in the English correspondence of the Asantehene. The standardization of procedures for the preparation of documents was likewise evidence of the trend towards professionalism.

Similarly, it was in the outcome of the move towards specialization that some individual envoys came to acquire their unique reputation: for example, Kwadwo Aberante as the envoy who "collected the King's Kostgelden," that is, payment in respect of the "notes," from the Dutch administration in the early nineteenth century; Tando as the "expert" on Wassa affairs; Owusu Koko Kuma as "the only channel for confidential communication with the coast;" Yaw Twumasi, initially a *batani* within the *Gyaase*, as the one who was usually sent in the 1860s to procure silken cloth and other articles from Fante for the Asantehene; Asante Agyei as being best suited for settling "hard palavers;" and so forth. Again, it is in the context of specialization that the diplomatic careers of certain office-holders must be seen: Asabi Antwi as an instrument of the oral retrieval of information; Kofi Bene and Boakye Tenten as *akyeame* celebrated for their commitment to peaceful policies; Gyakye Nantwi as a "specialist" in matters relating to capital punishment; and Bosommuru Dwira and Kofi Afrifa as "experts" in British affairs.

Specialization found expression not only at the individual level but also in the territorial jurisdiction of stools. Thus, the Butuakwa stool has from the early nineteenth century to the present day exercised responsibility for Fante while the Boakye Yam Kuma stool, of which Akyampon Tia and Akyampon Yaw, both paternal brothers of Kwaku Dua Panin, were among its noted occupants, acquired specialization in Elmina and Dutch affairs. The existence and utilization of avenues for upward mobility (advancement) as well as downward mobility (demotion) would seem to give the nineteenth-century Asante foreign service a touch of professionalism.

Professionalism was evident in other spheres as well. The conduct of embassies followed established lines that insisted upon efficiency, honesty, and integrity. Throughout the century, emphasis was placed upon the transmission of letters and the conveyance of messages by *afenasofo* as officials specializing in such activities. As early as 1817 a new law was promulgated insisting that "all persons sent on the King's business shall no longer seize provisions in any country," a regulation that sought to end extortion of goods and food by envoys for their sustenance.[36]

The rationale for Asante's external relations with its African and non-African neighbors was the search for cooperation towards the attainment of mutual goals. The continual recognition of this objective and its continuous application led to the intensification and standardization of practices and conventions associated with diplomatic appointments, communication, and representation. Yet, for the diplomat, beyond the exactitude of his instructions, his "code" of professional ethics was still largely unwritten and based on precedence rather than a codified system. The practices of his profession were sanctioned by long usage and conformity rather than a set of sanctions stipulated in writing. With the exception of career ambassadors, the Asante ambassador was regarded as such only when he was on duty or at post. He reverted to his original domestic position during periods of inter-diplomatic activity. Ambassadors could still undertake private business, for which reason Owusu Koko Kuma and his party, for example, were said to have arrived in Cape Coast in October 1872 in the "double capacity of traders and envoys." In the same vein Owusu Ansa, Sr. is known to have carried on "a little profitable business" while he was ambassador-at-large.[37]

However, the absence of the development of a full-time, paid diplomat who is not expected to engage in private business does not detract from the contention that nineteenth-century Asante ambassadors were professionals. The distinction between private and official life was known to and drawn by office-holders as far back as 1820. There was no question in the minds of foreign-office appointees and the appointing Asantemanhyiamu authority about the professional character of envoys. The notion that professionalism is dependent on full-time, salaried status is a twentieth-century concept that was non-existent in the nineteenth century.

A paradoxical situation existed within the area of written communication. Despite the growth of a chancery and the success with which "written diplomacy" came to be adopted, the channels for conveying messages remained largely conservative and uninnovative. The message-delay factor remained high. Asante could boast of nothing comparable to the "half-heads" (couriers) of Dahomey who impressed M'Leod so much and who were credited by Burton with the capability of covering a distance of 90 miles in three days.[38] It was R. J. Ghartey's disappointment at seeing how slowly some of the Asante envoys traveled that led him to recommend what he termed "posts of runners" to speed up the transmission of dispatches:

> The only way to get the quickest communications is to set up posts of runners for the purpose of conveying letters and messages at intervals, from the Protectorate boundary to the coast, the intervening distance not exceeding 10 to 12 miles, from the station of one post to another, the transposal of letters and messages.[39]

This suggestion, made in 1862, apparently went by unutilized, and diplomatic parties continued to traverse the Kumase-Cape Coast route at a great loss of time. The courier system was rejected, perhaps out of the fear that it might impair the accuracy of verbally transmitted messages or eliminate the grand scene of an envoy followed by his retinue, and the communications system remained conservatively slow.

Asante Diplomacy: An Assessment

Asante understood the concept of diplomacy in all its ramifications and promoted the principle of operating and adjusting its external relations through accepted diplomatic channels. The unabating efforts of Osei Tutu Kwame to work through the stipulations of the 1817 Bowdich Treaty, Kwaku Dua's determination to let his relations with the British administration be guided by the letter and spirit of the 1831 Maclean Treaty, Kofi Kakari's anxiety to operate through existing agreements in matters relating to Asen, and Mensa Bonsu's concern to abide by treaties regulating Asante-Dwaben relations are but a few examples in a century-long tradition of adherence to written and oral agreements by the Asante governments.

In the unceasing efforts of successive Asantehenes to work within the stipulations of agreements they had entered into with foreign governments; in the emergence of specific departments and individuals specializing in diplomatic activity; in the institution of standardized procedures regulating diplomatic appointment, conduct, representation, and communication; and in the growth of distinct governmental bureaus devoted to the preparation of diplomatic documents, there developed a veritable diplomatic practice in nineteenth-century Asante.

GLOSSARY OF PRINCIPAL ASANTE TWI

WORDS AND TERMS

This glossary provides meanings and translations for the principal Asante Twi words used in the text. Concern is shown throughout the translations for giving meanings for terms within the contextual sense in which they were used. Further, because of the absence of direct English equivalents for some Twi words, some of the translations represent nearest approximations rather than direct translations. Although the organization of the glossary is along general alphabetical lines, certain departures from Twi orthography were necessitated by reasons of simplicity and practicability. Firstly, the alphabetization does n0t take into consideration either the initial vowel or the initial nasal 'm-' or 'n-'. Thus, *aban* is listed under 'b' and *mpaboa* under 'p'. Secondly, the final 'ε', 'ɔ' or 'o' is also omitted. Hence, *abosodeε* is rendered as *abosode* *amantoo* as *amanto* and *akontaabuo* as *akontaabu*. Finally, throughout the text 'ε' appears as e and 'ɔ' as 'o'. Thus, *kɛtɛ* is rendered as *kete* and *okyeame* as *okyeame*.

B

obaa (pl. *mmaa*)	Woman; female.
abakomdwa	The stool of the heir apparent; the heir apparent.
aban	Castle; government.
abenase	King's wardrobe organization.
abenaseni	Officer of the wardrobe.
benkum	Left.
obirempon (pl. *abirempon*)	Literally 'big man' but usually divisional chief.
obofo (pl. *abofo*)	Envoy; messenger.
bone	Bad.
da bone	Bad day; a day regarded as impropitious for any major activity.
boode	Plantain.
boodedwani	"Cutter of plantain" (under Gyaase establishment).
abosode	Symbolic casting on sword.
Bosommuru	One of principal state swords.
bosommuruni	Officer of the Bosommuru sword.
obrafo (pl. *abrafo*)	Constabulary; sometimes used interchangeably with *adumfo*.

abrafomena   Bayonets.

D

da Day.
Adae   Festival celebrated twice every Asante
                                      month of forty-two days, when prayers
                                      and offerings are made to ancestors.
                                      Akwasidae is celebrated on Sundays
                                      and Wukudae on Wednesdays.
adamfo   Friend; patron or friend at court.
dampan   Office that usually opens on to the street.
danta   Loin cloth.
dawurofo/dawurubofo   Gong-gong beaters.Responsible for an-
                                      nouncing decrees.
Deboosohene   Head of entire *abenase* organization.
donko (p. unonkofo)   Slave, usually non-Asante acquired
                                      through purchase.
adumni (pl. *adumfo*)   Executioner.
odunsinni   Traditional physical; herbalist.
    (pl. *adunsinfo*)

Odwira   Most important annual festival; occasion
                                      for reviewing performance of state ad-
                                      ministrators.

F

Fekuo (pl. *nfekuo*)   Governmental department.
afena (pl. *afena*)   Sword.
afenakyem   Shield.
afenasoani   Swordbearer; envoy.
    (pl. *afenasoafo*)
nfohoofo   Roasters of meat under Gyasse.
fotosanni   Treasury official.
    (pl. *fotosanfo*)
fufuwoni   Pounder of fufu under Gyaase.

G

Gyaase   King's household organization.
Gysasewahene   Head of King's household attendants.
Gyaasewa   Exchequer.
ahemfie   King's palace.
    ahemfie adesua   "Court learning." Infomal education ac-

quired at court.

ohene — King, chief.

oheneba — Sons and daughters of kings, i.e., princes and princesses.

ahenkwaa (pl. *nkenkwaa*) — King's household servant.

ahenkwaakuma — Junior *ahenkwaa*.

ahohosomde — Gifts given to, or hospitality paid to, envoy by host.

K

kaneasoni (pl. *kaneasofo*) — Lamp-bearer.

kete — Bed.

Kete Kese — King's bed.

keteanomfena — Ceremonial swords used in rites connected with purification of king's soul or stools.

akoa (pl. *nkoa*) — Servant; subject of king or lord.

akonkonfo — Commercial entrepreneurs.

akontaabu — Accounting.

akonwasoani (pl. *akonwasoafo*) — Stool-carrier, under Gyaase.

okradwareni — "Washer of king's soul."

krakye — A person literate in English; clerk.

ohene krakye — King's secretary.

Kramo (pl. Nkramo) — Muslim

akuma — axe

akwammofo — Suppliers of chewing stick, under Gyaase.

nkwankwaa — Young men and commoners.

okyeame (pl. *akyeame*) — Often inaccurately translated as "linguist" or spokesman, but more accurately counselor.

Akyeamehene — Head of akyeame or counselors. In many cases, also Minister of Foreign Affairs and Chief of State Protocol.

M

oman (pl. *aman*) — State; nation.

omanhene — District king; king of *amanto*, that is, core

	Asante states.
mansufo	Providers of drinking water (under Gyaase).
amanto	The five states of Bekwae, Dwaben, Kokofu, Mampon and Nsuta, which form the core of Asante.
manwerefo	Supervisors of goldworks.
mma dwa	Stools of patrilineal descent.
mmamma	Sons and grandsons of occupants of appointive offices.
mmataho	Commissions accruing to functionaries from court fines and fees.
mmowerebubufo	Nail-cutters (under Gyasse).

N

ankobea	Royal bodyguard.
nifa	Right.

P

mpaboa	Sandals.
opanin (pl. *mpaninfo*)	Older person; elder; address of respect for senior persons.
patomni	Caretaker of drinks (under Gyaase).
peredwan	Gold weight of 8 ounces.
poma	Staff.
Mponponsu	One of principal state swords.
mponponsuni	Officer of the Mponponsu.

S

osa	War.
osahene	General.
Saana	Asantehene' s Treasury.
Saanahene	Asantehene' sTreasurer (Accountant).
nsabrane	Appellation.
safiesoni	Holder/keeper of drinks (under Gyasse).
Asantehemaa	Queen-mother.
Asantehene	King of Asante.
Asantemanhyiamu	Literally, "meeting of Asante nation," but used to refer to governing Council.
aseda	Thanks-offering; payments in respect of court proceedings.

sekan	Knife.
asemnie	Legal hearing or trial.
esen or *nsenieni* (pl. *nseniefo*)	Court crier or herald; envoy.
Nseniehene	Head of *nseniefo*.
sika	Gold; money.
Sika Dwa	The Golden Stool.
esom	Concept of service.
esom da	"Day of service." Day when a functionary is required to wait on the Asantehene.
esom dwa	Stool of service.
asomfo	Servants.
asomfomfena	Diplomatic swords.
somesisini	Waist-holder (under Gyaase).
Soodo (sodo)	Department of cooks.
Soodohene	Head of *soodofo*.
suman	Protective medicine.
nsumankwaani	Physician/spiritual caretaker. See also *adunsinfo*.

T

ataade	Dress.
aban ataade	Literally, "government dress," but in the instance cited, uniform.
atenefo	Torchbearers.
tie	Listen.
atumtuni	Gun-bearer.
Twafo	Advance guard in a military formation.

W

Awukudae	See under Adae.

Guide to Abbreviations

(As used in Notes and Bibliography)

ACBP   Asante Collective Biography Project

ADM   Administrative files

C.   Correspondence Papers presented to the United Kingdom

dd.   dated

encl.   enclosure

GNQ   Ghana Notes and Queries

IASAS   Institute of African Studies (Legon) Asante Stool History

JAH   Journal of African History

MMA   Methodist Mission Archives

Ms   Manuscript

NAG   National Archives of Ghana

NBKG   Nederlandsche Bezittingen ter Kuste van Guinea (The Hague)

n.d.   no date

PRO   Public Record Office

TGCTHS   Transactions of the Gold Coast and Togoland Historical Society

THSG   Transactions of the Historical Society of Ghana

NOTES

Chapter 1

1   Bowdich, 1821 (a), p. 28.
2   Dupuis, 1824, pp. 225-6.
3   *Idem.*
4   *Ibid,* p. 139.
5   Reade, 1873, p. 288.
6   *Affairs,* C. 3064, 1881, p. 134.
7   "The Gold Coast Chronicle," 19 November 1894; *Further Correspondence,* C. 7918, 1896, p. 13.
8   See Chapter 4 for a discussion of the missions of 1881 and 1894–95.
9   For an outline of Asante-British relations during this period, see Claridge, 1915, I, 303-18.
10 Dupuis, 1824, p. 149.
11 "The Royal Gold Coast Gazette," Cape Coast, 1 November 1823.
12 *Affairs,* C. 3064, 1881, p. 69: Dudley to Colonial Secretary, dd. Cape Coast, 17 February 1881.
13 Metcalfe, 1962, *passim.*
14 McCaskie, 1974, *passim.*
15 This view is universally expressed in traditional sources. Also see IASAS/99: Anwomaso; IASAS/103: Nfensi; and TASAS/105: Besiase, recorded by J. Agyeman-Duah. 14 September, 16 and 30 November 1963, respectively.
16 *Further Papers,* C. 456, 1855, p. 13.
17 C0. 96/27: Hill to Newcastle, dd. Cape Coast, 13 April 1853
18 See, for example, *Correspondence,* C. 670, 1872, pp. 26-7: Kofi Kakari to Salmon, dd. Kumase, 1 September 1874.
19 See, for example, *Despatches,* C. 907, 1874, pp. 6, 8, 12-13; *Further Correspondence.* C. 921, 1874, pp. 20-1
20 See, for example, *Despatches,* C. 907, 1874, p. 8: Kofi Kakari to Wolseley, dd. Kumase, 21 January 1874 and *Further correspondence,* C. 819, 1873, p. 3: Kofi Kakari to Harley, dd. Kumase, 20 March 1873.
21 *Despatches,* C. 907, 1874, pp. 12-3: Kofi Kakari to Wolseley, dd. Kumase, 27 January 1873.
22 *Papers,* C. 1402, 1876, p. 81: Mensa Bonsu to Governor-in-Chief, dd. Kumase, 11 June 1875.
23 *Ibid,* pp. 82-3: Mensa Bonsu to Governor, dd. Kumase, 16 July 1875.

24   *Further Correspondence,* C. 7918, 1896, p. 1: Telegram from Griffith to Ripon, received, 10 January 1895.

25   *Further Correspondence,* C. 7917, 1896, p. 172: Prempe to Hodgson, dd. Kumase, 7 February 1894.

26   *Further Correspondence,* C. 7917, 1896, pp. 201-2: Prempe to Governor, dd. Kumase, 28 June 1894.

27   The "Royal Gold Coast Gazette," Cape Coast, 15 November 1823.

28   *Papers,* C. 1402, 1876, p. 83: Mensa Bonsu to Governor, dd. Kumase, 16 July 1875.

29   Dupuis, 1824, pp. 225-6.

30   *Further Correspondence,* C. 7918, 1896, pp. 122-3.

31   Herskovits, 1950, p. 342.

32   Nicolson, 1958, p. 15.

33   *Ibid.,* p. 13.

34   Dupuis, 1824, introduction, pp. xix-xxiii.

35   This is the traditional view. Although the rumors of a Gyaman victory were in themselves false, they were initiated in Kumase itself, where Adoma Akosua actually caused a funeral to be held for the presumed death of the Asantehene.

36   Dupuis, 1824, introduction, p. xxiii.

37   Beecham, 1841, pp. 39-41.

38   The Dutch sources indicate a similar concern with the problem of identifying the status of Asante diplomats, although success was equally limited. The Dutch apparently were no closer to resolving the difficulty and succeeded in distinguishing among only certain classes of diplomats, using expressions like "*voorloper*" for "herald," "*sabeldrager*" for "swordbearer," and "*groot vaandrig*" for "great officer." See, for example, Huydecoper, 1962.

39   The analogy in Roman Private Law is evident. See, for example, Rudolf Sohm, *The Institute: A Textbook of the History and System of Roman Private Law,* 1907, p. 219.

40   Such works include F. Boyle, *Through Fanteland to Coomassie: A Diary of the Ashantee Expedition,* 1874; H. Brackenbury, *The Ashanti War,* 2 vols., 1874; T. B. Freeman, *Journal of Two Visits to the Kingdom of Ashanti,* 1843; J. Gros, *Voyages, Adventures et Captivité de J. Bonnat Chez les Achantis,* 1884; C. A. Henty, *The March to Coomassie,* 1874; and H. M. Stanley, *Coomassie and Magdala: The Story of Two British Campaigns in Africa, 1874.*

41   A. B. Ellis, *A History of the Gold Coast of West Africa,* 1893.

42   C. C. Reindorf, *The History of the Gold Coast and Asante,* 1895, p. iii.

43 W. W. Claridge, *A History of the Gold Coast and Ashanti,* 2 vols. 1915. p. vii.
44 R. S. Rattray, *Ashanti,* 1923; *Religion and Art in Ashanti,* 1927; and *Ashanti Law and Constitution,* 1929.
45 First published as *A History of the Gold Coast,* 1948.
46 These include: I. Wilks (1961) *The Northern Factor in Ashanti History,* University College of Ghana; (1966) "The Position of Muslims in Metropolitan Ashanti in the Early 19th Century," *Islam in Tropical Africa,* ed., I. Lewis, London, 318-41; (1970) *Political Bipolarity in Nineteenth Century Asante,* Ninth Melville J. Herskovits Memorial Lecture, Edinburgh; and (1975) *Asante in the Nineteenth Century: The Structure and Evolution of a Political Order,* Cambridge.
47 J. K. Fynn, *Asante and its Neighbours, 1700-1807,* 1971.
48 T. C. McCaskie, "The Paramountcy of the Asantehene Kwaku Dua 1838-1867: A Study In Asante Political Culture," Ph.D. Thesis, Cambridge, 1974.
49 "Prince Owusu-Ansa and Asante-British Diplomacy 1841-1884," Ph.D. Thesis, Wisconsin, 1974.
50 T. Lewin, "The Structure of Political Conflict in Asante 1875-1900," Ph.D. Thesis, Northwestern, 1974. Also see Lewin, *Asante before the British,* Lawrence, Kansas, 1978.
51 Agnes Aidoo, "Political Crisis and Social Changes in the Asante Kingdom 1867-1901," Ph.D. Thesis, UCLA, 1975.

Chapter 2

1 The source base for this discussion of *nhemkwaa* is derived extensively, through not exclusively, from a survey that was conducted in Kumase in May-June, 1980. The survey was a study of *nhenkwaa* roles, status, views and perceptions. Forty *nhenkwaa* living at both *ahemfie* (Asantehene's palace) and outside Manhyia in Kumase were interviewed and their answers to a set of questions recorded. The 40 were drawn from *nfekuo* whose functions were known to include being sent on errands and missions. The survey was administered by this writer with the assistance of a public school teacher who was himself an *ahenkwaa* resident at *ahemfie.*
2 For Kwaku Bosommuru Dwira, see for example, *Affairs,* C. 3064, 1881, *passim.* Brackenbury, 1874, II, 331-1; and Wilks, 1975, pp. 406, 573. For his role in the Boakye Tenten mission of 1881, see Chapter 4.

3   Interview with Agya Kofi Anane, Deputy Mponponsuhene, dd. Kumase, 2 June 1980.

4   See, for example, Rattray, 1911, pp. 33-46

5   Imterview with Yaw Kobi, *atumtuni*, and Kofi Ampan, *bosotmmuruni*, dd. Kumase, 11 June 1980

6   Interview with Atwi Kwaku (Twenduase *odekro*), Yaw Kobi (*atumtuni*) and Kofi Tuo (*fotosani*), dd. Kumase, 29 May, 11 and 17 June 1980, respectively.

7   IASAS/15, Gyase Stool History, recorded by J. Agyeman-Duah, 2 November, 1962.

8   For a further discussion of the *soodo*, see Kyerematen, *Kingship and Ceremony,* n.d., p. 5.

9   Bowdich, 1819, p. 294. Compare with Bowdich 1821 (a), p. 18.

10   IASAS/96: Abenase Stool History, recorded by J. Agyeman-Duah 11 October 1963.

11   For brief discussions of the *abenase*, see Kyerematen, *Kingship and Ceremony,* n.d., p. 3 and McCaskie, 1974, *passim.*

12   The *afotosanfo* must be distinguished from the *manwerefo* (supervisors of goldworks) and *borumfo* (royal goldsmiths).

13   The British pound continues to be reckoned at ¢2 rather than the official conversion rate which is much higher than that. Thus, £20 is only ¢40. Moreover, the true monetary values can only be measured in terns of traditional Asante currency equivalents.

14   Ramseyer and Klühne, 1875. p. 143.

15   MMA, London, Ms. of an unpublished book by T. B. Freeman, C. 1860, p. 161.

16   Interview with Yaw Kobi, *atumtuni* and Kofi Ampan, *bosommuruni*, dd. 11 June 1980.

17   Interview with Agya Atwi Kwaku, dd. Kumase, 5 June 1980.

18   Interview with Okyeame Antwi Buasiako, dd. Kumase, 3 June 1980.

19   The example of the late Dr. A. A. Y. Kyerematen, former Director of the Cultural Centre, Kumase, who began life as an *mpaboani,* was commonly cited.

20   Interview with Asomfohene Kwaku Kankam II, dd. Kumase, 19 June 1980.

21   Interviews with Asomfohene Kwaku Kankam, dd. Kumase, 3 August 1976 and 19 June 1980. Home here is a house across Antas road in front of *ahemfie*, although the Asonfohene's home town is Kokobra, where he actually lives.

22   IASAS/76, Asomfo Stool History, recorded by J. Agyeman-Duah, 25 May 1963.

23 Interview dd. Kumase, 19 June 1980.
24 See, for example, Huydecoper, 1962: entries for 19, 22, and 24 June and 11 August 1816.
25 See, for example, Dupuis, 1824, pp. 74, 158.
26 Interviews with Nseniehene Kwasi Addal III and Asomfohene Kwaku Kankam II, dd. Kumase, 31 July and 3 August 1976.
27 Bowdich, 1819, p. 298.
28 *L'Explorateur,* 1875-76, II, 622.
29 Interviews with Kwasi Addai III, Nsenieheme, dd. Kumase, 31 July 1976 and 31 May 1980.
30 *Idem.*
31 Bonmat, *L'Explorateur,* 1875-6, II, 622.
32 Bowdich, 1819. p. 256.
33 *Idem.*
34 Interviews with Kwasi Addai III, Nsemiehene, dd. Kumase, 31 July 1976 and 31 May 1980. For ceremonies connected with the enstoolment of a new Asantehene, see Kyerematem, *Kingship and Ceremony,* n.d., pp. 20-28 and Rattray, 1911, p. 102.
35 The memorable missions he could cite were to Bekwae, Teppa Ahafo and Goaso Ahafo, all for the purposes of encouraging local development, although he could not even recall the years he made them.
36 "*Kra Kose*" literally means "take a message to deliver." For the early history of the *nsenie* stool, see IASAS/81, Nsenie Stool History, recorded by J. Agyeman-Duah, 4 July 1963.
37 Interview with Nsenieheme Kwasi Addai III, dd. Kumase, 31 May 1980.
38 IASAS!81: Nsenie Stool History, recorded by J. Agyeman-Duah, 4 July 1963.
39 Bowdich, 1819, p. 298.
40 Interview with Kwasi Addai III, dd. Kumase, 31 May 1980.
41 Ramseyer and Kühne, 1875, p. 7
42 Bowdich, 1819, p. 176.
43 Hutton, 1821, p. 130 and n. See also Bowdich, 1819, p. 40: the *nseniefo* wore "long hair hanging in twists like a thrum nop."
44 Interview with Kwasi Addai III, Nseniehene, dd. Kumase. 31 May 1980.
45 Casely Hayford, 1903, p. 68.
46 *Ibid,* pp. 68, 70.
47 *Idem.*
48 *Idem.*
49 "The Times," 29 July 1873

50 Casely Hayford, 1903, p. 69
51 Brackenbury, 1874, II, 332; Ramseyer and Kühne, 1875, p. 308.
52 Lee, 1835, p. 365; Dupuis, 1824, pp. 90, 152; Bowdich, 1819, p. 296; Ramseyer and Kühne, 1875, p. 308.
53 Bowdich, 1821a, p. 19.
54 Bowdich, 1819, p. 33.
55 Freeman, 1843, pp. 46, 123.
56 *Ibid.*, p 70
57 *Idem.*, pp. 57-62, 129-30, 138-41, 150-2, 175-7
58 *Idem.*
59 Brackenbury, 1874, II, 332; Ramseyer and Kühne, 1875, p. 308- Kwadwo Adusei Kyakya is referred to as "principal linguist" and "head linguist" in Hutton, 1821, pp. 240-1, and "chief linguist" in Hutchinson's Diary in Bowdich, 1819, p. 393.
60 Hutton, 1821, pp. 272-3 and *passim*.
61 Interviews with Mr. C. E. Osei and Baafour Akoto, dd Kunase, 24 and 30 July 1976.
62 Bowdich, 1819, pp. 235-6.
63 The number of *akyeame* has increased from the traditional twelve to fourteen, the most recent addition being Antwi Buasiako, who was elevated to *okyeame* status by Asantehene Opoku Ware II in 1977.
64 Interview with Baafour Akoto, dd. Kumase, 30 July 1976.
65 Interviews with Nsuase Poku and Okyeame Boakye Tenten, dd. Kumase, June 5 and 13, 1980.
66 Rattray, 1911, pp. 94-5.
67 Rattray, 1927, p. 278.
68 The emphasis here is on giving definition to his diplomatic status outside Kumase as opposed to his service in the foreign bureaus in Kumase, which is discussed in Chapter 5. For a biographical profile of Owusu Ansa, see Owusu Mensa, 1974.
69 *Gold Coast,* C. 266, 1873, pp. 160-1, encl. in no. 99: Salmon to Hennessy, dd. Cape Coast, 19 October 1872.
70 *Affairs,* C. 3064, 1881, p. 89: Owusu Ansa to Griffith, dd. Cape Coast, 9 February 1881.
71 MMA: Freeman to Osborne, dd. Cape Coast, 22 August 1854.
72 *Further Correspondence,* C. 3386, 1881, p. 8.
73 "The West African Herald," 31 March 1871; *Affairs,* C. 3064, 1881, p. 13; *Correspondence,* C. 670, 1872, p. 15; *Gold Coast,* C. 266-1, 1873, pp. 295-8; Wilks, 1975, pp. 616-21.
74 *Further Correspondence,* C. 3386, 1881, pp. 32-3.
75 For a biographical profile of Owusu Dome, see ACBP/39 in

Asantesem, 10 (January 1979), 9-15, complied by T. McCaskie and I. Wilks.

76 Hutton, 1821, pp. 129-31.
77 Dupuis, 1824, introduction p. xxvii; Hutton, 1821, pp. 128-32.
78 Ibid., pp. 131-2.
79 Ibid., pp. 154-5.
80 NBKG 315: entry for 11 February 1821.
81 Dupuis, 1824, pp. 187, 197.
82 NBKG 351: entry for 11 February 1821.
83 Reindorf, 1895, pp. 175-6.
84 Dupuis, 1824, introduction, p. xxviii.
85 Cruickshank, 1853, I, 340.
86 Dupuis, 1824, introduction, p. xi-xii.
87 For outlines of early career, see IASAS/170: Heman, recorded by J. Agyeman-Duah, 24 January 1966.
88 Dupuis, 1824, p. 50.
89 Oral information narrated to the writer by Barima Owusu Ansa, dd. Kumase, 23 July 1976.
90 Reindorf, 1895, p. 172.
91 Interviews with Barima Owusu Ansa and Baafour Akoto, dd. Kumase, 22 and 30 July 1976, respectively. For written accounts of the Gyaman mission, see West African Sketches, 1824, pp. 228-32; Bowdich, 1819, pp. 244-5; and Delafosse, 1908, pp. 213-2.
92 Interview with Barima Cwusu Ansa, dd. Kumase, 22 July 1976.
93 Bowdich, 1819, p. 79.
94 Priestley, 1969, passim.
95 Described in traditional accounts as wearing "aban ataade," that is, uniform.
96 Reindorf, 1895, pp. 180-1.
97 "Royal Gold Coast Gazette," Cape Coast, June 1823.
98 For additional information of biographical interest, see ACBP/3 in Asante Seminar, 2 (April 1975), 5-7 complied by I. Wilks.
99 See, for example, "Royal Gold Coast Gazette," Cape Coast, 11 and 18 March, and 7 June 1823.
100 Interview with Barima Owusu Ansa, dd. Kumase, 23 July 1976.
101 Wilks, 1975, p. 30.
102 Bowdich, 1819, p. 162; Dupuis, 1824, introduction p. xix.
103 In Twi, "da bone," bad day.
104 Huydecoper, 1962: entry for 11 August 1816.
105 Bowdich, 1819, p. 79.
106 Ramseyer and Kühne, 1875, p. 307.
107 Idem.

108   Dupuis, 1824, introduction p. xix.
109   Meredith, 1812, p. 152.
110   Interview with Okyeame Boakye Tenten, dd. Kumase, 1 August 1976.
111   Affairs, C. 3064, 1881, p. 48. For an analysis of Akyampon Yaw's resident ambassadorship, see Rene Baesjou, "An Asante Ambassador to the Gold Coast," Leiden, 1979.
112   Ramseyer and Kühne, 1875, p. 213.
113   "The African Times," xii, no. 140, 23 February 1873, p. 97.
114   Ramseyer and Kühne, 1875, pp. 57, 136; "African Times," 1 February and 1 March 1877, and 1 July 1881. For a discussion of capital punishment, see Wilks, 1975, pp. 355-6, 592-5, 638-9, and McCaskie, 1974, passim.
115   "African Times," xii, no. 140, 23 February 1873; Ramseyer and Kühne, 1875, p. 308.
116   Ramseyer and Kühne, 1875, p. 182; see also Gold Coast, C. 266-1, 1873, p. 160.
117   Ranseyer and Kühne, 1875, pp. 94 309; Brackenbury, 1874, II, 331; "The Times," 29 July 1873.
118   Furguson and Wilks: interviews with Baafour Akoto, dd. Kumase, 31 October and 2 November 1973, in Wilks, 1975, p. 563.
119   Dampans are "small halls which open on the streets": Ramseyer and Kühne, 1875, p. 53. Also see Bowdich, 1819, p. 305; Dupuis, 1824, p. 83; Stanley, 1874, p. 227; McCaskie, 1874, pp. 169-70; Wilks, 1975, pp. 381-3.
120   Interview dd. Kumase, 30 July 1976.
121   Interview with Nseniehene Kwasi Addai III, dd. Kumase, 31 July 1976.
122   Mpaninsen might be regarded as wisdon and knowledge acquired through the elders.
123   Interview dd. Kumase, 22 July 1976.
124   Casely Hayford, 1902, pp. 69-70.
125   Interview with Baafour Akoto, dd. Kumase, 30 July 1971.
126   Vol. xxiv, no. 266, 1 November 1883, p. 122.
127   Bowdich, 1819, p. 249.
128   Meredith, 1812, p. 19.
129   Hutton, 1819, p. 292.
130   Casely Hayford, 1903, pp. 70-71.
131   Dupuis, 1824, introduction p. xix.
132   Meredith, 1812, pp. 105-6.
133   Correspondence, C. 670, 1872, p. 23, encl. in no. 13: Salmon to Kennedy, dd. Cape Coast, 19 October 1871.

134 Casely Hayford, 1903, p. 70.
135 *Ibid.*, p. 69.
136 Interview with Barima Owusu Ansa, dd. Kumase, 22 July 1976.
137 Daendels, 1964, p. 168.
138 *Further Correspondence,* C. 7917, 1896, pp. 183-5.
139 PRO. CO. 96/64: Pine to Newcastle, dd. 9 January 1864.
140 Brackenbury, 1874, II, 44.
141 Bowdich, 1819, pp. 248-9.
142 Lee, 1835, p. 168.
143 Bowdich, 1819, pp. 392-3.
144 For a biographical profile of Asante Agyei, see ACBP/6 in *Asante Seminar (Asantesem),* 3 (June 1974), 5-7, compiled by I Wilks.
145 *Further Correspondence,* C. 7917 1896, p. 38.
146 Owusu Taseamandi was the son of the heir apparent Osei Kwadwo. His grandmother, Tamia, was a Gyaman royal (sister of Gyamanhene Adimkra), who was captured and taken to Kumase after the revolt of 1818-19. "Taseamandi," which literally means "squanderer of the state," might have originated as a nickname.
147 *Affairs,* C. 3064, 1881, p. 17.
148 Brackenbury, 1874, II, 266-70; *Further Correspondence,* C. 922, 1874, p. 45.
149 Hutton, 1821, pp. 129-131.
150 Dupuis, 1824, introduction, p. xxxii.
151 *Affairs,* C. 3064, 1881, p. 82. Compare with a similar statement made by Owusu Ansa on an earlier occasion to Griffith that no envoy would "dare to say anything in a message which had not been told him by the King:" *ibid.,* p. 50; and with Brackenbury's observation: "that envoys from a king such as the Monarch of Ashanti is represented to be should state anything they have not previously been told to say, seems incredible," *ibid.,* p. 75.
152 *Further Correspondence,* C. 7918, 1896, pp. 122-3.
153 Ramseyer and Kühne, 1875, p. 157.
154 For a further discussion of ceremonial swords, see Kyerematen, 1964, *passim.*
155 Interview with Kwaku Kankam II, Asomfohene, dd. Kumase, 19 June 1980.
156 Interviews with Asomfohene Kwaku Kankam, dd. Kumase, 3 August 1976 and 19 June 1980. The significance of the star is grounded in the Asante maxim: "*Nyankon nsoroma, Onte ne te; ote Nyame te,*" that is, "a child of the Sumprene Being. I do not depend on myself; my illumination is only a reflection of His."
157 Interviews with Yaw Boadu (*mpomponsuni*), Kofi Ampan (*bosom-*

muruni) and Kwabena Poku (*bosommuru denkyemni*), dd. Kumase, 6 June 1980, and with Kwaku Kankam, dd. Kumase, 19 June 1980.

158   Reindorf, 1895, pp. 127, 138-9.
159   Hence the saying, "*wode sekan twa na antwa a na yefa akuma,*" that is, "it is when a knife fails to cut that we use an axe."
160   Interviews with Asomfohene, Kwaku Kankam, dd. Kumase, 3 August 1976 and 19 June 1980.
161   Brackenbury, 1874, II, p. 51.
162   *Despatches*, C. 907, 1874, p. 6.
163   Meredith, 1812, pp. 147-8, 151; Dupuis, 1824, pp. 125, 140, 261; Freeman, 1843, p. 3.
164   Dupuis, 1824, introduction, n. xxix.
165   For a further discussion of symbols, see Reindorf, 1895, pp 124-8; Kyerematen, 1964, pp. 29-42.
166   Bowdich, 1819, p. 132.
167   *Affairs*, C. 3064, 1881, p. 138.
168   Interview with Barima Owusu Ansa, dd. Kumase, 22 July 1976.
169   Bowdich, 1819, p. 294.
170   Interview with Kwaku Kankam, Asomfohene, dd. Kumase, 3 August 1976.
171   Ellis, 1893, p. 252.
172   *Papers*, C. 1343, 1876, p. 55: Strahan to Carnarvon, dd. Cape Coast, 8 January 1874.
173   *Ibid.*, pp. 61-2.
174   Affairs, C. 3064, 1881, pp. 111, 115.
175   *Ibid.*, p. 14.
176   *Ibid.*, pp. 5-6: Griffith to Kimberley, dd. Elmina, 5 January, 1881.
177   Beecham, 1841, pp. 93-4.
178   Bowdich, 1819, p. 129.
179   Dupuis, 1824, p. 197.
180   Ellis, 1893, p. 174.
181   *Affairs*, C. 3064, pp. i, 14.

Chapter 3

1   Bowdich, 1819, p. 24.
2   *Ibid*, p. 25.
3   See, for example, Plange's Journal in Brackenbury, 1874, I, 43-48; Reade, 1874, pp. 100-101; *Further Correspondence,* C. 819, 1873; *Despatches*, C. 907, 1874, *passim.*
4   Interview with Asomfohene Kwaku Kankam, dd. Kumase, 19 June

1980.
5   Interview with Kofi Ampam (*bosommuruni*), Yaw Boadu
    (*mponponsuni*) and Kwabena Poku (*bosomuru denkyemni*), dd.
    Kumase, 6 June 1980.
6   Bowdich, 1819, p. 66.
7   Reindorf, 1895, p. 173.
8   Ricketts, 1831, p. 20.
9   Reindorf, 1895, pp. 181-2.
10 Lee, 1835, p. 365.
11 Bowdich, 1819, p. 176.
12 Rattray, 1927, pp. 12-4.
13 Dupuis, 1824, p. 211 and n.
14 Bowdich, 1819, p. 390.
15 Rattray, 1911, p. 81.
16 Daendels, 1964, pp. 119-29, entry for 7 June.
17 Dupuis, 1824, pp. 158-166.
18 Daendels, 1964, p. 89, entry for 20 April 1816.
19 Interviews with Yaw Boadu (*mponponsuni*), Kofi Ampam (*bosom-muruni*), and Kwabena Poku (*bosommuru denkyemni*), dd.
    Kumase, 6 June 1980.
20 Brackenbury, 1874, I, 317-9; *Further Correspondence,* C. 1006
    1874, pp. 1, 9, 11; Ellis, 1873, pp. 349-50.
21 *Affairs,* C. 3064, 1881, pp. 135-6, 150.
22 *Further Correspondence,* C. 7917, 1896, p. 20: Agyemnan
    Prempe to Governor-in-Chief, dd. Kumase, 7 April 1890.
23 Dupuis, 1824, introduction p. xxviii.
24 Bowdich, 1819, pp. 123-4.
25 Ramseyer and Kühne, 1875, p. 307.
26 Dupuis, 1824, p. 168. Hutton, 1821, pp. 128-32.
27 See, for example, Dupuis, 1824, introduction p. xxvii.
28 *Further Correspondence,* C. 1006, 1874; no. 1, p. 1. 29.
29 *Affairs,* C. 3064, 1881, p. 6.
30 *Ibid.,* pp. 70-1.
31 *Idem.*
32 *Further Correspondence,* C. 7917, 1896, p. 20: Agyeman Prempe
    to Griffith, dd. Kumase, 7 April 1890, and ibid., p. 23.
33 Daendels, 1964, p. 84: entry for 13 and 15 April 1816.
34 *Affairs,* C. 3064, 1881, p. 134.
35 *Idem.*
36 Ramseyer and Kühne, 1875, p. 306.
37 *Further Correspondence,* C. 7917, 1896, p. 23: report of pro-
    ceedings of meeting of the Kofi Apea mission with Holmes, dd.

Cape Coast, 8 July 1890. Yaw Boaten's identity is unclear. He could have been the Kra Boadu *okyeame.*

38 PRO. CO. 96/263: Maxwell to Chamberlain, dd. 28 December 1894.

39 Interview with Asomfohene Kwaku Kankan, dd. Kumase, 3 August 1976.

40 See, for example, *Affairs,* C. 3064, 1881, pp. 113, 134, 137-8; Dupuis, 1824, introduction pp. xxvii-xxix.

41 Interview with Baafour Akoto, dd. Kumase, 30 July 1976.

42 See, for example, *Affairs,* C. 3064, 1881, p. 101.

43 Brackenbury, 1874, II, 51-4.

44 *Despatches,* C. 907, 1874, p. 9.

45 PRO. CO. 267/52: Collier to Croker, dd. Cape Coast, 16 April 1820; Dupuis, 1824, pp. 180-190. For an analysis of the inconsistencies of British policy during this period, see Collins, 1962, pp. 79-137.

46 *Further Correspondence,* C. 7918, p. 15: Griffith to Asante embassy, dd. Cape Coast, 21 December 1894; pp. 18-9: Asante embassy to Governor, dd. Cape Coast, 29 December 1894.

47 See, for example, *ibid.,* pp. 59-61, 87, 97-8, 109, 122, 138.

48 For a similar conclusion, see Wilks, 1975, pp. 41-44.

49 Huydecoper, 1962, p. 27: entry for 18 June 1816.

50 For an extensive discussion of travel, distances and their impact on the central administration, see Wilks, 1975, pp. 29-36.

51 *Affairs,* C. 3064, 1881, p. 52.

52 Brackenbury, 1874, II, 38-42.

53 Daendels, 1964, p. 256.

54 *Ibid.,* pp. 148-9, entry for 11 July 1816.

55 Dupuis, 1824, introduction, p. xxvi.

56 Bowdich, 1819, p. 23.

57 *Affairs,* C. 3064, 1881, p. 13.

58 Dupuis, 1824, introduction pp. cviii-cix.

59 *Correspondence,* C. 670, 1872, p. 19.

60 Cruickshank, 1853, 1, 266. For a general discussion of Asante oaths, see Rattray, 1911, *passim.*

61 Hutton, 1821, pp. 311-11.

62 *Idem.*

63 See, for example, *Affairs,* C. 3064, 1881, p. 63.

64 Dupuis, 1824, p. 252; Beecham, 1841, pp. 39-41.

65 For an outline of the Asen rebellion, see Claridge, 1815, I, 237-54.

66 Kwaaten Pete, ACBP/52 by I. Wilks in *Asantesem,* 10 (Jan. 1979),

31-36.

67   Dupuis, 1824, p. 254. Also see *ibid.*, p. 7; Beecham, 1841 pp. 40-1; Freeman, 1844, p. 2.
68   Reindorf, 1895, pp. 174-5; Hutton 1821, pp. 122-39; Dupuis, 1824, introduction, p. xii; Beecham, 1841, pp. 56-7.
69   Reindorf, 1895, pp. 187-8.
70   PR0. CO. 96/68: Conran to Cardwell, dd. Cape Coast, 8 September 1865.
71   Brackenbury, 1874, I, p. 31.
72   *Gold Coast,* C. 266, 1873, no. 10, p. 6.
73   *Ibid.*, pp. 295-8. The Dutch appeared to have found a plausible justification for the rearrest of Akyampon Yaw in his failure to comply with his oath: Ramseyer and Kühne, 1875, pp. 131-2, 170.
74   Brackenbury, 1874, 1, 78.
75   *Papers,* C. 266, 1873, p. 380: Cwusu Ansa to Harley, dd. Cape Coast, 21 March 1873.
76   *Further Correspondence,* C. 7918, 1896, pp. 45-6.
77   Dupuis, 824, p. 165.
78   *Military Return,* C. 274, 1874, and *Further Despatches,* C. 804, 1873, *passim.*
79   Interview with Baafour Akoto, dd. Kumase, 30 July 1976.
80   Interviews with Barima Owusu Ansa and Mr. C. E. Ossi, dd. Kumase, 24 and 29 July 1979.
81   Interviews with Okyeame Boakye Tenten and Asomfohene Kwaku Kankam, dd. Kumase, 1 and 3 August 1976.
82   Interview with Okyeame Boakye Tenten, dd. Kumase, 1 August 1976.
83   Cruickshank, 1853, I, 341-2. See also *L'Explorateur,* 1875-76, II, 623; Gros, 1884, pp. 194-5; "The Royal Gold Coast Gazette," Cape Coast, 7 June 1823.
84   Wilks, 1975, p. 441. Also see Bowdich, 1819, p. 256.
85   Rattray, 1911, pp. 114-5, 111.
86   Interview with Barima Cwusu Ansa, dd. 24 July 1976.
87   Bowdich, 1819, p. 293.
88   *Affairs,* C. 3064, 1881, pp. 42-3.
89   *Ibid.*, p. 55: statement of hammockman Kwadwo Obimpe, dd. Cape Coast, 24 March 1879. Hammockman Tanfuben also added that it was the Gyamanhene who gave them subsistence money. For a further discussion of the Gyaman mission of 1878-9, see Wilks, 1975, pp. 621-5.
90   GNA, Accra, ADN 1/21461: Huydecoper to Smith, dd. 9 August

1979.

91 *Affairs*, C. 3064, 1881, pp. 52-3: Owusu Ansa to Ussher, dd. Cape Coast, 17 May 1880.

92 Interview with Asomfohene Kwaku Kankam, dd. Kunase, 19 June 1980.

93 Boyle, 1874, p. 157.

94 *Further Correspondence*, C. 7917, 1896, pp. 43-4: Agyeman Prempe to Griffith, dd. Kumase, 20 January 1891.

95 *Ibid.*, pp. 32-3.

96 *Ibid.*, pp. 43-4.

97 *Ibid.* p. 70: Agyeman Prempe to Governor, dd. Kumase, 7 May 1891.

98 *Further Correspondence*, C. 4906, 1886, pp. 1, 6.

99 *Further Correspondence*, C. 5357, 1888, pp. 4-5: Griffith to Queen Mother *et al.*, dd. Christiansborg, 27 August 1886.

l00 *Further Correspondence*, C. 5615, 1888, p. 19.

101 *Further Correspondence*, C. 3386, 1882, p. 1.

102 *Further Correspondence*, C. 7917, 1896, pp. 43-4.

103 *Ibid.*, and C. 7918, 1896, *passim*.

104 Bowdich, 1819, p. 134.

105 See, for example, Reindorf, 1895, p. 171.

106 Bowdich, 1819, pp. 71, 83, 89, 112.

107 Brackenbury, 1874, I, 81.

108 Dupuis, introduction pp. xvi-xvii.

109 Hutton, 1821, p. 125.

110 Bowdich, 1819, pp. 93-4. This official's identity is still unclear, even if the name "Ocranameah" is understood as perhaps Okra Nuama.

111 Hope-Smith to Bowdich, dd. Cape Coast, 25 August 1817 in Bowdich, 1819, pp. 123-5, 131.

112 Daendels, 1964, pp. 165-6: entry for 4 September 1816; pp. 275-7: Huydecoper to Daendels, dd. Kumase, 9 December 1819; p. 279: Osei Tutu Kwame to Daendels, dd. Kumase, 29 November 1816.

113 Bowdich, 1819, pp. 123-4.

114 Wilks, 1975, pp. 156-9.

115 Bowdich, 1819, p. 124.

116 *Ibid.*, p. 168. At least one source claims that Tando did not make his fortune in Wassa: Daendels, 1964, pp. 123-4.

117 Bowdich, 1819, pp. 123-4.

118 Ramseyer and Kühne, 1875, p. 208.

119 *Affairs*, C. 3064, 1881, p. 96.

120   Bowdich, 1819, p. 319
121   Rattray, 1911, p. 299.
122   Ramseyer and Kühne, 1874, pp. 261-2, 291.

Chapter 4

1   Interview with Okyeame Akoto, dd. Kumase, 30 July 1976.
2   Rattray, 1911, p. 92.
3   *Further Correspondence,* C. 7918, p. 108.
4   Interview with Agya Atwi Kwaku, dd. Kumase, 5 June 1980.
5   Rattray, 1911, pp. 40-1
6   *Ibid.*, p. 42.
7   Interview with Barima Owusu Ansa, dd. Kumase, 23 July 1976.
8   Bowdich, 1819, p. 277.
9   Numerous references appear in the NBKG series and in Daendel's *Journal*, 1964, for instance, regarding the King's "Accra" being sent to demand the "kostgeld" (groundrent).
10   NBKG, 351: entries for 16 and 17 February 1821 (trans. L. Yarak).
11   Dupuis, 1824, p. 168.
12   A problem becomes evident in interpreting the use of the word "slave" in the sources. In a number of instances the English translation of the Twi word "*akoa*" may be more accurately rendered as servant or "attendant" rather than "slave" in the literal sense of the word. A case in point involves Anno Panin who served on the staff of ambassador Owusu Dome in Cape Coast in 1820. Though he is described as a "slave," Anno Panin was in actual fact the Ananta *okyeame*, who also acted as *okyeame* ("spokesman") to the embassy. Anno Panin was engaged in independent diplomatic assignments from Owusu Dome to Asantehene Osei Tutu Kwame and is not known to have been a "slave," although Dupuis (1824, p. 197) and Hutton (1821, pp. 129-30) described him as such.
13   Further Despatches, C. 803, 1873, encl. 3 in no. 1: Dawson to Harley, dd. Kumase, 19 December 1872.
14   Ramseyer and Kühne, 1875, p. 49.
15   *Further Correspondence,* C. 5615, 1888. p. 148.
16   *Further Correspondence,* C. 7917, 1896, no. 13, p. 38.
17   *Ibid.*, no. 68 and encl. pp. 170-3.
18   Interview with Nsumankwaahene Dumfe Gyeabour III, dd. Kumase, 29, July 1976.
19   Brackenbury, 1874, II, 335-7.
20   Interview with C. E. Osei and Nsumankwaahene Dumfe Gyeabour

III, dd. Kumase, 29 July 1976.

21 The contemporary records lumped *nsumankwaafo* and "Asante Nkramofo" together as "fetishmen." While Sawu is not a traditional *nsumankwaa* name (like Dumfe, Ahene or Asabre), its Asante origin might possibly be taken as an indication that he was an *nsumankwaani* rather than a member of the "Asante Nkramo" who bore typically Muslim names.

22 Boyle, 1874, pp. 293-4; *Further Correspondence,* C. 1006, 1874, p. 11; Hutton, 1821, pp. 128-132, 323; Ramseyer and Kühne, 1875 pp. 269, 271.

23 For the general outlines of Akyaawa Yikwan's career, see ACBP/ 466 in *Asantesem*, (July 1979), pp. 30-37.

24 For a casualty list, see Ricketts, 1831, pp. 124-5.

25 Reindorf, 1895, pp. 140, 250, 285.

26 PR0. CO 267/95: Osei Yaw Akoto to Hingston, dd. Kumase, 12 April 1828.

27 For a copy of the treaty, see Claridge, 1915, 1, 409-411.

28 Reindorf, 1895, pp. 253-4

29 *Further Papers,* C. 456, 1855, pp. 9-10: Kwaku Dua to Hill, dd. Kumase, 28 November 1853.

30 *Idem.*

31 IASAS/76, Asomfo Stool History, recorded by J. Agyeman-Duah, 25 May 1963. Also see interview with Asomfohene Kwaku Kankam, dd. Kumase, 19 June 1980.

32 PR0. CO. 96/43, Bird to Newcastle, dd. Cape Coast, 27 August 1858.

33 *Idem.*

34 *Ibid.*, record of "palaver," dd. 25, 26, and 28 June 1858.

35 *Ibid.*, Bird to Newcastle, dd. Cape Coast, 27 August 1858.

36 *Ibid.*, minutes of a public meeting, dd. Cape Coast, 12 July 1858

37 For career profiles of Asabi Antwi, see Asante Seminar, 5 (November 1976), 26-8 and *Asantesem* 6 (December 1976), 14-20 compiled by J. Adjaye and I. Wilks, respectively.

38 *Further Correspondence,* C. 894, 1874, pp. 60-62: Wolseley to Kofi Kakari, dd. Praso, 2 January 1874.

39 *Despatches,* C. 907, 1874, pp. 5-6: Wolseley to Kimberley, dd. Praso, 13 January 1874; Ramseyer and Kühne, 1875, p. 270.

40 *Despatches,* C. 907, 1874, p. 1: Wolseley to Kimberley, dd. Adanse Hills, 24 January 1874; Ramseysr and Kühne, 1875, p. 265.

41 *Despatches,* C. 907, 1874, pp. 12-13.

42 *Further Correspondence,* C. 922, 1874, pp. 26, 44.

43 *Ibid.*, pp. 45-7; Brackenbury, 1874, II, 266-270.
44 *Further Correspondence,* C. 1006, 1874, p. 1: Maxwell to Kimberley, dd. 13 March 1874.
45 *Further Correspondence,* C. 1006, 1874, p. 9: Maxwell to Kimberley, dd. Cape Coast, 18 March 1874.
46 Kofi Nti attended Surrey County School in England. He subsequently served in the British colonial administration in Trinidad before returning to the Gold Coast. He was appointed clerk to Agyeman Prempe I and accompanied the Asantehene when he was exiled to the Seychelles.
47 *Affairs,* C. 3064, 1881, pp. 12, 16.
48 Reindorf, 1895, p. 165, *Affairs,* C. 3064, 1881, pp. 47-8.
49 *Affairs,* C. 3064, 1881, p. 14.
50 *Ibid.*, p. 12.
51 *Ibid.*, p. 17, encl. in no. 15.
52 *Ibid.*, pp. 154-55; Ellis, 1893, p. 365. Owusu Taseanandi thereafter quickly disappeared from the scene. He committed suicide, possibly to resist exile: Ellis, 1883, p. 311; Burton and Cameron, 1883, II, 321
53 *Affairs,* C. 3064, 1881, p. 12
54 *Ibid.*, p. 18.
55 PRO. CO. 96/58: Pine to Newcastle, dd. Cape Coast, 10 December 1862. Kwasi Gyani may also have been an assistant aide to the Bantamanhene: See MMA: West to Boyce, dd. Cape Coast, 11 March 1863.
56 There is also the possibility of an interpreter's distortion.
57 This explanation was reiterated by Okyeame Kofi Bene on 18 February. See *Affairs,* C. 3064, 1881. p. 87.
58 *Affairs,* C. 3064, 1881, pp. 69, 86.
59 Burton and Cameron, 1883, II, 319.
60 *Affairs,* C. 3064, 1881, p. 86.
61 *Ibid.*, pp. 70-2.
62 *Ibid.* p. 365-6.
63 *Ibid.* p. 88.
64 *Ibid.* pp. 111, 113-4.
65 *Ibid.*, p. 127. Also see ACBP/4, *Asante Seminar* 6 (Dec 1976) 5-13, complied by T. McCaskie and I. Wilks.
66 *Affairs,* C. 3064, 1881.
67 Interview with Okyeame Boakye Tenten, dd. Kumase, 8 April 1971. Also see J. Lewin, fieldnotes: interview with Kwadwo Afodo, dd. Kumase, 29 November 1970.
68 Boakye's identity has not yet been fully ascertained. He may not

have been an uterine brother since Boakye Tenten had only one full sibling, Yaa Amankwaa. Kwaku Dua was in reality an adopted son of Boakye Tenten. He was his wife's sister's son.

69   For a full list, see *Affairs*, C. 3064, 1881, pp. 135-6, 150.
70   Interview with Okyeame Boakye Tenten, dd. Kumase, 8 August 1976.
71   *Despatches,* C. 907, 1874, p. 8: Kofi Kakari to Wolseley, dd. 21 January 1874.
72   *Papers*, C. 1402, 1875, p. 114: Mensa Bonsu to Governor, dd. Kumase, 8 November 1876.
73   *Affairs*, C. 3064, 1881, pp. 137-8, 140.
74   *Ibid.*, pp. 134-5.
75   Ellis, 1883, pp. 306-11.
76   *Further Correspondence,* C. 4054, 1884, pp. 50, 82.
77   Gros, n.d., p. 152
78   *Affairs*, C. 3064, 1881, p. 4.
79   *Ibid.*, pp. 150, 153. In place of the Golden Axe, Boakye Tenten suggested that a silver-topped cane given by Queen Victoria to Asantehene Kwaku Dua Panin might be copied in gold and used by future envoys of Asante on missions to the British administrators at Cape Coast.
80   *Affairs*, C. 3064, 1881, pp. 152, 155, 190-1, 196.
81   Ellis, 1893, p. 369.
82   For general sketches of Boakye Tenten's career, see ACBP/4 in *Asante Seminar*, 6 (December 1976), 5-13, compiled by T. McCaskie and I. Wilks.
83   *Further Correspondence,* C. 7918, 1896, p. 1.
84   *Further Correspondence,* C. 7917, 1896, pp. 201-2.
85   Wilks, 1975, pp. 641-54.
86   *Further Correspondence,* C. 7918, 1896, p. 13.
87   *Ibid.*, pp. 54, 201-2.
88   *Ibid.*, pp. 122-3.
89   *Furrther Correspondence,* C. 7917, 1896, p. 234.
90   Interview with Barima Owusu Ansa, dd. Kumase, 22 July 1976.
91   For the general outlines of Kwame Boaten's career, see ACBP/8 in *Asantesem* (March 1978), 12-21, compiled by I. Wilks.
92   PRO. CO. 96/249 and *Further Correspondence,* C. 7918, 1896, pp. 2-4: notes of interview of Asante embassy with Governor.
93   *Ibid.*, p. 14.
94   *Further Correspondence,* C. 7917, 1896, pp. 47, 211.
95   *Further Correspondence,* C. 7918, 1896, pp. 5, 26-33.
96   *Ibid.*, pp. 14, 26-33.

97   *Further Correspondence,* C. 7917, 1896, pp. 201-2: Prempe to Governor, dd. 28 June 1894.
98   *Further Correspondence,* C. 7918, 1896, p. 56: Maxwell to Ripon, dd. Accra, 11 April 1895.
99   *Ibid.,* pp. 40-1: Asante embassy to Governor, dd. Cape Coast, 3 January 1895.
100   *Ibid.,* p. 15: Griffith to Asante embassy, dd. Cape Coast, 21 December 1894
101   *Ibid.,* pp. 18-19, 45-6, 56.
102   *Ibid.,* p. 22: Griffith to Ripon, received 12 February 1895.
103   *Ibid.,* pp. 41-2.
104   *Ibid.,* p. 54, 56, 59-61.
105   PRO. CO. 96/256: minutes by Branston, dd. 10 April 1895.
106   *Further Correspondence,* C. 7918, 1896, pp. 90-100: Meade to Owusu Ansa, dd. 9 September 1895.
107   Wilks, 1975, pp. 650-3.
108   *Further Correspondence,* C. 7918, 1896, p. 108: Harris to Selbourne, dd. London, 26 October 1895.
100   *Ibid.,* pp. 118-9, 121-2.
110   *Ibid.,* pp. 125-6.
111   PRO. CO. 96/262.

Chapter 5

1   Dupuis, 1824, p. 90.
2   Wilks, 1975, p. 40.
3   For a detailed discussion of Osei Tutu Kwame's reform in administration, see Tordoff, 1962, pp. 399-417; Hagan, 1971, pp. 43-62; Wilks, 1967, pp. 206-39; and Wilks, 1975, pp. 129-30, 332-3, 416-7, 468-70. Osei Tutu Kwame earned the appellation "Bonsu" by reason of his having been the first Asantehene to reach the Atlantic Ocean (ref. Twi: *bonsu,* to touch the water). The praise name " Bonsu" may also have originated from the Twi word meaning "whale."
4   Bowdich, 1819, p. 246.
5   Wilks, 1975, pp. 605-32, provides a detailed discussion of Owusu Ansa's contribution to the administrative reorganization of Mensa Bonsu.
6   Bowdich in a letter to Hope Smith, dd. Kumase, 9 July 1817, cited in Bowdich, 1819, p. 82.
7   *Ibid.,* p. 121.
8   Though Twi documents did exist in the nineteenth century, there

is no evidence as yet that a Twi wing of the chancery developed.

9   Reindorf. 1895, pp. 132-3.
10   Bowdich, 1819, p. 232. For a career profile of al-Ghamba', see ACBP/13, *Asantesem*, 2 (April 1975), 8-10.
11   Bowdich, 1819, p. 240.
12   *Ibid.*, p. 296.
13   NBKG. 350, f. 64: entry for 15 May 1817 (trans., L. Yarak).
14   Robertson, 1819, p. 151.
15   Rattray, 1929, pp. 109-10; Levtzion, 1966, p. 115; Wilks, 1975, pp. 344-5; Bowdich, 1819, pp. 232, 243-4; Huydecoper, entries for 29 and 30 April, 1816; Lee, 1835, pp. 164, 174; Dupuis, 1824, p. 250.
16   Dupuis, 1824, pp. 97-98. For Muslim role in Asante, see Levtzion, 1968, pp. 181-7; Wilks, 1961, pp. 14-29 and Wilks, 1966, pp. 318-41.
17   Bowdich, 1819, p. 228. Oral evidence widely confirms this prohibition.
18   NBKG. 350: Osei Tutu Kwame to Daendels, dd. Kumase, 29 November 1816.
19   Interview with Owusu Ansa, dd. 23 July 1976.
20   NBKG. 716: Governor to Minister of Colonies, dd. Elmina, 10 May 1859.
21   State Archives, Copenhagen. *Generaltoldkammerets Archiv* 1760-1848. Sager til Guineiske Journaler 1778-1859. No. 1729/1819: Letter from Reierson, dd. 16 March 1819.
22   *Ibid.*, no. 31/1821: Letter from Steffens, dd. 28 January 1821.
23   *Ibid.*, no. 1848/1820: Letter from Osei Tutu Kwame, dd. Kumase, 17 May 1819. Also see R. A. Kea, "On Preferential Trade Terms: A letter from Asantehene Osei Bonsu to the Danish Governor (1819)" in *Asantesem*, 10 (January 1979), 55-7.
24   Reindorf, 1895, p. 235.
25   Freeman, 1843, p. 143; Owusu Ansa was baptized as John, Owusu Nkwantabisa as William.
26   For examples of letters prepared by Owusu Nkwantabisa, see PRO. CO. 96/11: Kwaku Dua to Maclean, dd. Kunase, 17 April 1847.
27   *Despatches,* C. 703, 1853, Wharton to Osborne, dd. Cape Coast 13 July 1861.
28   *Despatches,* C. 703, 1853, p. 8: Owusu Ansa to Hill, dd. Kumase, 16 April 1853; see also PRO. CO. 96/27: Hill to Newcastle, dd. Cape Coast, 8 April 1853.
29   MMA, London: Freeman to Osborne, dd. Cape Coast, 22 August

1854 and Freeman to General Secretaries, dd. Cape Coast, 13 July 1861.

30   MMA, West African Biographical Material, Box 1, pp. 6-7: Tregaskis to Owusu Ansa, dd. London, 22 August 1877.

31   PR0. CO. 96/76, No. 34: Owusu Ansa to Ussher, dd. Kumase, 23 March 1868, in Kennedy to Buckingham, dd. Freetown, 13 May 1868.

32   Ramseyer and Kühne, 1875, pp. 7-8.

33   *Correspondence,* C. 670, 1872, pp. 11, 13.

34   Ramseyer and Kühne, 1875, p. 7.

35   "The West African Herald," 31 March 1871.

36   *Despatches,* C. 266, 1873, p. 86: Kakari to Salmon, dd. 20 February 1872, in Hennessy to Kimberley, dd. 1 June 1872.

37   Johnson, 1971, pp. 25-6.

38   *Papers,* C. 1402, 1876, p. 81, enclosure in no. 70: Mensa Bonsu to Strahan, dd. Kumase, 11 June 1875.

39   *Ibid.,* p. 81: Mensa Bonsu to Strahan, dd. Kumase, 11 June 1875.

40   *Ibid.,* pp. 82-3, enclosure 5 in no. 70: Mensa Bonsu to Straham, dd. Kumase, 16 July 1875.

41   *Ibid.,* pp. 71-2, enclosure 1 in no. 65: Mensa Bonsu to Lyall *et al.,* dd. Kumase, 19 July 1875.

42   *Ibid.,* pp. 86-7: Mensa Bonsu to Strahan, dd. Kumase, 26 August 1875.

43   PRO. CO. 96/126, No. 83: Owusu Ansa to Kay, dd. Kumase, 10, 15, and 16 March 1879, in Lees to Hicks-Beach, dd. Accra, 14 April 1879.

44   *Papers,* C. 1402, 1876, p. 92: Bonnat to Strahan, dd. Cape Coast, 30 September 1875.

45   This translation of the original text which first appeared in French in *L'Explorateur,* 1876, III, 238, is based on that of M. Johnson, 1971, p. 27. Wilks, 1975, n. 610 suggests that "Accrono" might well be "Akroso" and also confirms Owusu Ansa's authorship of this document.

46   ADM, 1/2/361: enclosure in Huydecoper to Smith, dd. Banda, 9 August 1879.

47   *Further Correspondence,* C. 7917, 1896, p. 216: interview between Owusu Ansa and Griffith, dd. Accra, 13 June 1889.

48   *Ibid.,* p. 217.

49   *Idem.*

50   *Ibid,* pp. 70-2.

51   PR0. CO. 96/344: Hodgson to Chamberlain, dd. 22 September 1899.

52   NAG, Accra, ADM 12/3/5: Griffith to Ripon, dd. Aburi, 31 May 1893; *Further Correspondence,* C, 7918, 1896, pp. 10-13.
53   NAG, Accra, ADM 11/1483: Hodgson to Broom, dd. Accra, 23 February 1894.
54   *Further Correspondence,* C. 7918, pp. 21, 40-41, 43.
55   *Further Papers,* C. 890, 1874, p. 8, no. 3: Harley to Kimberley, dd. Cape Coast, 14 April 1873.
56   Ramseyer and Kühne, 1875, pp. 172, 196-7.
57   *Despatches,* C. 266-1, 1873, p. 150, enclosure 2 in no. 90: Kofi Kakari to Hennessy, dd. Kumase, 24 September 1872.
58   For biographical sketches of George Blankson, see Sampson, 1969, pp. 45-7; Ephson, 1958, pp. 38-9; and J. M. Akita, "Biographical Sketch of George Blankson of Anomabu (1809-1898)," in *Transactions of the Gold Coast and Togoland Historical Society,* Vol. 1. part V (1955), 217-8.
59   Sampson, 1969, p. 47.
60   *Further Papers,* C. 456, 1855, enclosure 1 in no. 3: Kwaku Dua to Cruickshank, dd. Kunase, 28 November 1853.
61   *Further Correspondence,* C. 819, 1873, p. 3: Kofi Kakari to Harley, dd. Kumase, 20 March 1873.
62   Beecham, 1841, p. 311, citing Wrigley to Wesleyan Committee, dd. 17 October 1836.
63   Ramseyer and Kühne, 1875, p. 89.
64   See, for example, *Correspondence,* C. 670, 1872, p. 13: Kofi Kakari to Governor, dd. 14 November 1870.
65   Ranseyer and Kühne, 1875. p. 101.
66   *Ibid.,* p. 99.
67   *Papers,* C. 1402, 1876, pp. 71-2, enclosure in no. 66: Mensa Bonsu to Lyall *et al.,* dd. Kumase. 19 July 1875.
68   *Ibid.,* pp. 82-3: Mensa Bonsu to Governor, dd. Kumase, 16 July 1875.
69   *Idem.*
70   *Despatches,* C. 266, 1873, p. 3: Kofi Kakari to Salmon, dd. Kumase, 23 November 1871.
71   *Ibid.,* p. 86: Kofi Kakari to Salmon, dd. Kumase, 20 February 1872.
72   Ramseyer and Kühne, 1875, p. 308.
73   For examples of chancery correspondence undertaken outside Kumase, see *Despatches,* C. 266, 1873, p. 88; *Despatches,* C. 266-1, 1873, pp. 378-80; *Further Correspondence,* C. 4052, 1884, pp. 92-3.
74   For examples of chancery letters the embassy wrote, see *Fur-

ther Correspondence, C. 7917, 1896, pp. 233-4, 239; *Further Correspondence,* C. 7918, 1896, pp. 14-5, 18-9, 21, 40-1, 43, 45-7, 54, 57-61, 87, 97-8, 109, 122, and 128.

75   Bowdich, 1819, p. 144.

Chapter 6

1   PRO. CO. 96/25: Hill to Bart, dd. Cape Coast, 23 October 1852.
2   *Despatches,* C. 907, 1874, no 14, pp. 19-20: Wolseley to Kimberley, dd. Camp Agianum, 7 February 1874.
3   This view was widely confirmed in field interviews. Also see Free-man, 1843, 2nd Journal, pp. 150-2, 168-9. Also compare the adnlnistration's negative posture on Western education with its attitude on Muslim education, which was strikingly favorable. Asantehene Osei Tutu Kwame, for example, faced no opposition from the Asantemanhyianu when he sent his children to the Quranic schools established by Muhammad al-Ghamba'. Dupuis, 1824, p. 107.
4   Bowdich, 1819, p. 56.
5   *Ibid.,* pp. 67, 85
6   Dupuis, 1820, p. 154.
7   PRO. 96/30: Cruickshank to Newcastle, dd. Cape Coast, 12 Jan-uary 1854.
8   Bowdich, 1819. p. 69 and n. 69.
9   *Ibid.,* pp. 110-11.
10   *Ibid.,* pp. 68-72, 87-8, 120-1, and 149.
11   *Ibid.,* pp. 113, 126-8.
12   *Further Correspondence,* C. 1006, 1874, no. 10, pp. 9-11.
13   Problems of interpretation subsequently arose from the wording of this treaty with respect to the Dwabenhene, who was accorded the status of a sovereign power by the treaty.
14   *Further Papers.,* C. 456, 1855, pp. 13, 34-5; *Despatches,* C. 266, 1873, p. 150.
15   *Despatches.,* C. 266, 1873, p. 156.
16   *Ibid.,* p. 183.
17   *Despatches,* C. 907, 1874, p. 8, enclosure 1 in no. 8: Kofi Kakari to Welseley, dd. Kumase, 21 January 1874.
18   *Further Correspondence,* C. 921, 1874, encl. 1 in no. 14, p. 20: Kofi Kakari to Wolseley, dd. 4 February 1874.
19   Reade, 1874, pp. 100-1.
20   *Correspondence,* C. 670, 1872, p. 9: confidential report from Ussher to Nagtglas, dd. Cape Coast, 27 November 1870.

21   Plange's diary, cited in Brackenbury, 1874, I, 48.

22   Brackenbury, 1874, II, 332.

23   *Correspondence,* C. 670, 1872, p. 10: Ramseyer and Kühne to Governor and Bromwell, dd. Ebenezer, near Kunase, October 1870.

24   Ramseyer and Kühne, 1875, p. 91.

25   Interviews with Kwasi Addai III, Nseniehene, and Kwaku Kankam, Asomfohene, dd. Kumase, 31 July and 3 August 1976.

26   *Correspondence,* C 670, 1872, p. 24; enclosure in no. 13: Crawford to Ussher, dd. Kumase, 7 August 1871.

27   *Further Correspondence,* C. 819, 1873, p. 3.

28   *Correspondence,* C. 670, 1872, pp. 15-16: Laing to Freeman, dd. Kumase, 31 March 1853.

29   Ellis, 1883, p. 273.

30   Coombs, 1963, pp. 107-8.

31   Wilks, 1975, pp. 233-4.

32   See, for example, C. 670, 1872, pp. 1-2: Kennedy to Natgtglas, dd. 9 October 1870.

33   *Ibid.,* pp. 3-4: Nagtglas to Kennedy, dd. Elmina, 25 October 1870.

34   *Ibid.,* pp. 12-13: Ussher to Kennedy, dd. December 1870.

35   *Ibid.,* p. 37-8: Kimberley to Kennedy, dd. London, 11 March 1871.

36   *Ibid.,* pp. 3, 5-6, 8-10, 12, 17-22.

37   *Correspondence,* C. 670, 1872, p. 13.

38   *Ibid.,* pp. 19-20.

39   *Ibid.,* pp. 21-22.

40   *Ibid.,* p. 24.

41   *Ibid.,* 1872, pp. 34-5, sub-enclosure 2 to enclosure 3 in no. 16: Kennedy to Kimberley, dd. Sierra Leone, 16 December 1871.

42   *Ibid.,* pp. 26-9.

43   Ellis, 1883, p. 273.

44   Ramseyer and Kühne, 1875, pp. 184, 187.

45   On Asen, see *Correspondence,* C. 670, 1872, pp. 26-8; *Further Correspondence,* C. 819, 1873, p. 3. On Denkyira, see *ibid.,* p. 3. On Adanse, see *Further Correspondence,* C. 7917, 1896, pp. 16-7. On Akyem, see *ibid.,* p. 3. On Dwaben, see *Papers,* C. 1402, 1876, pp. 81-3, 86-7, 114. On Atebubu, see *Further Correspondence,* C. 7917, 1896, p. 160.

46   For examples of correspondence on extradition, see *Despatches,* C. 385, 1864, pp. 6-7; *Affairs,* C. 3064, 1881, pp. 47-8. On Asante independence, see *Despatches,* C. 907, 1874, pp. 8, 12; *Further Correspondence,* C. 921, 1874, p. 20; *Further Correspondence,* C. 7917, 1896, pp. 70-2, 211-2; *Further Correspondence,* C. 7918,

1896, pp. 98, 122-3.

47 For examples of correspondence relating to the detention of Ramseyer, Kühne and Bonnat, see *Gold Coast*, C. 266-1, 1873, pp. 86, 183, 150-6; *Despatches*, C. 907, 1874, pp. 6, 8. On capital punishment, see *Further Correspondence*, C. 3386, 1882, pp. 32-3; *Further Correspondence*, C. 7917, 1896, p. 212.

48 *Despatches*, C. 385, 1864, p. 7.

49 *Correspondence*, C. 670, 1872, p. 26.

50 *Further Correspondence,* C. 819, 1872, p. 3.

51 *Papers*, C. 1402, 1876, p. 81.

52 *Ibid.*, p. 83: Mensa Bonsu to Governor, dd. Kumase, 16 July 1875.

53 *Further Correspondence,* C. 7917, 1896, p. 16: Prempe to Hodgson, dd. Kunase, 17 December 1889.

54 See, for example, *Correspondence*, C. 670, 1872, pp. 26-734-5.

55 *Further Correspondence,* C. 7917, 1896, p. 34: Prempe to Griffith, dd. Kumase, 22 August 1890.

56 *Ibid.*, p. 71: Prempe to Griffith, dd. Kunase, 7 May 1891.

57 PRO. CO. 96/27: Kwaku Dua to Hill, dd. Kunase, 16 May.

58 *Further Correspondence,* C. 7917, 1896, p. 201: Prempe to Griffith, dd. Kumase, 28 June 1894.

59 *Ibid.*, p. 20.

60 *Ibid.*, pp. 32-3: Kofi Apea to Holmes, dd. Elmina, 25 July 1890.

61 *Ibid.*, p. 239.

62 *Further Correspondence,* C. 7918, p. 54: Brew to Colonial Secretary, dd. London, 6 May 1895.

63 *Further Papers*, C. 456, 1855. p. 13.

64 *Affairs*, C. 3064, 1881, p. 6.

65 *Despatches*, C. 703, 1853, p. 8.

66 *Correspondence*, C. 670, 1872, p. 11.

67 *Gold Coast*, C. 266-1, 1873, pp. 17-8.

68 NAG, Accra, ADM 1/2/361: enclosure in Huydecoper to Smith, dd. Banda, 9 August 1879.

69 *Further Correspondence,* C. 7918, 1896, pp. 122-3.

70 *Further Correspondence,* C. 7918. 1896, pp. 107,109. Wilks 1975, pp. 647-54.

71 *The African Times*, xxiv, no. 266. 1 November 1883, p. 122.

72 *Further Correspondence,* C. 7919, 1896, p. 172.

73 *Further Correspondence,* C. 7917, 1896, p. 201.

74 Kwaku Dua III was elected Asantehene in 1888, but his formal enstoolment as Agyeman Prempe I could not take place until six years later in 1894.

75 *Despatches*, C. 385, 1864, p. 6.
76 *Further Gold Coast Correspondence,* C. 4052, 1884, pp. 72-3.
77 *Further Correspondence,* C. 7917, 1896, p. 189.
78 *Further Correspondence,* C. 7918, 1896, pp. 45-6.
79 *Despatches*, C. 266-1, 1873, p. 86.
80 *Further Correspondence,* C. 819, 1873. p. 3: Kofi Kakari to Harley, dd. Kumase, 20 March 1873.
81 *Further Correspondence,* C. 7917, 1896, pp. 70-1.
82 *Correspondence,* C. 670, 1872, p. 23: Salmon to Kennedy, dd. Cape Coast, 19 October 1871.
83 *Further Papers,* C. 456, 1885, pp. 9-10.
84 Reindorf, 1895, p. 174.
85 *Further Correspondence,* C. 7918, 1896, pp. 3-4: interview with Griffith, Cape Coast, 12 December 1894.
86 *Further Correspondence,* C. 1006, 1874, p. 1; Brackenbury, 1874, II, pp. 317-9; Ellis, 1893, pp. 349-50.
87 For the possibility of an interpreter's distortion, see Ellis, 1893, p. 365; also see evidence of Chief Ando of Elmina in *Affairs,* C. 3064, 1881, pp. 87-8.
88 *Affairs,* C. 3064, 1881, pp. 87-8.
89 Dupuis, 1824, pp. 132-3; Hutton, 1821, pp. 179-81.
90 *Despatches*, C. 385, 1864, pp. 6-7.
91 *Idem.*
92 Reindorf, 1895, pp. 258-60.
93 Compare Wilke, 1975, p. 663.

Chapter 7

1 Cruickshank, 1853, I, 197.
2 The "Gold Coast Methodist Times" of 31 August, the "Cold Coast People" of 24 September, and the "Gold Coast Chronicle" of 30 November 1894.
3 *Further Correspondence,* C. 7917, 1896, p. 236. Also see *Further Correspondence*, C. 7918, pp. 59-61.
4 It is not intended here to provide a full discussion of the subject of capital punishment, or of judicial administration in general, for which the reader is referred to Wilks, 1975, pp. 385-6, 592-5. 638-9; Bowdich, 1819, p. 297; and Rattray, 1911 *passim.*
5 Hutton, 1821, p. 224.
6 Bowdich, 1819, p. 240.
7 PRO. CO. 96/255: Griffith to Ripon, dd. 19 February 1895.
8 Freeman, 1843, 2nd Journal, p. 164.

9   *Despatches* C. 907, 1874, no. 9, p. 10.
10   *The African Times*, xvii, no. 186, 1 February 1877, pp. 14-15.
11   The "Gold Coast Methodist Times," 29 September 1894. Also see *Further Correspondence*, C. 4052, 1884, no. 35, pp. 82-3. For Owusu Ansa Sr.'s view on the subject, see Debrunner, 1967, p.180.
12   Interview with Agya Atwi Kwaku, dd. Kumase, 5 June 1980, and Daendels, 1964, p. 57.
13   *Further Correspondence*, C. 7917, 1896, p. 41.
14   *Affairs*, C. 3064, 1881, p. 47.
15   PR0. CO. 96/67.
16   *Despatches*, C. 385, 1864, no. 1, p. 3.
17   Bowdich, 1819, p. 88.
18   *Despatches*, C. 907, 1874, and Brackenbury, 1874, II, 149-51. Compare with *Further Papers,* C. 456, 1855, p. 6.
19   PRO. CO. 96/28.
20   Bowdich, 1819, p. 266. Also see Dupuis, 1824, p. 213n, who estimated that out of the 365 days of the year, the proportion of good or lucky days was no more than 150 or 160.
21   Bowdich, 1819, p. 139; Hutton, 1821, p. 166; Dupuis, 1824, p. 143; *Further Correspondence,* C. 7917, 1896, p. 61.
22   *Further Correspondence,* C. 7917, 1896, pp. 201-2.
23   Bowdich, 1819, n. 71.
24   *Further Correspondence,* C. 921, 1874, pp. 21-2.

BIBLIOGRAPHY

A. Secondary Sources (Books and Articles)

Adjaye, J.K. "Asante Official Correspondence: A Quantitative Approach Through Content Analysis." *Asante Seminar* [Northwestern University, Evanston] 3 (June 1975): 24-8.

_____ "Asabi Antwi and Oral Retrieval Mechanisms in Asante Diplomatic Practice." *Asante Seminar* 5 (Nov. 1976): 26-8.

_____ "Asantehene Agyeman Prempe I and British Colonization of Asante: A Reassessment." *International Journal of African Historical Studies* 2, 22 (1989): 223-49.

_____ "Asantehene Agyeman Prempe I, Asante History, and the Historian." *History in Africa* 17 (1990): 1-29.

_____ "Time, Identity, and Historical Consciousness in Akan." In Adjaye, J. K. ed., *Time in the Black Experience,* Greenwood, (Conn.), 1994.

Agbodeka, F. *African Politics and British Policy in the Gold Coast 1869-1900.* London, 1971.

Agyeman-Duah, J. "The Ceremony of Enstoolment of the Asantehene," *Ghana Notes and Queries* 7 (1965): 8-11.

Allman, J. M., *The Quills of the Porcupine: Asante Nationalism in an Emergent Ghana.* Madison, (Wis.), 1993.

Arhin, K. "The Structure of Greater Ashanti (1700-1824)." *Journal of African History* VIII (1967): 65-85.

_____ "The Missionary Role on the Gold Coast and in Ashanti: Reverend F. A. Ramsayer and the British Take-over of Ashanti 1869-1894." University of Ghana *Institute of African Studies Research Review,* IV, 2 (1968), 1-15.

Baesjou, R., *An Asante Embassy on the Gold Coast: The Mission of Akyampon Yaw to Elmina, 1869-1872.* Leiden, 1979.

Beecham, J. *Ashantee and the Gold Coast.* London, 1841.

Bevin, H. J. "M. J. Bonnat: Trader and Mining Promoter." *The Economic Bulletin of Ghana,* 4 (1960): 1-22.

Boahen, A. A. "Ashante-Dahomey Contacts in the 19th Century." *Ghana Notes and Queries* 7 (1965): 1-3.

Bonnat, M-J. "Les Achantis, Moeurs et Coutumes." *L'Explorateur* II (1875): 621 *et seq.*

Bowdich, T. E. *Mission from Cape Coast Castle to Ashantee with a Statistical Account of that Kingdom and Geographical Notices of Other Parts of the Interior of Africa.* London, 1819.

Boyle, F. *Through Fanteeland to Coomassie: A Diary of the Ashantee*

Expedition. London, 1874.

Brackenbury, H. *The Ashanti War of 1873-74.* 2 vols. Edinburgh and London, 1874.

Burton, R. F. *A Mission to Gelele King of Dahome.* 2nd ed. 2 vols. London, 1984.

Burton, H. F., & Cameron, V. L. *To the Gold Coast for Gold.* 2 vols. London, 1883.

Cardahi, C. "La Conception et la Pratique du Droit International Privé dans l'Islam." *Académie de Droit International, Recueil des Cours, 1937* Vol. II. Paris, 1938: 511-646.

Carson, P. *Materials for West African History in the Archives of Belgium and Holland.* London, 1962.

Casely, Hayford, J. E. *Gold Coast Native Institutions.* London, 1903.

Christaller, J. G. *Grammar and Dictionary of the Asante and Fanti Lanuage Called Tschi.* Basel, 1881.

Claridge, W. W. *A History of the Gold Coast and Ashanti.* 2 vols. London, 1915.

Collins, H. "The Panic Element in 19th Century British Relations with Ashanti." *Transactions of the Historical Society of Ghana* V (1962): 79-137.

Coombs, D. *The Gold Coast, Britain and the Netherlands, 1850-1874.* Oxford, 1963.

Crooks, J. J. *Records Relating to the Gold Coast Settlements from 1750-1874.* Dublin, 1923.

Cruickshank, B. *Eighteen Years on the Gold Coast of Africa.* 2 vols. London, 1853.

Daaku, K. Y. *Trade and Politics on the Gold Coast 1600-1720.* London, 1970.

Daendels, H. W. *Journal and Correspondence of H. W. Daendels, Part I, November 1815 to January 1817.* ed. E. Collins. Legon, 1964.

Danquah, J. B. "The Historical Significance of the Bond of 1844." *Transactions of the Historical Society of Ghana* I (1957): 3-29.

Debrunner, H. W. *A History of Christianity in Ghana.* Accra, 1967.

Dumett, R. E. *Survey of Research Materials in the National Archives of Ghana.* Basel. 1974.

Duncan, J. *Travels in Western Africa in 1845 and 1846.* 2 vols. London, 1847.

Dupuis, J. *Journal of a Residence in Ashantee.* London, 1824.

Elias, T. O. *The Nature of African Customary Law.* Manchester, 1956.

Ellis, A. B. *The Land of Fetish.* London, 1883.

_____ *A History of the Gold Coast of West Africa.* London, 1893.

Fage, J. D. "The Administration of George Maclean on the Gold Coast,

1830-44." *Transactions of the Gold Coast and Togoland Historical Society* 1 (1955): 104-120.

Freeman, R. A. *Travels and Life in Ashanti and Jaman.* London, 1898.

Freeman, T. B. *Journal of Two Visits to the Kingdom of Ashanti.* London, 1843.

Fuller, F. C. *A Vanished Dynasty: Ashanti.* London, 1921.

Fynn, J. K. *Ashante and Its Neighbours 1700-1807.* London, 1971.

Goldziher, I. *La Dogma et la Loi de l'Islam.* Paris, 1920.

Gros, J. *Voyages, Adventures et Captivité de J. Bonnat Chez Les Achantis.* Paris, 1884.

Hagan, G. P. "The Golden Stool and the Oaths to the King of Ashanti." *Research Review* IV, (1968): 1-33.

_____"Ashanti Bureaucracy: A Study of the Growth of Centralized Administration in Ashanti from the Time of Osei Tutu to the Time of Osai Tutu Kwamina Esibe Bonsu." *Transactions of the Historical Society of Ghana* XII (1971): 43-62.

Henty, G. A. *The March to Coomassie.* London, 1874.

Herskovits, M. J. *Dahomey: An Ancient West African Kingdom.* 2 vols. Evanston, 1938.

_____*Man and His Works.* New York, 1950.

Horton, J. A. B. *Letters on the Political Condition of the Gold Coast.* London, 1870.

Hutton, W. *A Voyage to Africa.* London, 1821.

Huydecoper, W. *Huydecoper's Journal, Journey from Elmina to Kumasi 28th April 1816-18th May 1817.* ed. G. Irwin. Legon, 1962.

Ingham, K. *Foreign Relations of African States,* London, 1973.

Johnson, M. "M. Bonnat on the Volta." *Ghana Notes and Queries* 10 (1968): 4-17.

_____"Ashanti, Juaben and M. Bonnat." *Transactions of the Historical Society of Ghana* XII (1971): 17-41.

Kea, H. A. "Four Asante Officials in the Southeast Gold Coast (1808)." *Ghana Notes and Queries* 11 (1970): 42-47.

Kimble, D. *A Political History of Ghana: The Rise of Gold Coast Nationalism 1850-1928.* Oxford, 1965.

Khadduri, M. T*he Islamic Law of Nations: Shaybani's Siyar.* Baltimore, 1966.

Kruse, H. "Al-Shaybani on International Instruments." *Journal of Pakistan Historical Society* I (1953): 90-100.

Kyerematen, A. A. Y. *Panoply of Ghana,* 1964.

_____"The Royal Stools of Ashanti." *Africa* xxxix, I (1969): 1-10.

_____*Kingship and Ceremony in Ashanti.* University of Science and

Technology, Kumasi, n.d.

Lee, H. *Stories of Strange Lands, and Fragments from the Notes of a Traveller.* London, 1835.

Levtzion, N. *Muslims and Chiefs in West Africa.* Oxford, 1968.

McCaskie, T. C., *State and Society in Pre-colonial Asante.* Cambridge, 1995.

_____"Time and the Calendar in Nineteenth Century Asante: An Exploratory Essay," *History in Africa* 7 (1980): 179-200.

McIntyre, W. D. "British Policy in West Africa: The Ashanti Expedition of 1873-4." *The Historical Journal* 5 (1962): 19-46.

_____*The Imperial Frontier in the Tropics, 1865-75.* London, 1967.

McKay, V. ed. *African Diplomacy: Studies in the Determinants of Foreign Policy.* New York, 1966.

Meredith, H. *An Account of the Gold Coast of Africa: With a Brief History of the African Company.* London, 1812.

Metcalfe, G. E. *Maclean of the Gold Coast.* London, 1962.

_____*Great Britain and Ghana, Documents of Ghana History 1807-1957.* London, 1964.

Matthews, N., and M. D. Wainwright. *A Guide to Manuscripts and Documents in the British Isles Relating to Africa.* [ed., J. D. Pearson] London, 1971.

M'Leod, J. *A Voyage to Africa, with some Account of Manners and Customs of the Dahomian People.* London. 1820.

Nicolson, H. *Diplomacy.* London, 1958.

Nørregard, G. *Danish Settlements in West Africa, 1658-1850.* [Trans., S. Mammen] Boston, 1966.

Priestley, M. "The Ashanti Question and the British: Eighteenth Century Origins." *The Journal of African History* II (1961): 35-59.

_____*West African Trade and Coast Society: A Family Study.* London, 1969.

Priestley, M., and Wilks, I. "The Ashanti Kings in the Eighteenth Century: A Revised Chronology." *The Journal of African* History 1, (1960): 83-96.

Queller, D. H. T*he Office of the Ambassador in the Middle Ages.* Princeton, 1967.

Ramseyer, F. A., and Kühne, J. *Four Years in Ashantee.* London, 1875.

Rattray, R. S. *Ashanti Law and Constitution.* Oxford, 1911.

_____*Ashanti.* Oxford, 1923.

_____*Religion and Art in Ashanti.* Oxford, 1927.

Reade, W. W. *The Story of the Ashantee Campaign.* London, 1874.

Reindorf, C. C. *History of the Gold Coast.* Basel, 1895.

Ricketts, H. J. *Narrative of the Ashantee War.* London, 1831.

Robertson, G. A. *Notes on Africa.* London, 1819.

Sarbah, J. M. *Fanti National Constitution.* London, 1906.

Satow, Sir Ernest. *A Guide to Diplomatic Practice.* London, 1932.

Smith, H. "Peace and Palaver: International Relations in Precolonial West Africa." *Journal of African History* XIV, 4 (1973): 599-621.

Sohm, R. *The Institute: A Textbook of the History and System of Roman Private Law.* Trans., J. C. Ledlie. New York, 1970.

Stanley, H. M. *Coomassie and Magdala: The Story of Two British Campaigns in Africa.* New York, 1874.

Tordoff, W. "The Exile and Repatriation of Nana Prempeh I of Ashanti (1896-1924)." *Transactions of the Historical Society of Ghana* IV, 2 (1960): 33-58.

_____ "Brandford Griffith's Offer of British Protection to Ashanti (1891)." *Transactions of the Historical Society of Ghana* VI (1962): 31-49.

Van Dantzig, A. "The Dutch Military Recruitment Agency in Kumasi." *Ghana Notes and Queries* 8 (1966): 21-24.

Ward, W. E. F. *A History of Ghana.* Rev. 2nd. ed. London, 1958.

Wilks, I. *The Northern Factor in Ashanti History.* University College of Ghana, 1961.

_____ "The Position of Muslims in Metropolitan Ashanti in the Early Nineteenth Century." In *Islam in Tropical Africa,* ed. I. Lewis. London, 1966: 318-341.

_____ "Aspects of Bureaucratization in Ashanti in the Nineteenth Century." *Journal of African History* VII (1966): 215-232.

_____ "Ashanti Government." In *West African Kingdoms in the Nineteenth Century,* ed. D. Forde and P. Kaberry. London, 1967: 206-238.

_____ *Political Bi-Polarity in Nineteenth Century Asante.* Edinburgh, 1970.

_____ *Asante in the Nineteenth Century: The Structure and Evolution of a Political Order.* Cambridge, 1975.

_____ "Dissidence in Asante Politics: Two Tracts from the Late Nineteenth Century." In *African Themes: Northwestern University Studies in Honor of Gwandolen N. Carter,* ed. I. Abu Lughod. Evanston, 1975: 47-63.

_____ "Land, Labour, Capital and the Forest Kingdom of Asante: A Model of Early Change." In *Evolution of Social Systems.* ed. J. Friedman and M. Rowlands. London, 1978: 487-534.

_____ "The Golden Stool and the Elephant Tail: The Rise of the Asante Middle Class." *Studies in Economic Anthropology.* Vol II.

ed. G. Dalton. Greenwich, Conn., 1979.

_____ *Forests of Gold: Essays on the Akan and the Kingdom of Asante,* Athens, Ohio, 1993.

Yarak, L. W. *Asante and the Dutch 1744-1873.* Oxford, 1990.

B.   *Newspapers*

The African Times (London)
The Gold Coast Chronicle (Accra)
The Cold Coast Methodist Times (Cape Coast)
The Gold Coast Times (London)
The Royal Gold Coast Gazette (Cape Coast)
The Times (London)
The Western Echo (Cape Coast)

C.   *Documents (Archives and Libraries)*

Items from the following classifications were consulted:

(i)   Public Record Office:

Colonial Office—C.O. 96: Gold Coast: Original Correspondence

(ii)   Methodist Missionary Society.Gold Coast CorrespondenceWest African Biographical Material.

(iii)   National Archives of Ghana, Accra, and Kumasi:
ADM 1/1—Series: Original Correspondence (including dispatches, telegraphic cablegrams and other communications) from Governors of the Gold Coast to Secretaries of State for the Colonies in London.

ADM 1/2—Series:Original Correspondence from Governors of the Gold Coast to Secretaries of State of London.

ADM 3/—Series Schedule of Out-Letters from Governors of the Gold Coast to Secretary of State, London.

ADM 9/—Series: Parliamentary Papers.

ADM 12/—Series: Confidential Prints.

(iv)   *Balme Library*, University of Ghana, Legon:

Furley Collection of translations and abstracts of Dutch archival material:

> *Dutch Journal* (N Series)
> *Journal* (N series)
> *Confidential Dispatches* (N series)

Institute of African Studies:

IASAS: Asante Stool Histories recorded by Joseph Agyeman-Duah.

1:	Asokwa, recorded 3 February 1963
2:	Ankobia, recorded 7 January 1963
3.	Ananta, recorded 25 February 1976
5.	Adum, recorded 13 February 1963
15:	Gyase, recorded 2 November 1962
22:	Nsumankwaa, recorded 26 October 1962
23:	Boakye Yam, recorded 3 March 1963
73:	Boakye Yam, recorded 6 June 1963
75:	Akankade, recorded 27 May 1963
76:	Asomfo, recorded 25 May 1963
81:	Nsenie, recorded 4 July 1963
95:	Adonten, recorded 17 July 1963
96:	Abenase, recorded 11 October 1963
106:	Akyampim, recorded 2 September 1963

(v)   *Manhyia Archives*, Kumasi:

A manuscript of Ashanti History narrated by King Prempeh I alias Nana Agyaman Duah whilst in Seychelles Island, 1907 (Unnumbered file).

(vi)   *Basel Missionary Society:*

P. Jenkins, *Abstracts from the Cold Coast Correspondence of the Basel Mission,* 1970. (Material is held at the Balme Library, University of Ghana, Legon.)

(vii)   *NBKG* - Archives of the Dutch Settlements on the Coast of Guinea series (Trans., Larry Yarak).

(viii)   *Parliamentary Papers,* U.K:

C. 551-II, 1842: *Report from the Select Committee on the West Coast of Africa, Part II* (X11).

C. 703, 1853: *Dispatches from Major Hill, the Governor of the Gold Coast Relating to the Warfare between the Fantis and the Ashantis* (LXV).

C. 456, 1855: *Further Papers Relating to the Warfare between the Fantis and the Ashantis* (XXXVI).

C. 385, 1864: *Dispatches from the Governor of the Gold Coast, Explaining the Cause of War with the King of Ashanti* (XLI).

C. 170, 1865: *Report of Colonel Ord, Appointed to Enquire into the Condition of the British Settlements on Western Coast of Africa* (XXXVII).

C. 670, 1872: *Correspondence Relative to the Cession by the Netherlands Government to the British Government of the Dutch Settlements on the West Coast of Africa* (LXX).

C. 266-1, 1873: *Gold Coast: Part II: Dispatches from Mr. Pope Hennessy Respecting the Transfer of the Dutch Possessions on the Gold Coast, etc.* (XLIX).

C. 819, 1873: *Further Correspondence Respecting the Ashanti Invasion* (XLIX).

C. 890, 1874: *Further Papers Relating to the Ashantee Invasion* (XLVI).

C. 891, 1874: *Further Correspondence Respecting the Ashantee Invasion* (XLVI).

C. 892, 1874: *Further Correspondence Respecting the Ashantee Invasion* (XLVI).

C. 893, 1874: *Further Correspondence Respecting the Ashantee Invasion* (XLVI).

C. 894, 1874: *Further Correspondence Respecting the Ashantee Invasion* (XLVI).

C. 921, 1874: *Further Correspondence Respecting the Ashantee Invasion* (XLVI).

C. 922, 1874: *Further Correspondence Respecting the Ashantee Invasion* (XLVI).

C. 1006, 1874: *Further Correspondence Respecting the Ashantee Invasion* (XLVI).

C. 1139, 1875: *Correspondence Relating to the Queen's Jurisdiction on the Cold Coast, and the Abolition of Slavery within the Protectorate* (LII).

C. 1140, 1875: *Correspondence Relating to the Affairs of the Gold Coast* (LII).

C. 1343, 1876: *Papers Relating to Her Majesty's Possessions in West Africa* (LII).

C. 1402, 1876: *Papers Relating to Her Majesty's Possessions in West Africa* (LII)..

C. 3064, 1881: *Affairs of the Gold Coast and Threatened Ashanti Invasion* (LXV).

C. 3386, 1882: *Further Correspondence Regarding Affairs of the Gold Coast* (XLVI).

C. 3687, 1883: *Further Correspondence Regarding Affairs of the Gold Coast* (XLVIII).

C. 4052, 1884: *Further Correspondence Regarding Affairs of the Gold Coast* (LVI).

C. 4477, 1885: *Further Correspondence Respecting the Affairs of the Gold Coast* (LV).

C. 4906, 1886: *Further Correspondence Respecting the Affairs of the Cold Coast* (XLVII).

C. 5357, 1888: *Further Correspondence Respecting the Affairs of the Gold Coast* (LXXV).

C. 5615, 1888: *Further Correspondence Respecting the Affairs of the Gold Coast* (LXXV).

C. 7917, 1896: *Further Correspondence Relating to Affairs in Ashanti* (LVIII).

C. 7918, 1896: *Further Correspondence Relative to Affairs in Ashanti* (LVIII).

D. *The Asante Collective Biography Project (ACBP;* based at Northwestern University, Evanston)

Asante Seminar, 1975–76
Asantesem, 1977–79

INDEX